THE COMPLETE
KITCHEN COMPANION

Barbara Chandler and Annette Yates

illustrated by Ken Astrop

Galley Press
in co-operation with
British Gas

General editor: Jackie Fortey

GALLEY PRESS
Copyright © 1980 Ventura Publishing Ltd, London
Created, designed and produced by Ventura Publishing Ltd,
44 Uxbridge Street, London W8 7TG, England
in co-operation with British Gas.
First published in 1980, under the title
The Gas Kitchen Companion, by Ward Lock Ltd,
116 Baker Street, London W1M 2BB, a Pentos Company.

Published in this edition 1984 by Galley Press,
an imprint of W.H. Smith & Son Limited,
Registered No. 237811 England.
Trading as WHS Distributors, St John's House,
East Street, Leicester, LE1 6NE.

ISBN 0 86136 790 1

Filmsetting by Tradespools Limited,
Frome, Somerset
Colour origination by D.S. Colour International
Limited, London
Printed and bound in Singapore by
Tien Wah Press (Pte.) Limited

Contents

Conversion tables

These are not exact, but 'rounded up'. When following recipes, always keep to the same set of measures (whether imperial, metric or American): never try to change in the middle from one to the other.

Capacities

1 fl oz	25 ml
2 fl oz	50 ml
¼ pt (5 fl oz)	150 ml
½ pt (10 fl oz)	300 ml
¾ pt (15 fl oz)	400 ml
1 pt (20 fl oz)	500–600 ml
1½ pt	900 ml
1¾ pt	1 litre
2 pt	1.1 litres
2½ pt	1.4 litres
3 pt	1.7 litres
1 gallon	4–5 litres

Spoon capacities

This refers to level spoons in each case.

¼ tsp	half 2.5 ml spn
½ tsp	2.5 ml
1 tsp	5 ml
2 tsp	10 ml
1 tbsp	15 ml

Weights

1 oz	25 g	16 oz (1 lb)	450 g
2 oz	50 g	1½ lb	700 g
3 oz	75 g	2 lb	900 g
4 oz	100–125 g	2½ lb	1.1 kg
5 oz	150 g	3 lb	1.4 kg
6 oz	175 g	3½ lb	1.6 kg
7 oz	200 g	4 lb	1.8 kg
8 oz	225 g	4½ lb	2 kg
9 oz	250 g	5 lb	2.3 kg
10 oz	275 g	5½ lb	2.5 kg
11 oz	300 g	6 lb	2.6 kg
12 oz	350 g	6½ lb	3 kg
13 oz	375 g	7 lb	3.2 kg
14 oz	400 g	7½ lb	3.4 kg
15 oz	425 g	8 lb	3.6 kg

Oven settings

These are not exact conversions but refer to dial markings. The thermostat setting or Gas Mark refers to the middle of the oven: it is warmer above and cooler below.

Gas Mark	°F	°C
Low	200	100
¼	225	110
½	250	120
1	275	140
2	300	150
3	325	160
4	350	180
5	375	190
6	400	200
7	425	220
8	450	230
9	475	240

When a recipe refers to a can of food, check that you use the size specified, as cans vary tremendously. Where imperial/metric conversions are given on can labels, they are exact and are not rounded up or down as are the tables above.

American measures

Dry measures

		Am
Butter, margarine	1 lb/450 g	2 cups
	1 oz/25 g	2 tbsp
Flour	1 lb/450 g	4 cups
	1 oz/25 g	¼ cup
Sugar	1 lb/450 g	2 cups
	1 oz/25 g	2 tbsp
Dried fruit	1 lb/450 g	3 cups
Rice	1 lb/450 g	2 cups

Liquid measures

(Water, stock, milk, cooking oil, etc.)

		Am
¼ pt/150 ml		⅔ cup
½ pt/300 ml		1¼ cups
1 pt/550 ml		2½ cups
2 pt/1.1 litres		5 cups

An imperial pint measures 20 fluid ounces, while an American pint measures 16 fluid ounces.

Preface

This is a cook book with a difference – it is not a recipe book. The authors and British Gas have sought to fill a noticeable gap by producing a compact reference book which concerns itself mainly with basic techniques. A quick glance at the contents page will show just how much ground has been covered.

At the time of publication there were some 15 million domestic gas customers in Britain, the majority of whom use gas for cooking. Indeed, research shows that gas is the preferred fuel for cooking by both housewives and the professional cook. Apart from being an inherently efficient fuel, it is easily and instantly controllable. Another plus is that today's gas cookers are designed for the economic use of fuel.

Over the years there has been a growing demand for gas and this is not likely to ease in the foreseeable future. Of course, cooking uses relatively small amounts of gas – for an average family about 80 therms a year. Much more gas is used for home heating – around 1000 therms a year is common for central heating, for example. Gas is now easily the most popular form of home heating. But this huge popularity has not meant a parallel increase in the total use of energy in homes. Despite the much higher standards of heating now taken for granted, the total heat used in the nation's homes has risen very little over the past decade – despite the fact that there are two or three million more homes to heat. The principal reason for this is the efficiency with which gas can be used. As a domestic fuel, gas has outstanding attributes. Apart from efficiency, it is a high quality fuel –

– and eminently suited to the domestic market, which is why British Gas' policy contains its use, as far as possible, to such premium applications.

Gas impinges little on our environment. It burns cleanly, and requires no storage at the user's home. From on-shore reception terminals to the customer, the gas is transported in underground pipelines, unseen and unheard. And even when gas installations, such as compressor stations, have to be built (more often than not in rural surroundings) great care is taken in their design to ensure the least possible impact on the environment. Various architectural awards are testimony to the care that the industry takes in this connection.

It is easy to take gas for granted. You turn on the tap and it is there at your bidding. But, as with all forms of energy and other commodities, gas has become more expensive and although gas is expected to retain its competitive position, it is prudent to expect that prices will continue to rise. So, apart from the national, and international, need to conserve energy, it is also in the housewife's own interest to practise economy in the use of fuel. For the less she uses, the less she has to pay.

A great deal of information on ways of saving energy is contained in the various leaflets and booklets freely available from every gas showroom. The remarkable thing is that the average house can quite easily attain energy savings of up to 20% by following a few simple procedures. Not to mention cash savings on fuel bills! Servicing of appliances, particularly central heating and fires, is another way of saving money on running costs, for an appliance which is not burning correctly is not efficient and is consequently wasting fuel. But there is another, even more important reason why regular servicing should be carried out. Safety.

Gas is a very safe fuel – at least as safe as any other. But like all sources of heat and power, it must be treated with respect if accidents are to be prevented. To help customers, British Gas regions have a number of regular servicing plans to meet the needs of every home. Ask at your local showroom for details. Remember, too, that only qualified people should service gas appliances and that it is against the law for anyone else to do so.

The laws about gas are very specific and it is worth repeating here the responsibilities that are placed on the consumer:

1 You must not use, or let anyone else use, any appliance you know, or suspect, to be dangerous.

2 Only competent people are allowed to install or service appliances or systems. You must not do it yourself if you are not competent.

3 If you suspect a gas leak you must turn off the supply at the main.

4 You must tell your local gas service centre immediately if an escape continues after you have turned off the main supply.

5 You must not turn on the gas or any appliance again until the escape or the appliance has been repaired by a competent person.

All the above are points of law and, if they are broken, you could be faced with a heavy fine.

Back to the subject of the gas kitchen. Today's gas cooker, in terms of both design and efficiency, is a sophisticated piece of equipment. Both the cooker manufacturers and British Gas (who in fact are *not* manufacturers) have development programmes to improve cooker standards. Work done at the world-famous British Gas Watson House Research Station in London has been responsible for many of the innovations on modern cookers. Efficiency, ignition and ease of cleaning are just some of the preoccupations for the highly qualified people who work there. These include home economists who, after the scientists and engineers have done their work, ensure that new devices and models actually *do* cook to the standards required – and that visually attractive features are also practical in everyday working kitchen conditions.

British Gas believes this book will help both new housewives and more experienced cooks to get the best out of their gas kitchens, and out of the nation's valuable energy resources.

The working kitchen

Good cooking starts with good planning, so spend a little time organising your kitchen in the best possible way. It is obviously easier to do this if you are installing a new kitchen from scratch, but some small changes in your existing kitchen can make a considerable improvement in working conditions.

A paper plan

Start by making a plan of your present kitchen layout. Using a steel tape, measure up the area of your kitchen in metric if possible (most kitchen units have now been metricated). Mark your measurements on a rough sketch. Now draw the kitchen area out on squared paper, using a scale of 1 cm: 20 cm. Mark the position of all doors (and the way they open), windows, gas point, electric power points, water supply, drainage and any equipment, like a boiler, that cannot be changed. Make a list of the faults of your existing kitchen, so that you can check back to see that your new ideas provide a satisfactory solution.

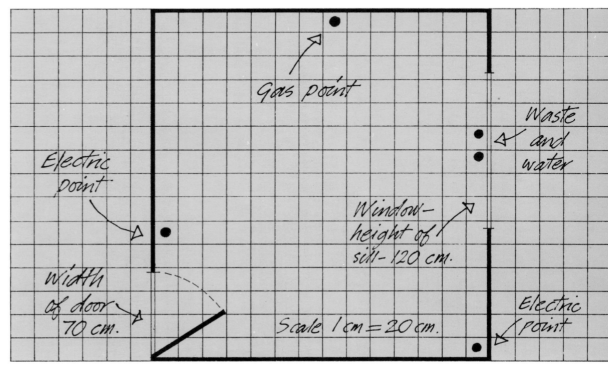

*Top: good cooking starts with good planning.
Bottom: make a plan on paper of your existing kitchen.*

Kitchen checkpoints

The answers to these questions will help you with your kitchen planning.

How much cooking must my kitchen cope with? (How much worktop? How much storage? Size of cooker?)

How many people, and how often, will be eating in the kitchen?

How much light does my kitchen get by day? By night?

How much money can I spend on my new kitchen/altering my old kitchen?

What equipment and furniture do I want to keep?

What from the following list is most important for me to buy now:

Cooker? (free-standing or built-in?)
Sink? (double?)
Fridge? (Freezer, fridge-freezer?)
Washing machine? (Dryer? Could these go in another room?)
Washing-up machine (on or under worktop?)
Kitchen units (kind and finish?)
Worktops? (made of what?)
Flooring (what kind?)

Do I need to improve ventilation?

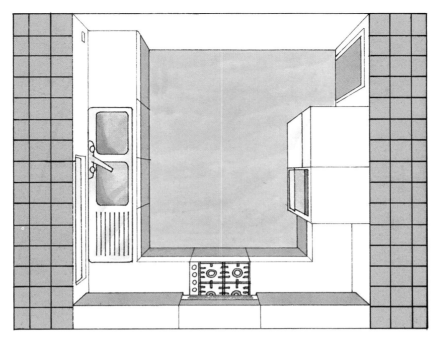

The work sequence

The most convenient arrangement of kitchen equipment is as follows: worktop/sink/worktop/cooker/(or built-in hotplate/worktop. This arrangement can be in a straight line, an L-shape or a U-shape. Avoid cramming the cooker or hotplate into a corner and plan for a worksurface on either side. Tall fridge-freezers and the popular tall oven-housing units should ideally come at the end of a run of work-surface so that they do not interrupt your work flow. The most-travelled route in the kitchen, known as 'the work triangle' by designers is between the sink, the cooker and the fridge. The distances between these three key appliances should be kept short, to save unnecessary leg-work. It is vital for family safety that the path between cooker and sink is not crossed by any through traffic, to the garden for example. This will help to avoid dangerous collisions when hot liquids are being carried about. It is useful to make cardboard cut-outs, to the same scale as the paper plan, of the equipment you already have and the units you are considering, so that you can move them around to find the best arrangement. Washing machines should be sited so that you can conveniently load and unload out of the way of other people walking through the kitchen. It is useful to have a shelf or compartment above or adjacent in which to keep your linen basket. Remember to leave space for future acquisitions (a dishwasher, for example).

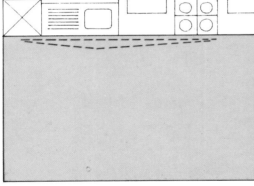
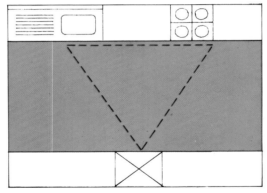
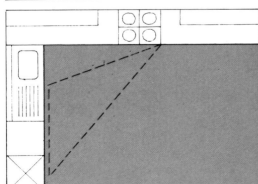
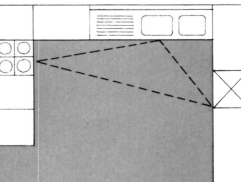

Top: planning a work sequence.
Bottom: kitchen equipment can be arranged in one straight line, two straight lines, an 'L' shape or a 'U' shape.

Worktop heights

Standard worktop height is 900 mm/ 36 in. This, of course, is a compromise height. Taller women may find it too low, particularly for the sink, where one effectively works in the bowl, below the level of the worktop. It is worth experimenting with a makeshift worktop to find the height that suits you best. As a general guide, stand in comfortable shoes with your arms bent and your lower arms relaxed: the position of your hands will indicate a comfortable worktop height for you. It is often possible to raise the height of new kitchen units by supporting them on a plinth.

Experiment to find the most comfortable worktop height.

The sink

The sink and the cooker (or built-in hotplate) should be linked by an unbroken worktop. In a conventional sink unit, the sink extends fully from front to back, and it is now possible to buy versions with a curved or 'rolled' front edge to match up with the newer worktops with rounded edges. Sinks with drainers on both or either side, and versions with double sinks are also available. 'Built-in' sinks look neater and more sophisticated but will be more expensive to install. They are contained within the worktop, and can be single or double, with or without drainers. Make sure you choose sinks with enough room to accommodate large items such as

Sinks can be single or double, 'sit-on' or inset, rectangular or round, with or without drainers.

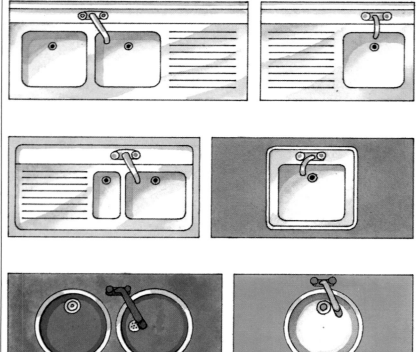

oven shelves, hotplate, pan supports, pastry boards, etc. Aim for double sinks where space and money permit: if either are in short supply, it is often useful to compromise with one full-size sink, with a second smaller sink alongside. If your kitchen is far from the dustbin (at the top of a block of flats, for example, or at the back of a terraced house), a waste disposal unit fitted into your sink is a blessing. Stainless steel is the most common material used for modern sinks, but versions are also available in coloured enamels, some with drainers to match. Continental round sinks look attractive but do make sure that they are large enough for all your needs.

Storage

Once you have worked out a satisfactory work sequence, you can turn your attention to storage. It is a good idea to make a list of items to be stored and to consider where they will go, while your kitchen is still at the paper-plan stage. Base units can provide storage below the work surface and shallower wall-hung units above it. The average kitchen is of limited size, and there are so many demands on space that precious storage must often be sacrificed. Washing machines and dishwashers, for example, may take up space below worktops; and worktops themselves reduce storage space. Storage cupboards should not be placed above a hotplate.

Storage zones: use the middle zone for things you need most, the bottom for those needed least and the top for your lightest items.

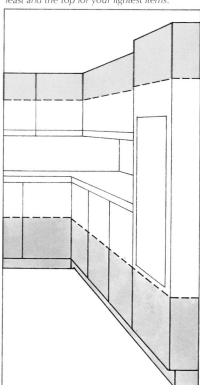

Food

Check that in your plan you are providing the various types of storage for different foods, bearing in mind the awkward heights of some items, such as cereal packets and bottles.

Dried goods e.g. flour, sugar, biscuits and tins	Dry cupboard
Semi-perishable foods e.g. bread, fresh fruit and vegetables	Well-ventilated cupboard
Perishable foods e.g. milk, cheese, meat and some salad vegetables	Refrigerator
Frozen food	Freezer or frozen food compartment of the fridge

Kitchen equipment

Now consider your kitchen equipment, including utensils, pans, and possibly cutlery and crockery. Remember that some items, like pressure cookers and deep-fat fryers, are large and tall. Provide a place on the plan for all those items that get forgotten: trays, pastry and chopping boards, tea and hand towels, rubbish containers, weighing scales and so on. Cleaning materials should be kept in a dry safe place out of the reach of children. There are several ways in which extra storage space can be squeezed out of the tiniest kitchen.

Below right: a free-standing gas cooker and range type.
Below: built-in storage units are designed to suit any size of kitchen and can be added to in stages.

Eating space

Most people like to provide space for eating in the kitchen, if only for snacks and breakfasts. A kitchen table with chairs that tuck away neatly, is one solution. If space is very restricted, consider a countertop the same height as the worktop, with stools that can be put away beneath, but remember that this arrangement is unsuitable for young children, who may topple off the stools. A table in a corner takes up less space with built-in bench seating, boxed in to provide extra storage. The position of the table should not be allowed to interrupt the basic work sequence, so that you need to walk around it to get from, say, cooker to fridge. Cutlery, plates and cups, jams, sauces and cereals and other items most used at the table should be stored near it. Use your table for extra work-surface for longer jobs, like preparing vegetables for a stew, and take the time to pull up a chair. Table tops should be easy to keep clean in a kitchen. An old table can be covered with plastic laminate, or the surface can be sanded clean and sealed with several coats of polyurethane varnish.

Cooking appliances

A free-standing upright cooker is still a popular choice for many kitchens. In a modern gas cooker, grill, hotplate and oven are all neatly combined in one unit which is easy to install, and can be taken if you move. Gas cookers vary in size from those suitable for making simple meals for one or two people, to large 'ranges' for big families, sometimes with two ovens. Some models have automatic timers, which will switch the oven on at the pre-arranged time. Other features available are push-button ignition, and oven linings which help to clean themselves. The arrangement of burners on the hotplate also varies: some models have raised individual pan supports with separate removable spillage bowls; others have a level one- or two-piece continuous grid to support your pans. Some models have special fast and/or slow burners, and many have a special control for simmering. Some new cookers incorporate the fan-assisted method of cooking (see p. 86). Rotisserie and kebab attachments are available for the grills of some cookers (see p. 87).

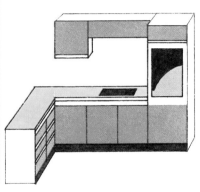

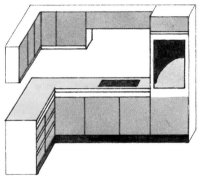

Worktops: in laminate with rounded front edge and curved upstand, in ceramic tiles with wood trim and in wood.

Built-in cookers

Many people who are investing time and money in installing a new kitchen are now choosing built-in cooking appliances rather than free-standing gas cookers. In this case, the hotplate is set into the worktop, while the oven is contained in a special tall cupboard (usually called a housing unit) and is at waist height to avoid tedious bending and stooping. A separate gas grill is usually mounted on the wall in the most convenient position. Built-in gas cooking appliances of this kind are more expensive to buy and install than a free-standing cooker, but are often more convenient to use. They look neater and more streamlined, and are easier to clean. Working heights are more comfortable, and the separation of oven, hotplate and grill enables you to adopt a more flexible kitchen layout.

Surfaces

Worktops

Plastic laminate is the most popular surface for worktops and does have many advantages. Prices are reasonable and tops are available in lengths up to at least 2440 mm/8 ft, sometimes longer. New-style tops have attractive rounded front edges and curved upstands at the back. Laminates are easy to wipe clean, and any stains can be removed with a weak solution of household bleach. There are now effective and subtle imitations of a wide range of natural materials, which include wood, cork, parchment, leather, marble and fabrics such as hessian. However, laminates will scratch if you cut directly onto their surface, and they can be damaged by very hot dishes. A stainless steel pan rest near your hotplate is a good idea. Ceramic tiles make an effective alternative to plastic laminates, but installation is likely to be more costly. Choose a hardwearing grade, and use a waterproof grout. Floor tiles, glazed or unglazed, such as quarries, are ideal. Wooden worktops look attractive and fit well with the current rustic look, but they must be expertly made from hardwood to avoid the opening of ugly joints and cracks. And they are less easy to keep clean. You could incorporate in your worktop a small area of marble – possibly the top from an old washstand – for pastry-making.

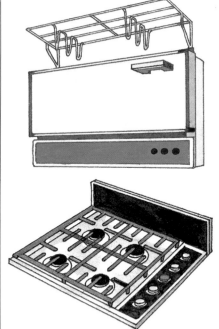

Built-in cooking: grill, hotplate and oven.

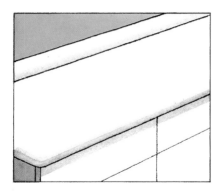
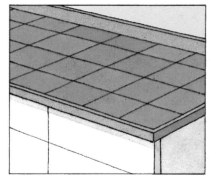
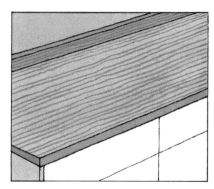

Walls

You will want your kitchen to stay bright and clean, so walls must be washable. Modern vinyl emulsions stand up well to grease and steam, provided they are applied to a sound dry, clean surface. Vinyl wall-coverings are hardwearing yet offer attractive patterns. Protect vulnerable areas behind cookers and worktops and sinks with ceramic tiles. Wood (for example, tongued and grooved pine boarding) makes a pleasant kitchen wall facing, but be sure to seal it well with several coats of polyurethane. A small area of cork or insulation board is useful as a pin-up place for recipes, messages, shopping lists and hints.

Top: tiled floor.
Bottom: well-sealed cork tiles.

Floors

Your kitchen floor should be easy to clean and comfortable to walk on. It also helps if it can deaden noise and disguise soiling to some extent. Modern cushion vinyls can be recommended on all counts, and for larger kitchens, the new wide widths are very easy to lay. Non-cushion sheet vinyls and vinyl tiles are less expensive and can be very attractive, but will be harder on the feet. Ceramic tiles, which may be glazed or unglazed (e.g. quarries), are expensive, noisy and very hard on the feet. Cork tiles feel pleasant and have an attractive natural appearance. They provide insulation against noise and heat loss to some extent, but do make sure they are well sealed. If possible, buy the type that have a clear vinyl wear layer applied at the factory.

Lighting and ventilation

Make sure that your kitchen has sufficient lighting. Exploit the natural light from the windows by siting the sink, main worktop or table beneath them. A single central pendant rarely provides enough artificial light, so incorporate strip lights over worktops and sink, or install spotlights at strategic points. Good ventilation is also essential. An extractor fan, preferably ducted to the outside, or a cooker hood, will draw out grease and steam-laden air, making working more pleasant and helping to preserve decorations.

Colour and atmosphere

Choose your kitchen colour scheme carefully. If it gets little sun, brighten it with warm colours based on reds, yellows or browns. A south-facing kitchen with plenty of natural light can take cooler schemes, with blues or greys. Lastly, remember that despite the emphasis on efficient working and planning, this is *your room* as much as anywhere else, and add your own personal touches. A comfortable chair, a pretty pot plant, or framed family photos – whatever pleases best.

Equipping your kitchen

Like many crafts, good cooking is easier if you have the right tools. For best results use the correct pans and utensils for each job, and buy the very best quality you can afford.

Saucepans

The ideal saucepan is made from a good heat conductor to cook food evenly (with no 'hot-spots' to cause sticking or burning) besides being durable and easy to clean. Good looks are an added bonus. Only experience can tell you exactly what type you prefer but here is the information to help you towards an initial choice.

Look for
1 **Thicker, heavier metals** to prevent food sticking.
2 **Well-fitting, sturdy lids.**
3 **Heat-resistant,** well-attached comfortable handles and knobs.
4 **Rounded insides** for ease of use and cleaning.

Always follow manufacturer's directions on preparing a new pan for cooking ('seasoning'). The following will cover the basic saucepan needs for a family of four.

One	2-pint/1.1-litre
Two	3-pint/1.7-litre
One	6-pint/3.4-litre
One	Milk pan with pouring lip (preferably non-stick)

These need not necessarily be a matched set. For example you may prefer the smaller sizes to be non-stick, but this is not necessary for the large sizes.

Keeping saucepans tidy
Some types stack. Otherwise you can use a saucepan rack, or hang pans from pegs or hooks, or from an 'S' hook over a rod. Use hooks or racks for lids where necessary.

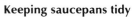

PAN POINTS
1 **Don't let handles stick out over hotplate edge – this is dangerous, especially to children.**
2 **Don't let handles stick out over uncovered adjacent burner – they will spoil.**
3 **Good quality pans can be heated on a high setting but then only need a low light to continue cooking.**
4 **In general do not heat an empty pan.**
5 **Do not put very hot pan straight into cold water or onto plastic laminate working surface.**

Saucepan types	Good points	Bad points	Care and cleaning
1 Aluminium Various gauges (thicknesses) available. Buy the heaviest you can. 'Cast' types are superior to 'pressed'	Good value: relatively inexpensive. Good heat conductors: cook food evenly. Hard-wearing. Easy to clean. Light to handle. Do not rust	Light-weight pans can distort over high heats – pans will wobble and lids won't fit. Discolours easily. Some foods react with the metal so cannot be used for storing food	Clean as soon after use as possible – food or fat left in can cause pitting. Use hot soapy water plus scouring pad. Do not use washing soda, it can cause corrosion. To remove discoloration, boil up a little water with lemon juice, vinegar or apple peelings
2 Enamel Smooth enamel coating can be applied to steel, aluminium or cast iron. Look for the Vitramel quality symbol	Hard smooth surface is hygienic and easily cleaned. Bright colours and attractive designs	Food may stick in light-weight pans so buy heavier qualities. Cheaper qualities can chip; a stainless steel rim provides good protection	Use nylon not metal scourers. Use wood or plastic utensils, not metal. Remove stains and food deposits by soaking overnight in water with a little biological washing powder added.
3 Stainless steel 18/8 and 18/10 refers to the nickel and chrome content and indicates best qualities	Light to handle. Strong and durable. Non-corrosive. Attractive brilliant finish does not rust or tarnish	Bad conductor of heat – food can scorch at sides. Look for pans with aluminium or copper base, or with '3-core sandwich' construction – mild steel or aluminium between two layers of stainless steel	Use hot soapy water but avoid scouring unless essential. For burnt deposits, soak for as little time as possible, as can cause pitting. Vinegar removes blue stains caused by overheating, or use a stainless steel cleaner
4 Cast iron Frequently coated with enamel outside and in, or with non-stick surface	Excellent conductor and retainer of heat, so that food continues to cook at low temperatures at an even rate, without need for stirring. Enamelled versions can be very attractive. Durable and long-lasting	If not coated will rust. Very heavy, so look for extra handles on large pans. Handles are frequently metal and will burn so always use oven glove. Can break if dropped on hard surface	Wash in hot soapy water and dry at once. If uncoated, rub with cooking oil to guard against rust. If coated, follow advice for 'enamel' (above) or 'non-stick' (below)
5 Copper Always lined with tin, tin nickel or stainless steel to prevent harmful reaction with food	Long-lasting and hard-wearing. Excellent conductor of heat, so cooks evenly. Very attractive	Lining wears in time (3–5 years, depending on use) and pans must be relined by cookware specialist. Discolours badly when heated. If handles are metal, will get very hot: use glove	Cook on lower heat than normal – heats up instantly. Overheating may bubble tin lining. Wash in hot soapy water while pan is warm. Avoid scouring. Soak off sticky or burnt deposits. To keep outside shiny use copper cleaner, or rub with cut lemon dipped in salt
6 Non-stick Usually aluminium coated inside with non-stick surface, e.g. Teflon, Fluon, SilverStone	Food does not stick: ideal for milk, sauces, etc. Easy to clean. Reasonably priced	Surface will wear off in time according to quality and use. Cheaper qualities may distort. See aluminium above	Do not overheat. Never use metal utensils: always wood or plastic. Wash in soapy water, rinse and dry thoroughly – small food particles left after cleaning could later burn and spoil surface
7 Ceramic glass Only special types, e.g. Corning Ware (formerly known as Pyrosil and Pyroflam) can be placed directly on hotplate	Inexpensive. Easy to clean. Attractive. Good retainer of heat, can be used on low settings. Can go from hotplate to table, and from freezer to oven. (Usually have detachable handles)	Poor conductors of heat so need careful heat control to prevent hotspots. Will shatter if dropped on on hard surfaces	Use hot soapy water. Soak off food deposits; if absolutely necessary use nylon scourer. Soak in solution of household bleach to remove stains

Frying-pan

Choose a heavy pan for even heating, in a good heat conductor such as heavy-gauge aluminium, which can be enamelled and/or non-stick, cast iron or copper-based stainless steel. A thin pan simply buckles when heated to become useless. A good average size is 8–10 in/20–25 cm.

Look for
1 **A comfortable heat-resistant handle.** A hanging ring or hole is useful for wall storage.
2 **Rounded insides** for easy use and cleaning.
3 **A matching lid** to prevent spluttering (an adjustable air vent is useful).

Omelette pan

Choose a thick-based pan, 6–8 in/15–20 cm to hold sufficient heat to cook egg immediately. (Non-stick heavy-gauge aluminium, cast iron or lined copper). Traditional heavy steel pans are also available, but keep lightly greased to prevent rusting. Rounded insides allow easy turning out.

Casseroles

These are deep dishes with well-fitting lids available in many shapes for cooking meat, vegetables and fish in the oven. Make sure you buy large enough for your particular needs. For 4 people a good choice would be: one 3½-pint/2-litre plus one 5-pint/3-litre.

Earthenware

Baked porous clay, usually glazed. Inexpensive, attractive. Used for traditional French cooking. Chips easily and will break if dropped.

Stoneware

A harder non-porous pottery, more durable than earthenware. Attractive designs.

TIP
To freeze a casserole, first cool. Then freeze in straight-sided casserole. Run hot water around pan sides to loosen, avoiding top. Turn out, wrap in freezer film or foil, and return to freezer. To heat, replace in original casserole, and place in low oven for about one hour.

Ceramic glassware

See notes under saucepans. Attractive designs, reasonably durable. The best types can be used on the hotplate to brown meat, and then transferred to the oven.

Cast iron enamelware

Very durable but rather heavy. More expensive than other types. Can be used on hotplate to brown meat.

Chip pan

Sensible size is 6-pint/3.4-litre with a wire basket, and well-fitting lid to keep out dust when not in use. A good choice is heavy-gauge aluminium.

Egg poacher

This is an aluminium pan with a lid, into which fits a tray to hold 3 or 4 individual removable metal cups (preferably non-stick), each to take 1 egg. For poaching methods, see p.21.

Steamer

This special pan cooks by steam from boiling water. You can save fuel by cooking a whole meal on one burner. Food remains whole since cooking is gentle (for example, whole fish). Good for Christmas and other puddings.

Steamed food is easily digested (good for infants and invalids). Little attention is needed for steaming: just check that there is enough water for the whole of the cooking time. A well-fitting lid is essential to prevent steam escaping and the pan drying up. At the same time you can cook in the base as well as in the steaming tier, but make sure the base is large enough to take your basin on a trivet (rack), plus steaming tier. Also make sure the steamer is large enough to cook the things you normally wish to cook, like a long roly-poly and whole fish. You can buy a steaming section to fit a general-purpose base. Sauces and garnishes are often needed to make the finished dish attractive.

Roasting tins

These are usually supplied with a new cooker and are the largest size that can be used in the oven for even cooking results. If you buy a roasting tin, choose heavy-gauge aluminium. Thin metal buckles under high heats and becomes useless. Tins with lids can be used for 'enclosed' roasting – see p. 27. A rack is useful for roasting meat out of its juices – to give a better, more even result.

Kettle

Choose a sturdy design in aluminium with or without enamel finish, preferably with a heat-resistant handle. A whistle to fit over the spout will serve as a handy reminder when it boils. An electric kettle gives you more room on your hotplate and keeps tea-making away from cooking. Keep all types of kettle free from hard water scale for maximum efficiency. You can buy descaling agents from your hardware store.

Kitchen tools

Here is a selection of the most basic items you will need for everyday cookery. There are of course countless other implements, dishes and gadgets you can add as your cooking skills develop.

General cooking and serving

Wooden spoons Unlike metal, these stay cool while cooking. You will need at least four. One with a long handle copes with deep pans; the flat spatula type is useful for getting into the edges of a saucepan. Keep a separate spoon for very spicy mixtures such as curries.

Ladle for serving soups and stews, and for potting jams.

Basting spoon with a long handle is for spooning hot fat over meat joints in the oven.

Fish slice If possible buy one with heat-resistant plastic blade for use in non-stick pans. Choose a flexible blade. In spite of its name, use for general frying (e.g. eggs, sausages, bacon) as well as fish.

Tongs Easiest way to turn and serve grilled and fried food. Keeps food whole, thus conserving valuable juices.

Palette knife for easing baked cakes and pastries out of tins; for smoothing icing, cream, etc; also for turning and serving small items of fried foods, e.g. eggs.

Pudding basins Three sizes are needed: 1-pint/550-ml, 1½-pint/900-ml, 2-pint/1.1-litre in heat-resistant china or glass. Use for steaming puddings, and mixing and storing small amounts of food.

Oven glove Traditional long 'glove', well padded, with pockets at each end and hole for hanging, protects both hands and is essential for heavy dishes. One-hand gloves are useful for light-weight pans.

Mixing and beating

Mixing bowl(s) A good average size is 5-pint/3-litre. Ideally, you also need a smaller size for small amounts (of egg whites for example) plus a larger one for Christmas cake and puddings.

Whisk A wire balloon whisk is what the professionals use. But you may prefer a rotary whisk with handle to turn the blades. Also used for beating are wooden spoons and metal forks.

Spatula This ingenious gadget has a flat flexible rubber blade that removes every last scrap of mixture from bowl or pan.

Measuring

Scales should have imperial and metric measurements for convenience. Traditional balance scales give longest-lasting accuracy. Spring types with a pointer in various designs can be free-standing or fixed to wall.

Measuring spoons Buy a set of imperial and metric spoons if you can (some are double-ended). Otherwise you must have at least: 1 teaspoon, a 5-ml spoon, 1 tablespoon and a 15-ml spoon.

Measuring jugs Buy two if possible: ½-pint/300-ml and 2-pint/1.1-litre. Look for comfortable handles and well-shaped pouring lip, graduated in imperial (fl oz and pints) and metric (ml and litres). Heat-resistant glass is best.

Cutting and chopping

Knives Good sharp knives prevent much frustration in the kitchen. Buy the best you can – it is better to have a few good ones than an extensive set of cheaper knives. Look for sturdy, comfortable long-lasting handles, with rivets to hold the blade firmly in place. Wood looks nice and feels good but plastic will go in dishwashers. For a basic set of knives choose:

Carving knife for cutting meat.

Bread knife with serrated edge.

Large cook's knife for cutting meat and cutting and chopping vegetables, including chipping potatoes. Can be from 7 in/175 mm to 10 in/250 mm; choose the size you find most comfortable.

Utility knife for general cutting and dicing of vegetables and meat, filleting fish, etc. From 4 in/100 mm to 6 in/150 mm.

Paring knife Small and neat with blade around 3 in/75 mm long to peel fruit and vegetables.

Sharpening steel and carving fork with guard.

Storage Do not store your knives loose in a drawer. You will blunt them, and you or your family could cut yourselves. Use a rack.

Carbon steel can be sharpened frequently to a razor edge, but stains and rusts easily.

Stainless steel holds a sharp edge longer, but do not allow it to become too blunt. Touch up regularly on a steel.

Chopping board Use a wooden board as knives will blunt easily on a laminated surface.

Kitchen scissors Choose a sturdy, comfortable pair and keep only for kitchen use – cutting string, paper, herbs, food (fish fins, tails, etc, chicken between the joints). Blades should be rust-proof and scalloped or serrated to prevent food slipping. Some are multi-purpose with serrated hand grips for opening screw-top jars, and a hook for opening bottles.

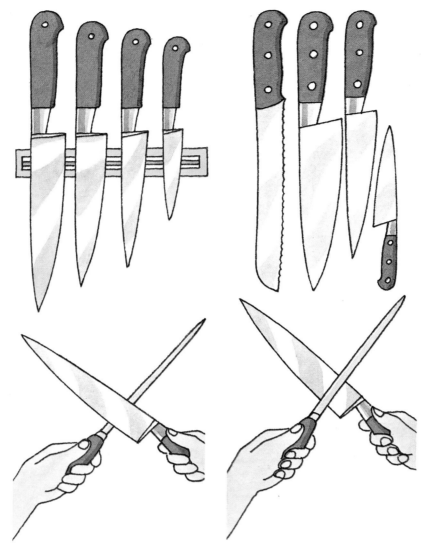

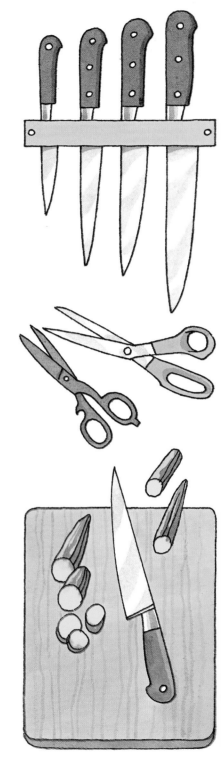

Sharpening a knife: draw whole length of blade from hilt to tip across front of steel.

Repeat across back of steel for other side of blade.

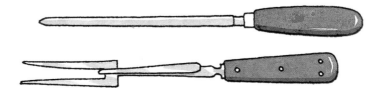

TIP
To sharpen a knife, hold steel firmly. Place knife blade at very shallow angle to steel (around 10°). Draw whole length of blade from hilt to tip across front of steel, and then repeat across back of steel for other side of blade. Repeat process about ten times. A good edge will slice effortlessly through a tomato.

Grating, grinding, squeezing, mincing

Grater Old-fashioned four-sided metal box grater is inexpensive, versatile and easy to use. Use coarse and medium sides for cheese and vegetables. Fine side is for nutmeg, lemon rind, etc. The slicing edge is handy for cucumber, potatoes and so on.

Pepper mill Choose a sturdy wooden design to provide freshly-ground pepper from whole peppercorns – this has much more flavour than factory-ground pepper.

Lemon squeezer (for oranges too) Old-fashioned glass type works fine. Or there are plastic versions with an underneath screw-on cup to catch the juice.

Mincer Traditional version that clamps onto working surface in tinned cast iron is still the best. Types with suction pads can slip.

Straining and sifting

Colander Choose a metal one with comfortable handles – plastic types melt if exposed to heat or hot surfaces. Aluminium is long-lasting. Enamel is attractive but tends to chip.

Sieves Metal types are more durable than plastic. Small size is useful for gravy and making vegetable purées, etc. Larger size is good for straining vegetables and sieving flour. (Make sure sieve is really dry after washing.) Or you can keep a fine-meshed plastic sieve just for sieving flour and icing sugar.

Baking

Baking sheet Should be solid and flat to avoid buckling when heated. A non-stick surface is a good idea.

Sandwich tins are for sandwich cakes: you will need two. A good size is 7–8 in/18–20 cm. Buy non-stick if possible or line with greased greaseproof paper.

Pie/tart plate A good size is 8–10 in/20–25 cm for pies, tarts, quiches, etc.

Pie dish for fruit or meat pies, 1½-pint/1-litre serves about four people.

Cake tin for larger cakes. Good average size to choose is 8 in/20 cm. Non-stick is especially good for fruit cakes – no greaseproof lining needed. Otherwise choose type with removable base.

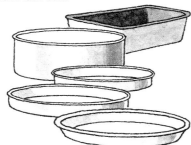

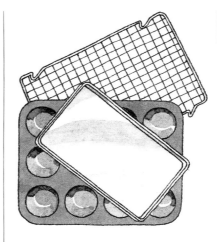

Bun pan/patty tin 12-hole (not 9-hole) non-stick type is best to save time.

Loaf tin Preferably choose non-stick type for easy removal of bread. One 1 lb/450 g and one 2 lb/900 g.

Cooling tray A wire grid, for cooling cakes, etc.

Pastry-making

Rolling-pin Usually wooden. Some expensive types in plastic or glass can be filled with cold water to keep pastry cool. A good size is 16–18 in/41–46 cm. Ones without handles are easier to use.

Flour dredger A metal or plastic container with a perforated lid to sprinkle flour evenly on your work surface before rolling out.

Pastry cutters These can be plain, or fluted or in different shapes. Sets usually range from 1 in/2½ cm to 3½ in/9 cm diameter. But you can make do by cutting round saucers, yoghurt cartons, jar tops, etc.

Pastry brush Use for brushing pastry with water, egg, milk or a sugar glaze. Choose a heat-resistant type that you can use for brushing cooking oil/melted butter, etc onto hot foods (e.g. kebabs). Also use for greasing pans with a little oil.

Timing and testing

Timer Essential for perfect pressure cooker or oven cooking. Many modern cookers incorporate a timer. If yours does not, buy one. Otherwise distractions from phone or children could ruin your cooking!

Thermometers A cook's thermometer ensures safe deep fat frying and efficient jam-making. A meat thermometer is useful to check when joints are cooked. Do not use in covered roasting pans.

Skewers Small straight skewers will test whether cakes, vegetables, meat joints, etc are ready. (For kebab cookery choose large flat type.)

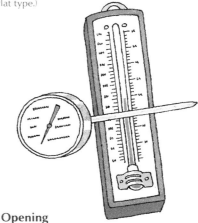

Opening

Can opener Can be hand-held, wall-mounted, suction-based or electric. Choose strong one which is easy to grip and easy to clean.

Bottle opener Simplest, inexpensive type is very efficient.

Cork screw Traditional type is most effective.

Eating for health

To stay healthy, you and your family should eat a mixed diet including a wide variety of foods. This will supply you with all the nutrients you need to provide energy, guard against infection, help growth, and maintain and repair the body. There are no hard and fast rules: sensible planning makes for sensible eating.

For sound nutrition and good health

Choose a wide variety of food according to the guide on this page and the 'food value' notes in each food section of the book.

Buy food which is fresh and in good condition. Follow our buying hints in each section.

Store food cleanly at correct temperatures according to the storage notes in each section. In general fresh foods should be kept at low temperatures.

Cook and/or prepare food correctly and hygienically according to the basic methods described in this book.

Nutrients in food

Nutrient	Used for	Found especially in
Proteins	Growth and repair. Some proteins are of higher quality than others, so eat a wide variety of protein-rich foods for a good balance	Meat, fish, eggs, milk, cheese, flour and bread, cereals, potatoes, nuts, pulses (dried vegetables), peas and beans
Carbohydrates	Providing energy, being also a form of fuel, and may be converted to body fat	In practice many foods contain carbohydrates, but the most important sources are bread and flour, rice and other cereals, potatoes, cakes, biscuits, confectionery, honey, treacle, jams. *Note* Sugar is pure carbohydrate and is only useful as a quick form of energy
Fats	Making energy, providing a concentrated form of fuel for the body	Butter, margarine, cooking oils and fats, fatty meat, fish (oily), eggs, cheese, cream, nuts
Vitamins	Regulating building and repair of the body and controlling the chemical reactions that take place in body cells.	
Vitamin A	Maintaining healthy eyes and good eyesight, and for general growth. Can be destroyed by high temperatures, for example by frying food	Butter, margarine, cheese, milk, eggs, fish (oily), meat (especially liver), fish liver oils, carrots, spinach, apricots, watercress, tomatoes
Vitamin B group This group includes thiamin (B_1), roboflavin (B_2), nicotinic acid (niacin, B_6)	Regulating the nervous system and releasing energy from food. Also assists in the building of blood.	Bread, cereals, meat (especially liver and kidney), milk, cheese, eggs, vegetables, wheatgerm, yeast, yeast extracts (e.g. Marmite) and meat extracts (e.g. Bovril). Vitamins of B complex are soluble so use as little water as possible in cooking, then preserve them by using cooking water in sauces and gravies

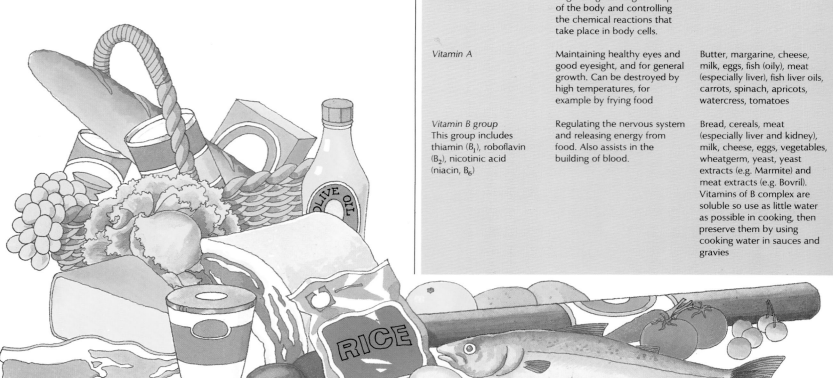

Nutrient	Used for	Found especially in
Vitamin C	Maintaining healthy teeth, gums, bones, blood and healing wounds. Also helps the body to make use of iron and calcium, so diets are beneficial which combine these nutrients (for example, orange juice followed by grilled kidneys and spring greens)	Black currants, strawberries, orange, lemon, lime, grapefruit, rosehip syrup, green vegetables and potatoes. Vitamin C is destroyed by light and heat, so store foods in a cool, dark place and cook in covered pan for as little time as possible
Vitamin D	Making and maintaining strong bones and teeth (Rickets can result from Vitamin D deficiency). Vitamin D comes mainly from our food but the body also makes some when exposed to sunshine	Margarine, butter, fish (oily), fish liver oils, milk, cream, cheese, eggs and green vegetables
Minerals *Iron*	Proper formation of blood. (An iron deficiency can lead to anaemia.) Iron is not easily absorbed by the body so needs replacing often	Black pudding, meat (especially liver and kidneys), cocoa, chocolate, dried apricots, bread, corned beef, beef, watercress and green cabbage
Calcium	Building and maintaining strong bones and teeth, particularly important for growing children, pregnant and nursing mothers. Our muscles need calcium to work properly	Milk, cheese, sardines, canned fish, yoghurt, watercress, white bread and flour

Basic eating plan

For convenience, foods are often classified into groups. The simplest way of ensuring an adequate intake of nutrients is to plan your meals to include foods from each of these four groups every day:

1 MEAT, INCLUDING BACON, SAUSAGES, OFFAL (e.g. LIVER AND KIDNEYS), COOKED MEATS, FISH AND EGGS.
2 MILK, CHEESE, YOGHURT, BUTTER, MARGARINE.
3 FRUIT AND VEGETABLES, INCLUDING POTATOES.
4 BREAD, RICE, PASTA, CEREALS, etc.

Meals

The number of meals you have in a day may vary from three to six (including snacks) according to your appetite, life style and personal preferences. But your overall intake of nutrients should meet your individual needs for each day/week. Breakfast is a very important meal, coming a long time after the previous meal. People work better (mentally and physically) on a good breakfast, particularly children going to school.

Dietary fibre (Roughage)

Although dietary fibre (also called roughage) is a mixture of fibrous carbohydrate which we cannot digest, it is an essential part of our diet. Lack of dietary fibre can lead to complaints such as constipation and various conditions of ill-health. Dietary fibre is present in vegetables, fruit, nuts, wholemeal bread and flour, and bran-based breakfast cereals. Include as many of these in your diet as possible.

Water

About two-thirds of our body weight is made up of water. It is essential for all our body processes. Apart from the water we drink, we also take in water from our foods and the body develops a small amount of its own. We lose water in our urine and faeces, in breathing and by evaporation from the skin.

Salt

As well as bringing out the flavour of food, salt is important to help maintain a correct balance of body fluids. It is also essential for the proper working of nerves and muscles. Babies and young children cannot take a lot of salt and it should not be added to their food. In general, older children and adults get as much salt as they need from a normal daily diet.

Convenience foods

It is important to eat a wide variety of as many fresh foods as possible, but there is a growing market for ready-to-heat and ready-to-eat foods. Canned, dried and frozen foods offer convenience as their major advantage. They also add variety to the diet and overcome seasonal fluctuations in supply. Their resemblance to fresh foods varies widely as regards flavour (some people prefer frozen peas to fresh, for example), but it is unlikely that there is any appreciable loss in nutritional value.

Eggs

Eggs are everybody's standby: ideal for quick nutritious main meals and an essential ingredient in a whole variety of other recipes.

Food value

Eggs are an inexpensive source of protein and, being easy to digest, are particularly suitable for special or invalid diets, meals for the elderly and young children.

Buying eggs

Eggs are easily obtainable all the year round. For fresher eggs, choose a place where there is a quick turnover of stock.

Size

The old labelling system (large, standard, medium, small) has been replaced by a new grading system based on egg weights. Size 3 is a useful size for everyday use.

Old	New	Uses
Large	Size 1 70 g or over Size 2 65–70 g	boiling, poaching, frying, i.e. when egg is to remain whole
Standard	Size 3 60–65 g Size 4 55–60 g	omelettes, cake-making, scrambling, sauces, baking, frying, poaching
Medium	Size 5 50–55 g	preserving, scrambling, freezing, sauce-making, omelettes
Small	Size 6 45–50 g Size 7 under 45 g	go mainly to the catering trade

Quality and freshness

By law, egg boxes must be stamped with the number of the week in the year in which they are packed (e.g. Week 30). To keep track of the relevant week, keep a small diary handy. Class A eggs are excellent quality, Class B, fair. 'Extra' marked on a Class A egg box indicates that the eggs have been packed for less than 7 days (the date of packing must be stated).

When a fresh egg is broken, the yolk is full and firm and the white is thick, edged by a small amount of thinner white. As an egg gets older the white becomes thinner and more runny, the yolk tends to break and the contents evaporate. The egg weighs less as the small air pocket in the broad end of the egg expands. A fresh egg placed in water sinks quickly and lies flat; if it is stale it turns upright; if it is bad it will float.

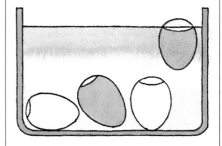

Colour

Brown eggs may cost a little more than white, but remember you are paying extra for the colour alone – inside, they are just the same.

Storage

Store eggs in a cool place, with the pointed ends downwards. Their porous shells can absorb smells, so keep them away from strongly flavoured foods (e.g. onions, strawberries, cheese, fish). They will keep for 7–10 days in a cool larder. In the fridge, whole eggs will keep for about 2 weeks (place them away from the ice compartment); egg yolks, covered with cold water, and egg whites, in a covered basin, will keep for up to 2 days; beaten whole eggs, covered, for up to one day; hard-boiled eggs in their shells for 2–3 days (but remember to mark them!). Keep a few eggs at room temperature in a small basin or rack, for making cakes and boiling.

Freezing

Whole eggs will only freeze satisfactorily if broken and blended. Egg whites can be frozen in ice cube trays, then stored in the freezer in plastic bags. Before freezing, yolks should be mixed with $\frac{1}{2}$ tsp/2.5 ml spoon of salt per yolk for use in savoury recipes, $\frac{1}{2}$ tsp/2.5 ml of sugar for sweet. Thaw in unopened container before use. Remember to keep a note of the number of eggs frozen. Cooked eggs will *not* freeze satisfactorily.

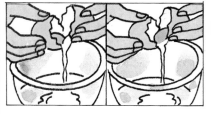

TIP
To separate an egg, break the shell in half against the side of a bowl and pass the yolk from one shell half to the other, letting the white fall down into the bowl. Put the yolks in a separate bowl.

Using eggs in cooking

Uses	In
Thickening (to avoid curdling mixture should not boil after eggs added)	Sauces, soups
Emulsifying (i.e. combining liquids)	Mayonnaise
Binding (holds ingredients together)	Fish cakes, rissoles
Coating (prevents absorption of fat)	Fried fish, rissoles, fish cakes
Raising (eggs hold air when beaten)	Cake and batter mixes, meringues, soufflés
Decorating	Pastry (glazed with beaten eggs). Cold meat/fish (with sliced hard-boiled eggs)

Using eggs for meals

Boiling

Eggs which have been stored at room temperature are less likely to crack. Piercing the shell at the broad end of the egg with a needle also helps to prevent cracking.
1 **Fill** a small pan with water and bring to the boil.
2 **Place** egg gently into water, using a spoon, and immediately lower heat to simmer.
3 **Cook** size 3 eggs for 3–4 min; larger eggs for slightly longer.
For *hard-boiled* eggs, use the same method, but cook for about 8 min and cool immediately in cold water to avoid a dark ring forming around the yolk (this is unsightly, but harmless). When cool, crack shell and peel.

Coddling

Coddled eggs have a creamy white suitable for small children and invalids.
1 **Place** eggs in pan of boiling water, cover and take off heat.
2 **Leave** for from 5–7 min (sizes 3 and 4).

Poaching

If fresh eggs are used, the white is less likely to separate from the yolk.
1 **Half-fill** a poaching pan with water.
2 **Put** a small piece of butter in each metal dish.
3 **Bring** water to the boil, break eggs into dishes, season lightly with salt and pepper and cover.
4 **Simmer** gently until eggs are set (about 3 min).
5 **Loosen** with blunt knife before turning out onto, for example, hot buttered toast.

This method gives an even, rounded shape.
or
1 **Fill** a small frying-pan with 1½ in/4 cm of water.
2 **Bring** to the boil, then lower heat until just simmering.
3 **Break** each egg gently into the water (a buttered metal pastry cutter can be used to hold eggs in place).
4 **Cook** for about 3 min (sizes 2 or 3). (A pinch of salt and a few drops of vinegar in the water help the egg white to set.)
5 **Remove** with draining spoon and drain on kitchen paper before serving.
Do not boil water furiously after eggs have been added, as they will break up.

Scrambling

Allow 1½ to 2 eggs per person.
1 **Beat** together eggs with a fork (do not use a whisk) with salt and pepper and 1½ tbsp/30 ml of milk for every 2 eggs.
2 **Melt** a knob of butter in a heavy pan (preferably non-stick).
3 **Coat** the base of the pan well, but do not let the butter brown.
4 **Pour** eggs into the foaming butter, and stir well over a gentle heat using a wooden spoon.
5 **Lift** the eggs away, as they thicken and set on the bottom of the pan, and cook until evenly thick.
6 **Remove** pan immediately from heat and serve at once – the eggs will go on cooking if left in hot pan.
For *flavoured* eggs, you can add fried mushrooms, chopped grilled bacon or flaked cooked fish.

Frying

1 **Heat** enough cooking or vegetable oil, or bacon fat, to cover base of frying-pan.
2 **Break** egg into pan, when fat is hot (but do not allow to brown).
3 **Allow** to start to set, and then spoon fat over the egg continuously until cooked (this helps the yolk of the egg to cook evenly with the white). If you like eggs with crispy edges, use hotter fat than for eggs with smooth white edges.
4 **Use** something flexible such as a fish slice or palette knife to get the egg out of pan, or it will break.

Baking

1 **Place** small buttered ovenproof dishes (often called ramekins) on a baking tray and break an egg into each.
2 **Season** with salt and pepper.
3 **Bake** in an oven for 5–8 min (Mark 4–5/350–375°F/180–190°C) until eggs are just set. If you wish, you can add a knob of butter and/or 1 tbsp/15 ml of cream to each egg before cooking and then increase cooking time to 6–9 min.

Omelettes

Use a thick frying-pan, about 6–8 in/15–20 cm, preferably non-stick with rounded sides. Use 2 eggs for 1 person and 3–4 eggs for 2 people. Larger omelettes tend to break. Use butter for best flavour, but margarine, cooking oil or bacon fat can also be used.
1 **Beat** 2 eggs together (for 1 person) gently (never whisk), season with salt and pepper to taste and add 1 tbsp/15 ml of water to help lighten the mixture.
2 **Gently heat** pan. Add knob of butter and melt to spread over bottom of pan. Let the butter foam but not brown.
3 **Pour** in eggs, tilting pan so that surface is covered.
4 **Stir** gently once or twice with a fork or spoon. The eggs should be in the pan for the shortest possible time. Leave a few seconds, then lift mixture away from sides so that raw egg mixture runs underneath the cooked parts. Do this until the omelette is set, being golden underneath but still moist on top. Add filling if wished.
5 **Tilt** pan so that omelette slides to one side, and use palette knife or spatula to fold into centre. Slide unfolded part onto warmed plate and flip folded part on top to fold again (three layers).
Serve immediately: omelettes toughen if left.
Fillings Use chopped fresh herbs, parsley, chives, grated cheese, tomatoes (peeled and chopped), grilled chopped bacon, fried sliced mushrooms, cooked chopped meat, cooked flaked fish, cooked vegetables, or use up any suitable left-overs.

Flour

Flour comes from grains of wheat, finely crushed or 'milled'.

Food value

Each wheat grain is made up mainly of starch, with outer layers of bran, plus the tiny but important germ. The amount of the original wheat left after processing varies according to the type of flour, and is described as a percentage by the term 'extraction rate'. Different types of baking need different flours for good results (see chart).

Storage

Keep flour in bags on a cool, dry, airy shelf. If the kitchen is steamy, transfer into large jar or tin with lid, but do not add new flour to old.

Flour type and extraction rate	Colour, flavour, texture	Use for	Food value
Wholemeal or **wholewheat** (these are the same). 100% – nothing is added or taken away	Bran gives wholemeal baked goods brown colour and close texture. Germ provides 'nutty' flavour. 'Stoneground' refers to a traditional milling process – no nutritional significance	Bread, heavier types of pastry and cakes, dumplings, scones, biscuits and crumbles (either on its own or mixed with wheatmeal or white flour)	The wheatgerm provides valuable quantities of nutrients including carbohydrate, protein, Vitamin B complex and iron. Wholemeal flour is an excellent source of dietary fibre
Wheatmeal or **Brown** 85 to 90% (10 to 15% of grain removed)	Unbleached with part of bran removed to give lighter texture' than wholemeal; 'nutty' flavour	Bread, pastry, cakes, dumplings, scones, biscuits and crumbles	
White 70 to 74% (26 to 30% of grain removed)	Removal of bran and wheatgerm makes flour whiter to give lighter, finer texture		In the milling of white flour certain of the nutrients above are removed with the outer parts of the grain and so, by law, Vitamin B, nicotinic acid and iron are added back in prescribed quantities. Calcium is also added
1 strong plain flour	High gluten content adds 'body' to baking (gluten is a protein). It absorbs water and gives dough elasticity.	Bread, puff and flaky pastry	
2 plain flour	Softer, 'weaker' flour with less gluten	Thickening sauces and casseroles. Coating meat, fish, rissoles, fish cakes. Binding fish cakes, rissoles, hamburgers. Cakes, sponges, shortcrust pastry, scones, Yorkshire pudding, pancakes, dumplings	
3 self-raising flour	Plain flour with added raising agent	Cakes and sponges. Suet crust pastry	

Type	Keeps for
Wholemeal/brown	up to 2 months (may go rancid – buy in small quantities)
Strong and plain white	4–6 months
Self-raising	2–3 months

TIP
To thicken a casserole or stew, mix about a tbsp/15 ml of flour with water to make a smooth but runny paste. Turn heat down very low and add to the stew a little at a time. Bring to the boil, stirring well. Repeat, if necessary, for a thicker stew.

Bread

Bread, one of the oldest foods known to man, is as essential today as ever.

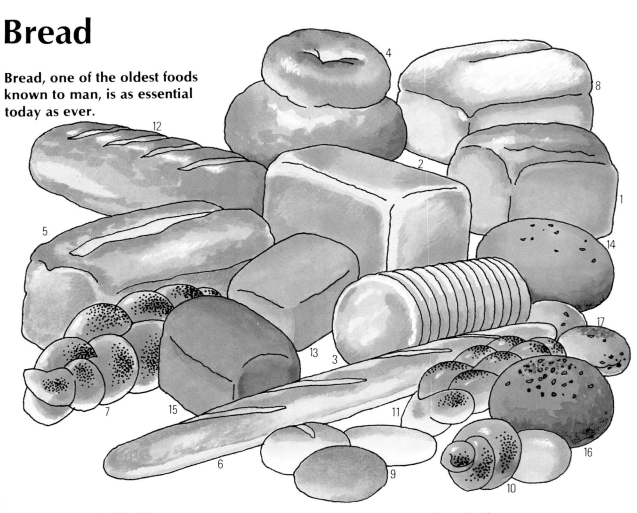

Food value

Since bread makes up a large part of our daily diet, it is a good source of energy and protein and provides valuable quantities of calcium, iron and B vitamins.

Buying bread

Try to buy from shops that take a daily delivery, or better still from where bread is baked on the premises. A wide variety of bread of all shapes and sizes is available.

Storage

To keep bread soft, moist and free from mould, store at normal room temperature in clean, well-ventilated, dry container, which should not be airtight – a bread-bin or crock, for example. Do not store in the fridge. Very crusty bread (e.g. French stick) is best eaten the same day. Loaves with softer, thinner crusts and moister crumb (e.g. sandwich loaf) will keep 2–3 days. Milk breads and those enriched with fat or eggs will keep up to 4 days. Keep wrapped bread in packaging loosely tied, or folded on top.

Freezing

Fresh bought or home-baked loaves will keep (wrapped) in the freezer for 4–6 weeks. Sliced bread can be toasted from frozen. In the freezer, par-baked loaves keep for 4 months, risen dough for 2 weeks, unrisen for up to 1 month, according to type.

White breads (unenriched dough)
1 *Tin loaf* Everyday bread sold unwrapped or wrapped, unsliced or sliced in three different thicknesses. Good for sandwiches and toast.
2 *Sandwich loaf* Flat top gives even, square slices and may be white or brown.
3 *Barrel* Fluted cylindrical shape, ideal for slicing. Is also called pistol, rasp, landlady's or lodger's loaf.

Crusty white breads
4 *Cottage* A traditional, hand-made round loaf with top, baked on the oven bottom.
5 *Split tin* Given a deep cut down the centre before baking. Also *cob* – round, baked out of tin.
6 *French stick* Long thin baton, thick crisp crust with or without poppy seeds, at its best a few hours after baking.
7 *Poppy-seed plait* Very crusty plaited loaf decorated with poppy seeds.

White breads (enriched dough: eggs and/or milk and/or fat are added)
8 *Farmhouse* Baked in tin with rounded corners, dusted with flour and cut down middle before baking. Sometimes wrapped and sliced.
9 *Flat loaves (Baps)* Names vary: e.g. Scotch bap, Irish bap, Devon flat, Essex paddle. Oval or round with a thin soft crust.
10 *Milk loaves* Shapes include winkles, batons, barrels, oval and rounds. Enriched with milk and usually glazed. Often decorated with poppy seeds.
11 *Cholla* A rich plaited Jewish bread, glazed and topped with poppy seeds. Egg, fat and sugar give a soft yellow crumb. Keeps and toasts well.
12 *Bloomer* Long loaf with rounded ends. Top is slashed several times so that the loaf can 'bloom' up or rise better.

Brown breads
13 *Wholemeal* A true wholemeal is made from flour from the whole wheat grain. Close texture, good nutty flavour. Shapes include cobs, pots and batons.
14 *Wheatmeal* Tin or cob-shaped, made from a mixture of white and wholemeal flour, lighter in texture than wholemeal.
15 *Wheatgerm* Tin shape, made from white or brown flour with wheatgerm added. Sold under brand names such as *Hovis, Vitbe.*

16 Rye breads
Great variety of shapes. Vary from the very heavy dark Russian rye to a light caraway-flavoured kümmel. Strong flavour.

17 'Tea' breads and buns
Fruit breads, richly or lightly fruited, sugary or plain. Malt bread with its characteristic flavour and moist crumb may be plain or fruited.

Using bread in cooking

Bread slices can be used for puddings such as summer pudding, bread pudding and fruit charlotte. Breadcrumbs can be added to rich fruit puddings to lighten the texture. Also use crumbs for savoury stuffings for meat, poultry, game and fish; or to make toppings for casseroles, vegetables, pasta or fish. (Sprinkle over dish and then crisp under hot grill for 3–5 min or in hot oven for 10 min.)

Fresh crumbs Use bread 1 or 2 days old. An electric blender is quickest, or for coarser crumbs use an ordinary grater. Store in clean polythene bag in fridge for 2–3 days or in freezer for 3 months.

'Raspings' are bread slices (or crumbs) dried in cool oven until golden brown, then crushed with rolling pin. Will keep in covered container for 1–2 weeks.

Buttered crumbs can be used to top sweet or savoury dishes, for coating meat, fish, croquettes, or as a basis for stuffings. Melt 1 oz/25 g butter in a pan and add about 5 oz/150 g fresh breadcrumbs. Stir well. Spread on baking sheet and place in cool oven, Mark ½/250°F/120°C and allow to dry without browning. Will keep in the fridge in airtight container for up to 2 months.

Toast is better made with bread 1 or 2 days old. For thick toast, with soft middle, cut ¼–½ in/5–10 mm slices and toast quickly on each side under a hot grill, or use electric toaster. For crisp toast, cut bread ¼ in/5 mm thick and turn often during toasting.

Melba toast Cut slices of stale bread ⅛–¼ in/3–6 mm. Dry in oven, Mark 2–3/300–325°F/150–160°C, on a baking sheet until lightly and evenly browned, crisp and curling. Turn 2 or 3 times. Takes about 35 min. Cool and store in airtight tin. Serve cold instead of bread with any meal.

TIP
For hot garlic bread, make diagonal slashes in a long French loaf and insert in each a little butter mixed with crushed garlic. Wrap in foil and place in hot oven for 10 min.

Fried bread makes a breakfast of eggs and/or bacon into a more substantial meal, and is also a good base for snacks. Use cooking oil or bacon fat and before you put in bread slices (cut in half) make sure that the fat is hot enough to brown a cube of bread in 15 seconds.

Sandwiches

The classic 'quickie snack', easy to prepare, with countless possible variations, hot and cold. A good sandwich can be a satisfying, well-balanced meal, often better food value than a hot dinner. The secret is in the fillings. Choose body-building foods such as eggs, cheese, meat or fish, together with lettuce, tomato, watercress or other vegetables.

Bread can be white, brown, wholemeal or rye, one day old for easy cutting. Ready-sliced bread (thin and fresh) saves time and effort. A large loaf gives 20–24 slices, a small, 10–12.

Butter or margarine should be soft, not oily (to make it go further beat in some warm milk – 2 tbsp/30 ml to 4 oz/100 g). Spread over one side of slice to the edges. You need about 8 oz/225 g for a large loaf. Spread some filling on the buttered side of one slice and top with another bread slice, buttered side down. Using sharp knife, cut crust off (if liked) and cut into squares, fingers, triangles or use fancy cutters.

Rolled sandwiches Cut crusts off new bread. Butter one small slice and place at one end a slice of suitable filling (e.g. cooked meat such as ham with cooked asparagus piece). Roll up (like a Swiss roll) and serve.

Alternatively cut crusts off a sandwich loaf, using a sharp knife. Slice thinly lengthwise (instead of across) to make long, narrow slices. Spread with butter and a soft filling. Roll up each slice, wrap in foil or polythene and cool in fridge for a few hours. Just before serving cut across to form pinwheels (about ½ in/1 cm thick).

TIP
Always cover sandwiches with foil or cling film until ready to serve, otherwise they quickly dry out.

Open sandwiches are made with thick slices of firm bread – white, brown, wholemeal, rye, etc, buttered with filling on top, colourfully decorated. They are good for using up small amounts of food, and best served on a plate with knife and fork.

Toppings (on their own or combined): slices of cold meat, cheese, eggs, salami, pâté, flaked fish, cream cheese, cottage cheese, scrambled egg, caviare. Decorate with lettuce, tomato, cucumber, green or red pepper, radish, onion, gherkin, anchovy, capers, parsley, mayonnaise, lemon slices or twists, parsley, olives, chopped nuts or thick sauces on meals.

Toasted sandwiches Toast a sandwich brown on both sides or make two slices of hot toast and then butter and fill. Serve on plate with knife and fork.

Sandwich fillings should be well-flavoured and easy to handle. Take filling right to edge of bread. Avoid foods that make bread soggy.

TIP
Most sandwiches can be frozen (for packed lunches, for example) if well wrapped, except for those with fillings made from salad, tomatoes, hard-boiled eggs and mayonnaise.

Use	With
Savoury	
Egg, hard-boiled, sliced or chopped or scrambled	Parsley, gherkin, tomato, cucumber, grilled crisp bacon
Cheese, sliced or grated Cottage cheese	Pickle, apple, tomato, onion, walnuts (chopped), gherkin, radish, carrot, chives
Cream cheese	As above, also chopped pineapple, raisins
Fish, cooked flaked/canned	Gherkins, cucumber, salad, mayonnaise
Meat, sliced or chopped finely	Chutney, horseradish (beef), mustard (beef and ham), watercress (chopped)
Chicken, sliced or minced	Ham, tomato, pineapple, salad
Pâté	Tomato, cucumber, salad
Sweet	
Apple	Celery, raisin, salad dressing
Banana	Honey, cinnamon
Peanut butter	Apple

To make bread you need:

1 Flour (see previous page).
2 Yeast A living plant which needs food (from sugar and flour) and warmth to grow, producing bubbles of carbon dioxide to raise and lighten the dough. Yeast works more quickly in warmth but dies at a high temperature so that when the bread is baked, rising stops. Freezing stops growth but does not kill yeast.
Fresh yeast Quick and easy, but often difficult to buy (try health food shops or bakers). Should be a putty-like creamy colour, firm and easy to break. Store in a loosely tied polythene bag, lidded glass jar, cling film or foil in the fridge, for up to 2 weeks; in the freezer in individual foil-wrapped ($\frac{1}{2}$ oz/15 g or 1 oz/25 g) cubes packed in a sealed container, for 4–6 weeks. To use, thaw at room temperature for 30 min. Never blend fresh yeast with sugar.
Dried yeast Available as small hard granules in tins and small sachets from grocers, chemists and health food stores. Follow maker's instructions. Yeast should froth up when added to the water. No froth means stale yeast: do not use. It keeps for 4 months in an airtight container. Transfer to a smaller container as yeast is used. 1 oz/25 g fresh yeast is equal to $\frac{1}{2}$ oz/15 g dried yeast. Yeast quantities vary according to the type of dough (bread). On average, use 1 oz/25 g fresh yeast ($\frac{1}{2}$ oz/15 g dried) to 3 lb/1.4 kg flour white; and 2 oz/50 g fresh yeast (1 oz/25 g dried) to 3 lb/1.4 kg wholemeal flour.
3 Salt, an essential for flavour; it also regulates action of yeast but too much can kill yeast.
4 Sugar to provide food for dried yeast.
5 Fat to enrich dough and add bulk; also delays staling, and improves softness and colour. Use butter, vegetable fat or lard.

> **TIP**
> **To cover dough, put a few drops of oil into polythene bag and crumple it up.**

Basic method

This is for white bread. Use the same method for wholemeal but double the yeast quantities, and increase water to about 1 pt/550 ml. Makes 2 small loaves.
1 Weigh out $1\frac{1}{2}$ lb/700 g strong plain flour, 2 tsp/10 ml salt, $\frac{1}{2}$ oz/15 g lard, all at room temperature.
2 Mix together flour and salt into a large bowl and rub in lard. (As for pastry, see p. 68.)

3 Either blend $\frac{1}{2}$ oz/15 g fresh yeast in $\frac{3}{4}$ pt/ 400 ml hand-hot water **or dissolve** 1 tsp/5 ml sugar in $\frac{3}{4}$ pt/400 ml tepid water and sprinkle on 2 tsp/10 ml dried yeast. Stir and leave for about 10 min until frothy.
4 Add yeast liquid to the dry mix and work to a firm dough with wooden spoon or fork, or hands. Dough should leave sides of bowl clean. Add a little flour if the mixture is too wet.
5 Knead dough for a well-risen loaf with an even crumb texture:
(a) by hand – on a lightly floured surface fold the dough towards you then push it down and away with the palm of the hand or knuckles, stretching and pummelling with a rocking movement. Give the dough a quarter turn and repeat process until the dough feels smooth and elastic (firm, not sticky). Takes about 10 min.

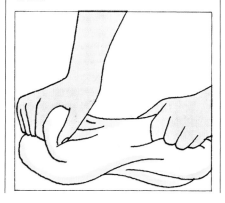

(b) by mixer – use dough hooks according to manufacturer's instructions. Place yeast liquid and dry ingredients in bowl, turn to lowest speed and mix 1–2 min to form dough. Increase speed slightly and mix for further 2 min to knead.
6 Shape kneaded dough into a ball and place in a large lightly oiled polythene bag, tied lightly, or leave in bowl inside oiled polythene bag or covered with cling film or damp tea cloth.

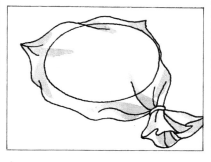

7 Leave to rise to twice its original size. The slower the rising the better.
45–60 min in a warm place (but too high temperature will kill yeast)
2 hrs at room temperature
12 hrs in cold room or larder
24 hrs in fridge.
8 Knock back the dough on a smooth surface; flatten with knuckles to reduce to original size.

9 Shape or mould the dough. Divide into two pieces, each as wide as the tin, and twice as long. Flatten each piece and fold in three, tucking the ends under to fit (well-greased) tin exactly. To avoid spoiling texture and colour of crust, do not use much flour. Place each tin in a lightly oiled polythene bag, tied loosely or with ends tucked under.

10 Prove (allow to rise for a second time) until the dough has doubled.
11 Remove polythene bags and bake in a hot oven, Mark 8/450°F/230°C for 30–40 min or until loaves shrink slightly from tin sides and crust is golden. Loaves should sound hollow when tapped underneath.
12 Cool the loaves (before storing), out of tin on wire rack.

> **TIP**
> **To freshen stale bread, place loaf tightly wrapped in foil in hot oven (Mark 8/ 450°F/230°C) for 5–10 min. Cool in foil. Serve while still warm.**

Meat

Meat is the most important (and most expensive) part of most families' diet. Master the secrets of cooking it properly and you are well on the way to being a good cook.

Food value

Meat is a prime body-building food, a good source of high-quality protein, also iron and B vitamins, and rich in fat (although the content varies according to type and cut).

Buying meat

Meat is expensive so it pays more than ever to shop wisely. The best place to buy is from a knowledgeable and friendly butcher who keeps a well-labelled display in a clean, orderly shop. Many supermarkets have a butchery counter, with wrapped meat labelled with the name of cut, weight and price. You can deliberate for as long as you like, but you may not get expert advice.

Prices vary with supply and demand. Tender, popular cuts are higher priced but cheaper tougher cuts have much the same food value, except that they usually contain more fat. Imported meat is usually less expensive than home-killed.

Quality and freshness

Colour is not a good guide. Meat only has a strong red colour if it has been recently *cut*. After some time meat goes browner, without loss of eating quality. The colour of the fat varies according to the breed of animal and its feed. In general look for finely textured meat with a little firm fat.

> **TIP**
> **Open-freeze cubed meat for casseroles, pack into polythene bags and use quantities as needed.**

Storage

Always take meat home and put in the fridge as soon as possible. Remove shop wrappers, and store meat on a clean plate in the coolest part of the fridge, which is the shelf just below the freezing compartment. Cover with foil or cling film. Joints should have wet surfaces wiped with kitchen paper before storing. Beef and lamb joints will keep for 3–5 days, pork for 2–4 days. Chops and steaks will keep for 2–3 days, mince for 1–2 days. Cooked meat will keep for 2–3 days in the fridge, but cover to prevent drying up.

Freezing

All meat must be well wrapped and sealed to exclude all air in thick polythene bags, heavy duty or double thickness foil, or freezer film.

Joints

Beef joints will keep for up to 1 year, lamb joints for up to 9 months, pork joints for up to 6 months. Thaw boned and rolled joints before cooking and joints to be pot-roasted and braised. Thawing times are as follows:

Weight	In fridge	Room temperature
less than 3 lb/1.4 kg	3–4 hrs per lb/450 g	1–2 hrs per lb/450 g
more than 3 lb/1.4 kg	6–7 hrs per lb/450 g	2–3 hrs per lb/450 g

Other joints can be cooked from frozen:

Beef	30–40 min per lb/450 g
Lamb	+ 30–40 min extra at Mark 4/350°F/180°C
Pork	40–45 min per lb/450 g + 40–45 min extra at Mark 5/375°F/190°C

Chops and steaks

Trim away surplus fat, and pack in usable quantities. Wrap individually in heavy duty or double layer foil, or freezer film, and then pack in polythene bag and seal, or interleave with freezer film, or polythene or waxed paper and overwrap; will keep for 9 months to 1 year. Mince and cubed stewing steak, etc, can be frozen in polythene bags or in plastic containers; mince will keep for about 3 months, stewing and braising meats for about 8–12 months.

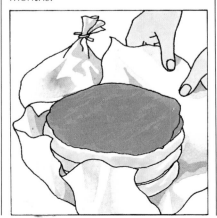

Cooking methods

Use our charts on the next pages for exact cooking times for different cuts. Roasting times are for 'slow' method which usually is better.

Roasting

This is only suitable for prime, tender cuts. Meat in the oven is heated by radiation and convection of the hot air. *Slow* roasting is cleaner, minimizes shrinkage, and gives better flavour. *Fast* roasting may be more convenient, but meat will shrink.

1 Weigh the meat and calculate the cooking time:

	Slow Mark 4/350°F 180°C	Fast Mark 7/425°F 220°C
Beef	20–25 min per lb/450 g + 20–25 min extra	15–20 min per lb/450 g + 20 min extra
Lamb	25–30 min per lb/450 g + 25–30 min extra	20–25 min per lb/450 g + 25 min extra
Pork	30–40 min per lb/450 g + 30–40 min extra	25–30 min per lb/450 g + 30 min extra

NOTE For Yorkshire pudding (see p. 72) with beef, use fast roasting method. When using automatic oven allow extra time for oven to reach correct temperature.

2 Tie or skewer into shape if necessary. Place meat on wire rack in roasting tin with fat (cooking oil, lard or dripping). Season with pepper and mustard and add herbs if liked, but no salt because this draws out the meat juices (except for pork: salt on skin makes crisp crackling).

3 Baste (spoon over) meat with the hot fat about every 20–30 min during cooking. *Enclosed* roasting in a meat dish with lid, parcel of foil or roasting bag needs no basting, keeps oven clean and gives a moister joint with soft, less-tasty outside. Cooking times are the same as above, and for a crisper, browner joint, open up for the last half hour.

Grilling

This cooks meat quickly with minimum fat by radiant heat under gas or electric grill. Use only for prime tender cuts.

1 Preheat grill.
2 Trim off excess fat.
3 Brush the meat and grill pan rack with cooking oil or melted fat. This helps browning and prevents meat drying out and sticking.
4 Season if liked.
5 Place meat underneath on grill pan when grill is at its hottest. Turn once during cooking.

Frying

Frying is suitable for tender cuts. Meat is cooked half-covered in shallow fat. Some fatty 'meats', such as bacon rashers and sausages, provide sufficient fat which melts during cooking, and therefore need no extra. Use a heavy frying-pan, saucepan or flameproof casserole. The type of fat you use affects the food flavour. Butter, margarine, dripping and olive oil give good flavour but start smoking at a lower temperature than cooking oils and fats, which are preferable.

1 Trim off excess fat, with scissors/sharp knife.
2 Heat enough fat in pan to reach half-way up sides of meat.
3 Test fat for correct temperature: a small piece of bread should brown in 15 seconds.
4 Put meat in fat, one piece at a time (use tongs and take care to avoid splashing).
5 Brown one side of each piece then turn over with tongs and brown the other side.
6 Reduce heat and fry gently until meat is cooked.

Pot roasting

This method is used for cheaper, less tender cuts that need moist, slow cooking, in a heavy pan or flameproof casserole on hotplate, or in an ovenproof casserole in oven. Use a well-fitting lid since meat cooks in its own steam.

1 Weigh meat and calculate cooking time:

Beef	30–40 min per lb/450 g + 30–40 min extra
Lamb	25–30 min per lb/450 g + 25–30 min extra
Pork	30–35 min per lb/450 g + 30–35 min extra.

2 Heat enough cooking oil, lard or dripping to cover bottom of a heavy pan.
3 Brown the meat all over (for improved colour and flavour). Vegetables can add extra taste: prepare according to kind and cut into large chunks and also brown in the fat, e.g. carrots, onions, swede, parsnip, celery. Season with salt, pepper and herbs.
4 (a) Reduce hotplate heat, cover pan and cook gently for calculated time or
(b) Transfer to casserole if necessary, cover and place in oven, Mark 4/350°F/180°C, for calculated time.
5 Turn joint occasionally but open pan for as little time as possible.
6 Remove meat (and vegetables) and pour off all but a little fat – use remaining fat and juices in pan to make gravy.

Braising

This is used for cheaper cuts, not sufficiently tender to roast, and is a combination of pot-roasting and stewing. Meat is cooked slowly in a covered container on a bed of root vegetables and herbs ('mirepoix') with a little liquid to provide steam. You need a heavy saucepan or flameproof casserole for hotplate cooking, or an ovenproof casserole for oven cooking. A well-fitting lid is essential to avoid loss of steam.

1 Trim off excess fat, weigh meat and calculate cooking time which is the same as for pot roasting.
2 Prepare vegetables of any mixture (potatoes, carrots, celery, swede, parsnip, turnip, onion, sliced or cubed).
3 Heat sufficient cooking oil or fat, lard or dripping to cover bottom of heavy pan. Brown meat all over to improve colour and flavour. Remove meat.
4 Lightly brown vegetables in same fat. Add sufficient stock to just cover and bring to the boil.
5 (a) Place meat on top of vegetables, cover, reduce heat and cook gently for calculated time or
(b) Transfer vegetables to casserole if necessary. Place meat on top of vegetables, cover and cook in oven, Mark 4/350°F/180°C, for calculated time.
6 Transfer meat to serving dish, keep warm.
7 Vegetables may either be served with meat, and remaining juices used to make gravy; or blended and used to thicken the juices as a gravy; or kept for a soup.

Stewing/casseroling

This uses cheaper, less tender cuts not suitable for other methods. The meat is covered in liquid, and vegetables and herbs are added for flavour. Cooking is done slowly on a hotplate in covered heavy pan or flameproof casserole (usually called a stew) or in a covered ovenproof casserole in the oven (usually called a casserole). Both need tight-fitting lids to prevent loss of steam and drying up.

1 Trim off excess fat and cut meat into individual portions, or into cubes (1 in/25 mm).
2 Prepare vegetables according to kind and slice or cube.
3 For a thicker stew, toss the meat in flour seasoned with salt and pepper.
4 (a) For a white stew (with a light colour) Put the meat into the pan along with vegetables and stock or water (about ½ pt/300 ml to each lb/450 g meat) or
(b) For a brown richer stew Heat a little cooking oil or fat, lard or dripping in the pan and brown the meat well all over. Add vegetables and brown for a few min longer. Add stock or water (amount as above).
5 Bring to the boil and cover.
6 Reduce heat and cook gently on hotplate or in oven, Mark 3/325°F/160°C, until tender:

Beef	2½–4 hrs
Lamb	1½–2½ hrs
Pork	2–3 hrs.

7 Adjust seasoning to taste.

TO MAKE GRAVY FOR A ROAST JOINT

1 Pour off all but 2 tbsp/30 ml of fat from roasting tin.
2 Stir in 1 tbsp/15 ml of plain flour. Cook, stirring well until brown.
3 Gradually stir in ½ pt/300 ml of hot vegetable water or stock.
4 Bring to the boil, stirring well, and season to taste.

Beef

Joints
Serve as a substantial main meal, Sunday lunch for example, and for entertaining.

Steaks
Use for main meals, special occasions and entertaining.

Stewing steak
Cut into pieces and use for casseroles, stews, pies, puddings and curries. Mince and use for spaghetti bolognese sauce, shepherd's pie, meat balls, hamburgers, etc.

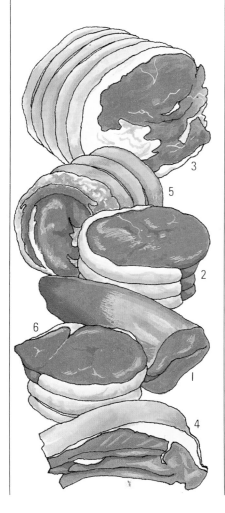

Cuts	Buying	Cooking	Serving
Joints			
1 Fillet Prime quality strip of meat (boneless) from beneath sirloin	Expensive, tender and lean. Sold whole. Allow 4–8 oz/125–225 g per person	*Roast* for 20–25 min per lb/450 g + 20–25 min extra	*Hot* and sliced with gravy, Yorkshire pudding, mustard, horseradish sauce. Roast and/or boiled vegetables or serve (hot or cold) with green salad
2 Topside Lean meat from hindquarter. Used for Boeuf Bourguignonne and Beef Olives	Economical, usually sold boned and rolled. Allow 5–8 oz/150–225 g per person	*Pot roasting* and *braising* are best, 30–40 min per lb/450 g + 30–40 min extra. Lacks flavour compared to e.g. sirloin. Or *roast*, 20–25 min per lb/450 g + 20–25 min extra	*Cold* with salad (mixed), mayonnaise, coleslaw, potato salad, etc, or with hot buttered vegetables *Cooked left-overs* Chop or mince to make shepherd's pie, pasties, rissoles
3 Sirloin Large joint from ribs, from hindquarter	Tender, good flavour. Can be bought on bone. Allow 7–12 oz/ 200–350 g per person. Or boned (fillet removed) and rolled. Allow 5–8 oz/150–225 g per person	*Roast* for 20–25 min per lb/450 g + 20–25 min extra	
4 Rib Large joint including rib bones, from forequarter	Fore-ribs are prime quality, back and top ribs are medium quality. Can be bought on bone. Allow 7–12 oz/200–350 g per person. Or boned: Allow 5–8 oz/150–225 g per person	Fore-rib: *roast* 20–25 min per lb/ 450 g + 20–25 min extra. Back and top ribs: *pot roast* or *braise* 30–40 min per lb/450 g + 30–40 min extra	As for fillet, topside and sirloin
5 Brisket Joint of coarse meat layered with fat – from forequarter	Economical, excellent flavour. Usually sold boned and rolled. Can be bought salted. (Soak overnight and rinse before cooking.) Allow 5–8 oz/150–225 g per person	*Braise* for 30–40 min per lb/450 g + 30–40 min extra. Or *boil*: joints up to 3 lb/1.4 kg, 30 min per lb/450 g + 30 min; joints over 3 lb/1.4 kg, 45 min per lb/450 g + 45 min	Try braising in cider, wine/stock, fruit juice (orange)/stock. *Serve hot* with: boiled potatoes, dumplings, boiled and/or braised vegetables; mustard, horseradish
6 Silverside Boneless joint from hindquarter	Should be lean. Can be bought salted. (Soak overnight and rinse before cooking.) Allow 5–8 oz/ 150–225 g per person	*Braise* for 30–40 min per lb/450 g + 30–40 min extra, or boil as for brisket	As for brisket or traditionally as 'boiled beef and carrots'
Steaks			
7 Fillet Undercut of sirloin, very lean, tender	Expensive, usually weigh 6–7 oz/ 175–200 g. Allow 1 steak per person	*Grill* for 7–12 min *Fry* for 7–10 min $\frac{3}{4}$–$1\frac{1}{4}$ in/2–3 cm thick medium rare	Traditionally served with parsley butter. Other suitable accompaniments: fried or baked potatoes, fried or grilled mushrooms, fried or grilled tomatoes, fried onion rings, mustard, horseradish sauce, watercress, dressed green salad
8 Rump Prime quality steak cut from next to sirloin. Use for Boeuf Stroganoff	Most common type usually sold in thicker slices than other cuts. Good flavour. Should have thick edge of fat. Allow 5–8 oz/175–225 g per person	*Grill* for 7–12 min *Fry* for 7–10 min $\frac{3}{4}$–$1\frac{1}{4}$ in/2–3 cm thick, medium rare	

Nos. in charts on this and following pages refer to illustrations.

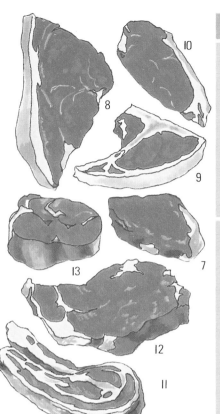

Cuts	Buying	Cooking	Serving
Steaks (continued) **9 Sirloin** Prime quality	Cut about 1 in/25 mm thick, called T-bone if left on bone. Allow 5–8 oz/150–225 g per person. Minute steak (from upper part of sirloin) very thin, weighs 4–6 oz/125–175 g. Should have little or no fat. Allow 1 steak per person	*Grill* for 7–12 min plus *Fry* for 7–10 min plus $\frac{3}{4}$–$1\frac{1}{4}$ in/2–3 cm thick, medium rare	As for fillet and rump
10 Entrecôte Cut from between ribs or sometimes from sirloin	Look for steaks about 1 in/25 mm thick. Allow 5–8 oz/150–225 g per person	*Grill* for 7–12 min plus *Fry* for 7–10 min plus $\frac{3}{4}$–$1\frac{1}{4}$ in/2–3 cm thick, medium rare	As for fillet and rump
Stewing steak **11 Flank/Skirt** Coarse-grained meat from belly	Usually bought ready cubed or minced. Allow 5–8 oz/150–225 g per person	*Stew* or *casserole* for $2\frac{1}{2}$–4 hrs	Vary flavour of casseroles by adding: fresh or tinned tomatoes; fresh or dried herbs/spices; root vegetable stocks. Commercially prepared sauces, e.g. Tabasco, Worcestershire or Soy sauce, mustard. *Toppings* Scones (cobbler), dumplings (plain or with herbs or spices), pastry. You can serve warm (herb/garlic) bread instead of potatoes. *Garnishes* Orange, pineapple or apple (in curry). Cream or yoghurt garnish can be stirred in just before serving (do not boil)
12 Chuck/blade Less tender cut from shoulder	Cheaper cut. Should be fairly lean, sold in slices or cubed. Allow 5–8 oz/150–225 g per person	*Stew* or *casserole* for 2 hrs minimum. *Braise* for 2 hrs minimum	
13 Legs and shin Very lean but tough cuts	Usually sold cubed or minced	*Stew* or *casserole* for 3–4 hrs minimum. *Braise* for 3–4 hrs minimum	

Veal

Roasting joints are not widely available. The commonest types of veal in the butcher's shop are escalopes and pie veal.

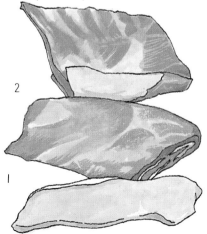

Cuts	Buying	Cooking	Serving
1 Escalopes Usually cut from the fillet, an expensive tender strip of meat. Use for special occasions and for entertaining	Thin slices with little or no fat. Butcher will beat them thin, or do at home with rolling-pin on board. Each escalope should weigh about 3 oz/75 g. Allow 1 per person	*Fry*, coated with beaten egg and breadcrumbs (see p. 37), for 8–10 min	Serve with grilled bacon rolls, tomatoes and/or mushrooms, fried/boiled potatoes, green vegetables/green salad, or with watercress/parsley butter/lemon slices. Or serve in sauces, e.g. wine, mushroom, tomato or mustard. Or after frying, top with slice of ham and grated cheese and place under grill until cheese is melted
2 Pie veal or stewing veal is for stews and casseroles, pies and puddings	Economically priced small offcuts of breast, shoulder, neck and knuckle sold cut into cubes or pieces ready for use	*Stew* or *casserole* for 2–3 hrs	Before serving, stir cream or egg yolks into casseroles, ragouts, etc, but do not boil. Use for vol-au-vent (pastry cases) filling. Serve pies hot or cold with green vegetables/green salad. *Fillings* Mix veal with bacon, liver or sausage meat. *Toppings* for pie: shortcrust, hot water crust or puff/flaky pastry.

Pork

Pork must always be well cooked; season well and do not add extra fat.

Joints

Serve whole as substantial meal for Sunday lunch, entertaining etc, or cut in cubes for casseroles.

Chops/cutlets

Serve for midweek main meals and grills.

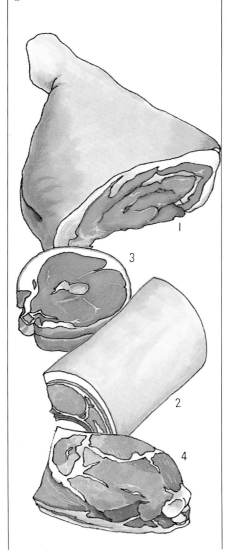

Cuts	Buying	Cooking	Serving
Joints			
1 Leg Large joint of lean meat	Usually sold cut into 2 pieces, or can be boned and rolled (give butcher notice). Allow 8–12 oz/ 225–350 g per person (with bone). Ask butcher to score skin well, for good crackling	Roast for 35–40 min per lb/450 g + 35–40 min extra. Stew or casserole for 2–3 hrs	Hot roast slices with: apple sauce, gravy (thin). Roast and/or boiled vegetables. Cranberry/red currant jelly. Grilled tomatoes/mushrooms. Stuffings Sage and onion; apple and raisin. Garnishes Fried apple rings, watercress.
2 Loin Prime cut often including kidney	Expensive, but superb. Look for thin layer of fat (½ in/15 mm), not a thick white coating. Usually bought on bone – ask butcher to 'chine' (loosen thick end of bone to assist carving). Can be boned and stuffed. Skin must be well scored (see above). Allow 8–12 oz/ 225–350 g per person (with bone)	Roast for 35–40 min per lb/450 g + 35–40 min extra	Cold with chutney/pickle, apple sauce, various salads, buttered new potatoes. To vary seasoning: cut off rind and rub fatty side with salt/pepper/ mustard mix or salt/pepper and rosemary before cooking
3 Fillet Lean cut from top of hind leg	Most expensive cut, very tender with no fat or skin, so no waste	Roast for 30–35 min per lb/450 g + 30–35 min extra. Grill for 3–5 min. Fry for 3–5 min. Stew for 2–3 hrs	Coat fillet steaks in egg and breadcrumbs, before frying. Garnish Fried apple rings
4 Bladebone Cut from top of foreleg	Buy on bone for good flavour. Or ask butcher to bone ready for stuffing. Allow 8–12 oz/225–350 g per person (with bone)	Roast for 30–35 min per lb/450 g + 30–35 min extra. Pot roast, 30–35 min per lb/ 450 g + 30–35 min extra	To make crispy crackling: score skin well – use sharp point of knife to cut slits. Salt well. Do not add fat
5 Spare rib Collar. Cut off bone for casseroles and pies, etc	Economical, with good flavour, tender and quite lean	Roast for 30–35 min per lb/450 g + 30–35 min extra. Pot roast, 30–35 min per lb/ 450 g + 30–35 min extra. Stew/casserole for 2–3 hrs	Try Chinese style with: bean sprouts/bamboo shoots/soy sauce/ vinegar/peppers. Serve with rice
6 Hand and spring Foreleg	Excellent flavour and very economical. Look for large joint (preferably over 3 lb/1.4 kg) with plenty of meat at thick end, thin layer of fat. Score well to give plenty of crackling. Can be boned and stuffed. Allow about 12 oz/ 350 g per person (with bone)	Roast for 30–35 min per lb/450 g + 30–35 min extra. Braise for 30–35 min per lb/ 450 g + 30–35 min extra	Add chopped apples and rosemary to the bed of vegetables when braising
7 Belly Fatty cut but sweet. Can be bought sliced as rashers	Very economical. Look for thick cut of belly with good layers of meat and fat. Score skin for good crackling	Roast for 30–35 min per lb/450 g + 30–35 min extra. Braise for 30 min per lb/450 g + 30 min extra. Grill rashers 10–15 min. Fry rashers 10–15 min	When braising, try apple juice instead of stock

Cuts	Buying	Cooking	Serving
Chops/cutlets			
8 Chops Cut from loin	Chump chops and loin chops often have a piece of kidney in them. Allow 1 chop per person	*Grill* for 15–20 min. *Fry* for 15 min	Serve with apple sauce, cranberry/red currant sauce, fried/boiled potatoes, green vegetables, green salad, grilled tomatoes/mushrooms.
	Spare-rib chops have little or no bone – economical, tasty buy. Allow 1 chop per person	*Grill* for 15–20 min. *Fry* for 15 min. *Braise* for ¾–1 hr. *Roast* in foil for ¾–1 hr	*To stuff thick chump or loin chops:* slit to the bone to make a pocket for stuffing, e.g. sage and onion; apple and rosemary. Close filled pocket with wooden cocktail stick
9 Spare ribs Cut from belly	Look for ribs in one piece – with meat between ribs. Allow 8 oz/225 g per person. The ribs are separated before cooking	*Grill* for 15–20 min (must be charred). *Roast* for 1 hr at Mark 6/400°F/200°C on rack in roasting tin, and baste every 15 min with marinade	*Marinade* before cooking, and baste with sauce during cooking. To make marinade mix 2 tbs/30 ml of vinegar or lemon juice, cooking oil, and tomato purée with ¼ pt/150 ml white wine. Season and add crushed garlic if wished. For a sweet sauce add honey, brown sugar or jam

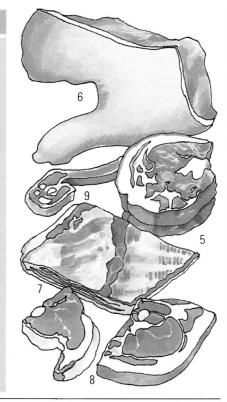

Cuts	Buying	Cooking	Serving
Bacon joints			
Gammon (1) Hind leg, very large prime joint – often called ham	Sold whole (weighing 12–14 lb/5–6 kg) or cut in pieces: *middle gammon* (best); *corner gammon* and *slipper* (triangular pieces); *knuckle* (end piece). Allow 7–12 oz/200–350 g per person on bone, 5–8 oz/150–225 g per person off bone	*Roast* for 20 min per lb/450 g + 20 min extra. *Boil* for 20 min per lb/450 g + 20 min extra. *Braise* for 35 min per lb/450 g + 35 min extra. *Casserole* (especially slipper) for 1–1½ hrs	*Hot* with roast potatoes/fried potatoes/boiled new potatoes/green vegetables, gravy/white sauce, red currant jelly *Cold* with hot buttered potatoes and vegetables. Or with various salads (e.g. wrap slices round asparagus). Good for picnics (sandwiches)
Middle cut From back – often called 'throughcut'	Reasonably priced. Good lean cut, often sold rolled. Allow 5–8 oz/150–225 g per person	As above	*For a change* Boil in apple juice. Remove rind and roast joint – ½ hr before end of cooking, coat fat with crushed pineapple, demerara sugar or honey
Forehock (2) Front leg	Inexpensive when bought whole with bone. Often sold as foreslipper (fairly fatty), middle cut and butt or knuckle both very economical. Can be boned and rolled. Allow 7–12 oz/200–350 g per person (on bone), 5–8 oz/150–225 g per person (off bone)	*Roast* for 20 min per lb/450 g + 20 min extra. *Boil* for 20 min per lb/450 g + 20 min extra	*Left-overs* Use for bacon in the hole' (batter), omelettes, quiches (flans) in flavoured white sauce with rice or noodles *Garnishes* Pineapple rings, orange slices, fried apple rings or wedges, watercress. Cut off rind and coat fat with breadcrumbs or crushed cornflakes

Bacon

Bacon, available smoked or unsmoked, comes from the cured (salted) meat of specially bred pigs. There is usually little waste because most cuts are boneless.

Buying bacon

Smoked bacon is milder, and less salty than unsmoked, with a better (firmer) texture, and pinker colour with distinct smoky flavour and smell. Buy from a shop with a good turnover, as bacon dries very fast after cutting. Bacon which looks dry and a dark colour is probably stale. Specially-cured bacon is sold in vacuum packs. These should be tight and intact, not loose.

Storage

In the fridge, fresh joints wrapped in foil or cling film will keep for 5–7 days; fresh rashers/steaks/chops

wrapped in foil or cling film, for
7–10 days; vacuum-packed joints
and rashers, for 1 week (once
opened 4–5 days); boil-in-the-bag,
for 3–5 days.

Freezing

The bacon must be fresh. Do not
wrap in foil as salt may make tiny
holes in the aluminium. Use freezer
film or polythene. Vacuum packs can
be frozen as they are. Smoked and
unsmoked joints keep for 3 months;
vacuum-packed for 4 months;
cooked for 1 month. Smoked and
unsmoked rashers, steaks and chops
keep for 1 month; vacuum-packed
for 3 months. Cooked bacon can be
frozen but it dries out and loses
flavour fast. Cooked casseroles keep
for 1 month.

Soaking joints

To remove salt either (a) soak for
1–3 hrs in plenty of cold water, or
(b) place meat in a large pan, cover
with cold water and bring slowly to
the boil. Discard water and cook
joint as normal (dry before roasting).

Cooking methods

Bacon can be roasted, braised, fried
or grilled, see general methods, p. 27.

Boiling

Use heavy pan with tight-fitting lid.
1 **Weigh joint** and calculate cooking time:
20 min per lb/450 g plus 20 min extra.
2 **Place meat** in pan and cover with cold
water. Bring slowly to the boil.
3 **For unsoaked** joints, discard water and
cover with fresh cold water.
4 **Bring** slowly to the boil again.
5 **Reduce heat,** cover and simmer gently for
calculated time, topping up with boiling water
during cooking if necessary.
Do not allow bacon joint to cool in the liquid.

Baking

Calculate cooking time as for boiling and then
follow steps 1–5, but only simmer for half the
cooking time.
6 **Remove joint** from pan, wrap in foil and
place on baking tray.
7 **Cook** in preheated oven, Mark 5/375°F/
190°C, for rest of cooking time.

Cuts	Buying	Cooking	Serving
Bacon joints (continued) **Collar (3)** From behind neck	Sold as *prime collar* (better part) or *end collar* (inexpensive). Allow quantities as for forehock	*Roast* (prime) for 20 min per lb/ 450 g + 20 min extra. *Boil* for 20 min per lb/450 g + 20 min extra. *Braise* for 35 min per lb/450 g + 35 min extra. *Casserole* for 1–1½ hrs	As for gammon, middle cut, back and forehock
Streaky Thin layers of lean and fat from belly	Economical – more fat in proportion to meat than other cuts. Can be bought in slices	*Boil* for 20 min per lb/450 g + 20 min extra. *Roast* without adding fat for 20 min per lb/450 g + 20 min extra	As for gammon, middle cut, back and forehock piece. Slices: form circles, secure ends with wooden cocktail stick, filling with stuffing
Chops/steaks/rashers			
Chops Cut from back	Usually ¼–½ in/½–1 cm thick – or thicker. Good value. Choose lean ones. Allow 1 per person	*Grill* for 10–15 min. *Fry* for 7–12 min	Serve with pineapple slices, fried apple rings, banana, onion sauce.
Gammon steaks (4) From hind leg and Collar steaks from collar (behind neck)	Should not be less than ¼ in/½ cm thick. Allow 1 per person	*Grill* for 10–15 min. *Fry* for 7–12 min. Snip rind with scissors at regular intervals to prevent curling	As above
Back (5) Prime rashers	Most expensive. Allow 1–2 rashers per person	*Fry* Arrange in pan (with little or no fat), lean parts lying on top of fat on next rasher *Grill* Arrange fat parts lying on top of lean part of next rasher. 1–3 min each side depending on thickness	Serve with fried egg, fried/grilled tomatoes and mushrooms. As part of mixed grill. In flans (cooked and chopped) or omelette. With corn fritters and fried banana. On toast, toasted sandwiches
Middle cut (6) (Throughcut) long rashers, back and streaky joined	More economical. Allow 1–2 rashers per person		
Streaky (7) Thin rashers cut out of streaky joint	More economical, more fatty	*Fry* Preferably without fat. Place in cold pan and heat until sizzling with fat running out. *Grill* until crisp, about 2 min each side	As above or good for garnish – roll up and grill to make bacon rolls/curls. Use cooked and chopped to fill jacket potatoes, in omelette, savoury flan.

Chops/steaks/rashers

Use chops for a light meal or supper
midweek; steaks for a main meal or
entertaining; rashers for breakfast,
lunch or snacks.

Bacon and ham joints

Use for: entertaining (gammon if
large-scale), Christmas, substantial
family meals, Sunday lunch and cut
up for kebabs, casseroles, stews
and pies.

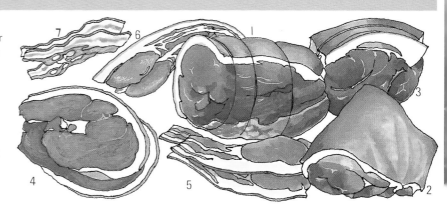

Lamb

Joints
Serve whole as a substantial meal for Sunday lunch, entertaining, etc, or cut in cubes for pies, stews, casseroles, curries and kebabs.

Chops/cutlets
Use for main meals and grills.

Stewing lamb
Cut in pieces and use for casseroles (e.g. Irish stew, Lancashire Hot Pot) and broth.

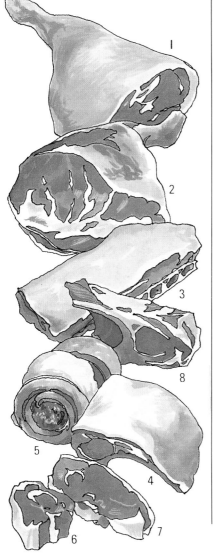

Cuts	Buying	Cooking	Serving
Joints			
1 Leg Lean meat, can be small or large. Use for kebabs	Tender. Expensive but good buy. Look for thin outside layer of firm fat. Can be bought boned, ready for stuffing (give butcher notice). Allow 8–12 oz/225–350 g per person (on bone), 5–8 oz/150–225 g per person (off bone)	*Roast* for 25–30 min per lb/450 g + 25–30 min extra. *Casserole* (cut in cubes) for 1½–2 hrs. *Braise* for ¾–1½ hrs. *Grill* for 10–15 min (cubed as kebabs)	*Hot*, sliced with gravy, mint sauce or jelly, redcurrant jelly, onion sauce, new potatoes, buttered carrots and other vegetables. *Garnishes* Watercress, orange slices. *Cold* with salads *Left-overs* Chop or mince to make pasties, moussaka, pie fillings (with flavoured white sauce).
2 Shoulder Large joint of sweet meat, interlayered with thin fat. Use for kebabs	Economical, often with more flavour than leg. Difficult to carve: use a sharp knife. Can be bought whole, or boned for stuffing (give butcher notice), or as a half shoulder. Allow 8–12 oz/225–350 g per person (on bone), 5–8 oz/150–225 g per person (off bone)	*Roast* for 25–30 min per lb/450 g + 25–30 min extra. *Stew* for 1½–2 hrs. *Braise* for ¾–1½ hrs. *Grill* for 10–15 min (cubed as kebabs)	*Stuffings* for boned or rolled joints: sage and onion; apricot and walnut; orange; date and apple
3 Loin Prime cut from middle of back (saddle)	Can be bought on bone or boned and rolled (with stuffing). Allow 8–12 oz/225–350 g per person (on bone), 5–8 oz/150–225 g per person (off bone)	*Roast* for 25–30 min per lb/450 g + 25–30 min extra	As for leg and shoulder
4 Best end of neck Cut from next to loin. Use for Crown Roast and Guard of Honour	Needs thorough cooking to melt fat throughout. Very good flavour. Allow 8–12 oz/225–350 g per person	*Roast* for 30–35 min per lb/450 g + 30–35 min extra	As for leg and shoulder
5 Breast Fatty cut of good flavour	Good amount of fat and bone. Usually cheaper. Bone, stuff and roll. Allow 8–12 oz/225–350 g per person	*Roast* for 30–35 min per lb/450 g + 30–35 min extra	As for leg and shoulder
Chops/cutlets			
6, 7 Chops Cut from loin	*Loin* chops have small T-shaped bone. *Chump* are meatier with small round bone. Allow 1–2 chops per person	*Grill* for 10–15 min. *Fry* for 10–15 min. *Braise* for ¾–1 hr	*Hot* with mint sauce/jelly, fried or baked potatoes, grilled or fried mushrooms, grilled or fried tomatoes, watercress, buttered new vegetables, parsley butter, salad (green). *Cold* with salads.
Cutlets Cut from best end of neck. Good for mixed grills	Have a long curved bone with an 'eye' of lean meat. Allow 1–2 cutlets per person	*Grill* for 7–10 min. *Fry* for 8–10 min	Cutlets, being easy to eat, are good for picnics
Stewing lamb			
8 Middle and scrag end of neck	Cheaper cuts. Much fat and bone but good flavour	*Stew* or *casserole* for 1½–2½ hrs. *Pot roast* for 25–30 min per lb/450 g + 25–30 min extra	For casserole ideas, see beef. For toppings, see beef, plus chopped mint for flavour. *Garnish* with cream or yoghurt: swirl in before serving (do not boil)

Liver

Liver is an excellent source of protein, iron and vitamin A.
Allow 4–6 oz/125–175 g per person.
Store in fridge on covered plate, 1–2 days.
Freeze in usable quantities, raw or cooked as casserole for 3 months. Thaw before cooking.
Prepare by washing well and drying. Remove any large tubes and cut into thin slices.
Serve fried (toss first in seasoned flour and add onions and herbs), or grilled as main meal with bacon rashers, and grilled/fried tomatoes, or include in mixed grill. Try frying thin slivers with chopped onion and stir in lemon/orange juice and chopped parsley. As an alternative to potatoes serve with buttered noodles or green salad.

TIP
Liver is easier to slice while partially frozen.

Kidneys

Kidneys have a similar food value to liver.
Store in fridge on covered plate, 1 day.
Freeze raw or cooked as casserole for 2–3 months.
Prepare by removing thick surrounding layer of fat (if any) and peel off transparent skin. Cut kidneys in half along their length, and cut out the 'core' in the middle.
Serve stewed with steak and onions in traditional puddings or pies or as part of a mixed grill or in sauce on toast, or with rice or noodles or curried. Grilled kidneys and bacon make a good breakfast dish.

Sausages

Sausages make substantial, economical speedy meals or snacks.
Buying sausages
Pork are the most expensive but usually taste better. Best quality (premium) with a high proportion of meat will cost a little more but are worth it.

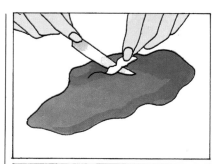
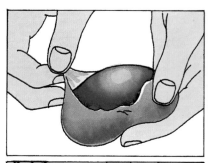
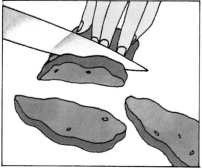

Liver

Calf's	The best and the most expensive with a delicate flavour	Grill, fry, stew, casserole, braise
Lamb's	Cheaper with a slightly stronger flavour	As above
Pig's	Strong flavour, softer texture, good for pâté	Stew or casserole
Ox	The cheapest with a strong flavour, coarse texture	Stew or casserole
Chicken's	Not always available unless frozen	Good for pâté

Kidneys

Lamb's	Best, good flavour	Grill or fry whole or halved
Pig's	Larger than lamb's, not so tender	Grill, fry, stew or casserole
Calf's and Ox	Cheapest, very strong flavour	Stew or casserole

Beef are less expensive with a different, stronger taste. Also available is a mixture of beef and pork.
Some sausages are strongly flavoured with herbs. You get about 8 large sausages to the lb/500 g, and 16 small ones, called chipolatas. Skinless sausages cook quickly, with a drier texture and are good for casseroles.
Allow about 4 oz/125 g per person.
Sausagemeat can be used for stuffing, 'toad-in-the-hole' (sausage in batter), sausage rolls, scotch eggs and pies.
Storage Sausages will keep in fridge if wrapped for up to 5 days if fresh; if packed, follow sell-by/use-by date.
Freeze meal-sized quantities, interleaved with freezer film, polythene or waxed paper and overwrapped. It is best to thaw before cooking. Otherwise, grill gently under low heat.
To cook Never pierce skins, because juices escape. Fry or grill (medium heat), turning occasionally with tongs to brown evenly. Allow 10–20

min, according to thickness. Alternatively bake in greased roasting pan in oven at Mark 6/ 400°F/200°C for 20–30 min (useful when cooking large quantities).
Serve hot with vegetables, or as hot dog (long roll with fried onions) or cook in batter as Toad-in-the-Hole or add to a mixed grill. Good cold for picnics.

Beefburgers

Beefburgers (also called hamburgers) are flat cakes of minced beefsteak.
Allow 1–2 per person.
Store wrapped in fridge for 2–3 days if fresh; if packed, follow sell-by/ use-by date.
Freeze interleaved with freezer film, polythene or waxed paper and overwrapped for up to 3 months.
To cook Fry or grill until done to liking (from rare to well done). Time depends on thickness.
Serve with fried potatoes, fried or grilled tomatoes and/or mushrooms; or as part of a mixed grill; or in flat bread rolls with fried onions (with relish, mustard and/or ketchup).

Poultry

Poultry includes chicken, turkey, goose and duck and is readily available all year round. It is economical and versatile with little fat but lots of bones.

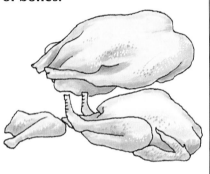

Food value
Poultry is an excellent source of protein.

Buying poultry
Younger, more tender birds have flexible breastbones and wing tips, and feet, and smooth legs, with plump breasts and legs and little fat. Before cooking, always wash well inside and out under running water, and dry thoroughly.

Storage
Poultry keeps fresh wrapped loosely in fridge for 3 days, but store giblets (innards) separately for 1–2 days. Keeps cooked for 1–4 days, covered.

Freezing
Only freeze freshly killed poultry (keep only 4–6 hrs before freezing). Freeze giblets separately (3 months). Home-frozen chicken keeps 12 months, turkey for 6 months. Or store ready-frozen (with giblets inside for 3 months. *Always* thaw poultry completely in original wrapping before cooking.

Type	Buying	Cooking	Serving
Chicken			
Roasting About 8 months old. Use for Sunday lunch, main meal	Weight ranges from 3–5½ lb/ 1.4–2.4 kg. To serve 4, buy 3 lb/ 1.4 kg or allow 12 oz/350 g per person. To serve 6, choose 5 lb/ 2.3 kg	*Roast* for 20 min per lb/450 g + 20 min extra	*Hot* with gravy, bread sauce, bacon rolls, chipolata sausages, seasonal vegetables, roast/fried potatoes, boiled potatoes, stuffing *To roast:* add flavour – put garlic clove/lemon wedge/bunch fresh herbs in cavity.
Boiling Elderly laying hen over 1 year old	Weight ranges from 4–8 lb/ 1.8–3.6 kg. Allow 12 oz/350 g per person. Excellent flavour, less tender	*Braise* for 1½ hrs. *Roast* for 20 min per lb/450 g + 20 min extra – but boil 1 hr first	*Season* with herbs: tarragon, rosemary, marjoram, lemon juice. *Left-overs* can be used to make stuffed pancakes, or in sauces (curry) or quiche. Use giblets to make gravy.
Capon Specially fattened chickens. Traditionally served at Christmas	Tend to be seasonal (Christmas). Weight ranges from 5–8 lb/ 2.3–3.6 kg. Serves 6–8	*Roast* for 20 min per lb/450 g + 20 min extra	*Stuffing* A stuffed bird will take longer to cook, do not pack too tightly. E.g. parsley and thyme, raisin and celery.
Poussin Baby chicken, 4–6 weeks old. Use for special entertaining	Weight ranges from 2–2½ lb/ 900 kg. Allow 1 per person if small. Cut 1 in half to serve 2, if large	*Roast* for 20 min per lb/450 g + 20 min extra. *Grill* for 10–20 min. *Deep fry* for about 15 min	Use carcass (raw or cooked) for soup/stock. *Cold* with salad, mayonnaise, or 'chaudfroid' (cooked with jellied sauce)
Spring/Frying 6–7 weeks old	Weight ranges from 2–3½ lb/ 900–1.6 kg. Allow 1 for 3 persons	*Roast* for 20 min per lb/450 g + 20 min extra. *Fry* (jointed) for 10–15 min	As for roast chicken
Joints Use for substantial casseroles	Quarters, breasts, drumsticks, wings, thighs. Allow 1 joint per person (but 2 drumsticks or thighs)	*Deep fry* for 15–20 min. *Shallow fry* for 15–20 min/side. *Grill* for 10–20 min. *Casserole* for 30–40 min	Dip in beaten egg and breadcrumbs (or batter) before frying. Serve with bread/tomato/ mushroom sauce, green salad, fried potatoes. Fried/grilled tomatoes/mushrooms, etc, or fruit such as peaches
Turkey Traditional Christmas bird	Weight ranges from 5–15 lb/ 2.3–6.8 kg. Allow 6–8 lb/2.1–3.6 kg for 8–12 persons, 10 lb/4.5 kg plus for 13–15 persons	*Roast* for 10–15 min per lb/450 g + 10–15 min extra	As for roast chicken plus cranberry sauce, chestnut stuffing (neck only, not cavity)
Turkey joints	Breast, thigh, wing, drumstick. Allow 1 joint per person	*Deep fry* for 15 min/side. *Shallow fry* for 15 min/side. *Grill* for 15 min/side. *Casserole* for 40–50 min	As for chicken. Cranberry/red currant jelly can be stirred into casseroles
Duckling Birds are 6 weeks to 3 months old, served for special meals	Buy birds of 3 lb/1.4 kg weight or more, because of high proportion of bone and fat. Allow 1 lb/450 g per person	*Roast* for 30 min per lb/450 g + 30 min, adding no fat, or joint and cook as casserole	Serve with apple sauce, orange sauce or cherries. *Stuffing* Sage and onion

Fish

Are you making the most of fish? Most types offer good value for money and make convenient meals, being quick to cook with little loss of weight.

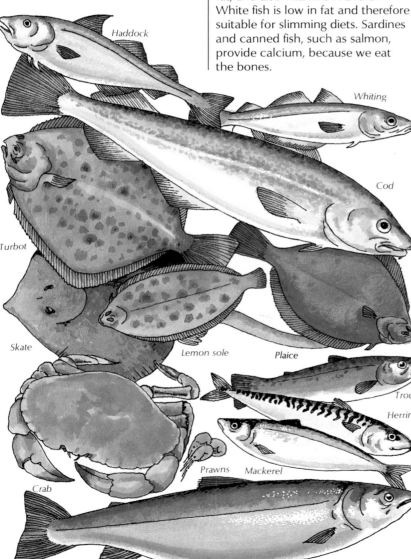

Haddock

Whiting

Cod

Turbot

Skate

Lemon sole

Plaice

Trout

Herring

Prawns Mackerel

Crab

Salmon

Fish types

These include white, oily and smoked fish, and shellfish. They can be fresh, or frozen (including boil-in-the-bag), canned or vacuum-packed (used for smoked fish).

Food value

Fish is an excellent source of protein containing only a little less than meat. Oily fish is a good source of fat, and also vitamins A and D. White fish is low in fat and therefore suitable for slimming diets. Sardines and canned fish, such as salmon, provide calcium, because we eat the bones.

Buying fish

A port is the ideal place to buy fish, but at fishmongers and supermarkets everywhere, you can find fish fresh or frozen; or filleted (with bones removed); or cut into cutlets or steaks (sections cut through the whole fish, including the middle bone). Buy from a clean, cool shop, with fresh water running over the display if possible. Whole fish should have bright clear eyes, bright firm scales (flaking scales are a sign of staleness) and red gills. Fish should smell pleasant and wholesome. The flesh of whole fish and of fillets should be firm and elastic, not flabby or watery, so that when pressed with a finger, there should be no impression left on the flesh. There should be no blood clots or dark patches, and smoked fish should be bright and glossy. The shells of lobster, prawns, and crab should be bright and hard; those of mussels and oysters should be closed, or should close when tapped.

Storage

Fresh fish should preferably be eaten on the day it is bought. Otherwise store in the refrigerator on a shelf under the freezing compartment, for 1 day. Smoked fish and Dover sole will keep for 2–3 days. Cover to prevent drying and the smell from affecting other foods.

Freezing

For home freezing, fish must be freshly caught. Bought fish has probably been frozen on its journey from a port: do not refreeze. Commercial quick-freeze methods are better than domestic freezing which tends to leave fish runny and flabby on thawing. Frozen fish keeps for about 3 months.

Preparing

Frozen fish or fish packed in supermarkets has always been cleaned and often filleted. Your fishmonger will usually clean and fillet your fish at no extra cost.

To fillet

Use a sharp knife with a thin blade to take the fish off the bones.
From flat fish, e.g. plaice: cut 4 fillets (2 from each side). First cut down backbone. Working from head to tail, cut and ease away left fillet; turn fish round and cut off other fillet from tail to head. Repeat on other side.
From round fish, like haddock cut 2 fillets. Cut down backbone. Ease fillet away with point of knife. Turn fish over, repeat.
Herring and mackerel are served whole. Cut off head, tail and fins; cut fish open on underside, remove insides, and remove inner skin by rubbing with fingers dipped in salt. Place fish on board, cut side down, press gently with fingers down back to loosen bone. Turn fish over and ease backbone away with fingers – removing as many small bones as possible.

Scaling

Remove scales by scraping them under water from tail to head, with blunt edge of knife.

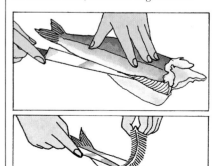

Skinning fillets

Place fillet on a board, skin side down. Hold corner of skin down firmly. Dip your fingers in salt to prevent slipping. Using a sharp knife, work from this corner with a sawing action, (not too heavily or you may cut the skin) holding the flat blade against the fish flesh.

Coating fish with egg and breadcrumbs

Use dishes large enough to take comfortably the foods to be coated, one piece at a time. Dip fish piece first in a bowl of beaten egg, then, using fingers, fork or tongs, lift out and allow excess egg to drain back into bowl. Place in bowl of breadcrumbs and turn to coat all over, then lift out, gently shaking so excess crumbs fall away. Egg and breadcrumb coating can be used for other foods before frying, such as veal escalopes and rissoles. **Batter coating** for fried fish (see p. 71). Chips are described on p. 43.

Cooking methods

In general, fish needs little cooking. When cooked, fish flakes easily, and translucent flesh turns opaque. For exact cooking times for different types, see our chart.

Shallow frying

Suitable for fillets, steaks and cutlets, small whole fish, shellfish and fish cakes. Use a heavy pan and cooking oil or a mixture of oil and butter (half and half) for better flavour. Before frying, fish can be coated with seasoned flour, oatmeal, or beaten egg and breadcrumbs.
1 Heat fat/oil in pan – use enough to come half-way up the sides of the fish.
2 Test fat for correct temperature: a small piece of bread should brown in 15 seconds.
3 Put fish in the fat, one piece at a time, fleshy side down, carefully using tongs or slice to prevent splashing.
4 Brown on fleshy side then turn over using fish slice or spatula to avoid breaking fish and brown on skin side.
5 Reduce heat and fry gently until fish is cooked.
6 Drain on crumpled kitchen paper.

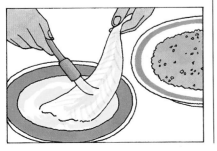

Deep frying

Deep frying can be used for fillets, small whole fish and for shellfish. Use a heavy deep pan and cooking oil. Before frying, the fish is usually coated with batter (see p. 71) or beaten egg and breadcrumbs.
1 Heat enough oil in pan to come one-third of way up side.
2 Test fat for correct temperature – 1 in/2½ cm cube of bread should brown in 1 min. Or to be safer use a thermometer: 370°F/188°C. If fat is too cool, fish will be soggy; if too hot, outside will brown before inside is cooked.
3 Lower fish carefully into fat (a little at a time to avoid lowering temperature) and cook until golden brown.
4 Lift out with a draining spoon and drain on crumpled kitchen paper.

Grilling

Used for fillets, steaks, cutlets, small whole fish and shellfish.
1 Brush fish and the bars of grill pan rack generously with melted butter.
2 Make shallow slits in the skins of whole fish to prevent splitting during cooking.
3 Preheat grill and put fish under on pan.
4 Turn once during cooking, using fish slice or spatula, and baste occasionally, with the butter.

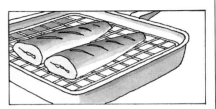

Fish type	Buying	Cooking	Serving
White			
Cod	Available all year, sold whole if small, or as fillets or steaks/cutlets. White flesh with not much flavour. Allow 6–8 oz/175–225 g per person or 1 steak 1 in/25 mm thick	*Shallow fry/grill* for 5–6 min each side (fillets/steaks). *Deep fry* for 5–10 min (fillets/steaks). *Bake* for 10–20 min (fillets), 20 min (steaks), 10–15 min per lb/450 g (whole).	For lunch and family meals, serve fillets or steaks with sauce. Or fry white fish with chips. Or use for fish pie. *To fry* white fish, dip in batter or in egg and breadcrumbs.
Haddock	Available all year, but best Sept–Feb. Sold whole if small or as fillets or steaks/cutlets. Firmer flesh, more delicate. Also sold smoked. Allow as for cod	*Poach* for 20 min (fillets/steaks), 10–15 min per lb/450 g (whole). *Steam* for 10–15 min (fillets/steaks). *Stew* for 10–30 min	*Sauces* Tartare for fried white fish; or tomato, or cheese, or parsley, or hollandaise with fillets or steaks. *Garnishes* Lemon wedges or slices, or chopped parsley or other herbs. *Stuffings* for steaks (remove bone) or rolled fillets include cheese and tomato, or chopped herbs, or eggs and parsley. Cube white fish for casseroles, sauces and curries. *Fish Florentine* is cooked white fish on a bed of spinach topped with cheese sauce. *Serve* white and oily fish with boiled new or fried potatoes, carrots, beans, broccoli, peas, creamed vegetables (spinach, sweetcorn, rice, salad)
Turbot	Available all year but best April–Aug. Flat fish sold whole or as fillets, steaks/cutlets. Creamy flesh, good flavour. Allow 1 per person if small or as for cod		
Hake	Best from June–Jan. Fillets, steaks/cutlets. Closer, whiter flesh – better flavour. More expensive. Does not keep well. Allow as for cod	*Shallow fry/grill* for 5–6 min each side. *Deep fry* for 5–10 min. *Bake* for 10–20 min (fillets), 20 min (steak). *Poach* for 20 min. *Steam* for 10–15 min. *Stew* for 10–30 min	
Coley/Saithe	Available all year. Fillets, steaks/cutlets. Pink/grey flesh turns white when cooked. Tends to be dry. Allow as for cod		
Huss/Rock Salmon	Available all year. Fillets, steaks/cutlets. Sold skinned. Pinkish flesh. Good with strong flavours. Allow as for cod	As for hake	As for cod

Steaming

This can be done in a perforated steamer on top of a pan of boiling water; or on the top of boiling vegetables; or on the rack of a fish kettle (see p. 14) with a little water in bottom; or on a covered buttered plate on a pan of boiling water. A gentle cooking method, good for retaining flavour and juices, and very suitable for children and invalids. Use for fillets or for whole fish.

1 Season fish and (if liked) place a dot of butter on top and sprinkle with lemon juice.
2 Wrap in a parcel of foil to help hold the fish together, and then cook over steam, as above.

Poaching

Fish is cooked by simmering in liquid on the hotplate or in the oven. Use for fillets, steaks/cutlets or for whole fish. As with steaming, this is a gentle cooking method.

1 Place liquid in saucepan, casserole or fish kettle. This can be salted water with vinegar or lemon juice, a bay leaf, and peppercorns; or a mixture of seasoned milk and water. Do not use too much; just enough to come about half-way up the fish when in the pan.
2 (a) Heat the liquid on the hotplate until just simmering. Put the fish in and bring back to simmer. Cover, reduce heat and cook very gently. Or:
(b) Put fish in the cold liquid, cover and cook in the oven at Mark 4/350°F/180°C. Calculate cooking time from time simmering begins. Approximate times: 10–15 min per lb/450 g for whole fish; 20 min for fillets, cutlets.
3 Drain before serving and use cooking liquid in sauce so that no goodness is wasted.

Baking

A good method for retaining flavour. Use for fillets, cutlets and for small whole fish.
1 Heat oven to Mark 4/350°F/180°C.
2 Place fish, which may be stuffed, in ovenproof casserole, season, dot with butter and sprinkle with a little lemon juice.
3 (a) Cook uncovered, basting frequently, or
(b) Wrap loosely in foil and place on baking tray. Fillets, 10–20 min; steaks/cutlets, 20 min; small whole fish, 25–30 min.

Fish type	Buying	Cooking	Serving
White (continued)			
Whiting	Available all year but best Nov–Feb. Whole or fillets. Good economical buy but does not keep well. Delicate flavour. Allow 1 for 2 persons or 6–8 oz/175–225 g per person	As for cod	As for cod
Sole – Dover	Available all year, whole or fillets. Grey-black skin. Flesh firm, delicate flavour: best of the flat fish. Allow 1 per person. At its best 2–3 days after catching	As for cod	As for cod
Sole – Lemon	Has lighter skin and a more pointed shape. Not so fine a flavour	As for cod	As for cod. Lemon or orange sauce go well with plaice and sole
Plaice	Available all year. Whole or fillets. Orange spotted brown skin. Soft white flesh, delicate flavour	As for cod	As above
Skate	Available all year, best Oct–March. Sold as 'wings' (sides of fish), usually skinned, Pinkish flesh. Allow 8–12 oz/ 225–350 g per person	*Shallow fry* for 5–6 min each side. *Deep fry* for 5–10 min. *Poach* for 20 min	'Black butter' is made from melted butter combined with vinegar and capers, and poured over skate. Or serve with tomato sauce.
Halibut	Available all year, best July–March. Usually sold as steaks/cutlets. Excellent flavour but tends to be dry. Allow as cod	As for cod but best wrapped in buttered foil and *baked* for 20 min. *Grill* for 5–6 min each side (use plenty of butter)	As for cod
Oily			
Herring	Available all year, best April–Nov. Whole usually 6–12 oz/175–350 g. Shiny with bright (not red) eyes. Creamy colour flesh with distinctive flavour. Allow 1 per person (fishmonger will fillet)	*Shallow fry/grill* for 5 min each side (whole), 5–6 min (fillet). Good coated with oatmeal and fried. *Bake* for 10–15 min	See note under white fish. Soused herring is cooked in flavoured vinegar and served hot or cold
Kipper (smoked herring)	Available all year. Sold on or off bone (whole or fillets). Allow 1 per person	*Grill* for 5–6 min each side. *Poach* for 5 min	Serve for breakfast. Or mix with butter and seasoning to make pâté
Mackerel	Available all year, best Feb–June. Sold whole (often smoked). Skin – blue-green stripes; flesh creamy with distinctive flavour. Does not keep long – avoid flabby fish with copper tinge. Allow 1 per person (6–8 oz/ 175–225 g)	Make 3 diagonal slits on each side. *Shallow fry/grill* for 5 min on each side. *Bake* for 10–15 min	With gooseberry sauce. Can be served soused. See above
Pilchard	Buy at coast if possible. Small round fish sold whole. Must be fresh (do not keep). Also available canned. Allow 1–2 per person	*Shallow fry/grill* for 5 min each side (whole)	Serve on toast as breakfast dish or for a snack. Serve with tomato sauce
Sardines (young pilchards)	As above. Also available canned. Allow more	As for pilchard.	As for pilchards, above

Stewing and casseroling

These methods produce fish soups and chowders. They are best for skinless and boneless fillets as all flavour and juices are retained. Use white fish for soups, stews and curries; shellfish for bisque (a rich creamy soup); clams, mussels, scallops for chowder (a thick stew with potatoes); a mixture for bouillabaisse (a fish soup speciality of the Mediterranean).

1 Cut fish into cubes 1 in/25 mm.
2 Prepare any vegetables according to kind and slice thinly or chop.
3 Toss fish pieces in seasoned flour for a thicker stew.
4 Heat a little cooking oil and butter in a pan and cook vegetables till brown.
5 Stir in the fish and add enough stock/water to just cover.
6 Bring to the boil and cover.
7 Reduce heat and cook gently on hotplate or in oven, Mark 4/350°F/180°C, until fish is tender, 10–30 min depending on ingredients (vegetables, etc).
8 Adjust seasoning to taste.

FISH FINGERS

They are best made from all cod, but can be a mixture of white fish such as cod/haddock/coley (often labelled 'Economy'). Cook from frozen. Fry or grill for 4 min each side.

FISH PIE

Cook some white fish in a covered pan in a little milk or milk and water and seasoning. Drain and flake the fish. Use the cooking liquid to make a thick white sauce (see p. 56). Stir in the fish and some chopped parsley. Pour mixture into ovenproof casserole, top with mashed potatoes mixed with milk and butter and sprinkle with some grated cheese. Cook in oven at Mark 6/400°F/200°C till golden on top, about 35 min.
VARIATIONS Add sliced hard-boiled egg, fried mushroom slices or peeled shrimps.

Fish type	Buying	Cooking	Serving
Oily (continued)			
Sprats	Available Nov–March. Smaller than herring – whole. Sometimes smoked	As for pilchard (3–4 min each side)	As for pilchard
Whitebait (family of herring and sprat)	Best Feb–Aug. Small silvery fish (about 1 in/25 mm long). Allow 8 oz/225 g per person	Rinse in cold salted water, do not gut or take off head. Coat in milk and flour. *Deep fry* for 2 min until crisp.	Serve as a starter. Garnish with cayenne pepper and lemon wedges
Anchovies (species of herring)	Usually sold salted in tins. Give piquancy to dish. Buy whole, very fresh	*Grill* for 3–5 min each side (whole)	Wash tinned anchovies in milk and dry on kitchen towel. Use in pizza, quiche and fish dishes
Freshwater			
Salmon	Available Feb–Aug. Whole or steaks. Most expensive. Oily, red, well-flavoured flesh – rich. Allow 1½ lb/700 g for 4 persons	*Poach* for 10–15 min per lb/450 g, 10–15 min (steak). *Steam* for 10–15 min (steak). *Grill* for 5–7 min each side (steak). Tends to dry on cooking – wrap in foil	*Special occasions* Use whole fish, e.g. trout and almonds, or salmon (hot or cold). Serve cold decorated with tomatoes, cucumber, gherkins, olives, etc, to make attractive patterns: or aspic – whole or as steaks. Hot salmon steaks can be served with hollandaise sauce or melted butter Cold steaks or whole fish can be served with mayonnaise and salad
Salmon trout (Sea trout, Sewin)	March–July. Whole. Less expensive than salmon. More delicate flavour. Flesh often more colourful than salmon; does not dry so much. Can be smoked. Allow 6–8 oz/175–225 g per person	As for salmon	
Trout	*Rainbow* – available all year. 6–12 oz/175–350 g whole, delicate white flesh. *Brown* – Feb–Sept. Not widely available. Often considered better than rainbow. Larger. Both relatively expensive. Sometimes sold smoked	*Grill/shallow fry* for 5–6 min each side. *Bake* for 10–15 min (whole) in foil	As for salmon
Shellfish			
Prawns Shrimps	All year. Usually sold boiled (prawns often in shells). Shrimps smaller, less expensive. Still sold in pints. Allow 1 pt of prawns for 4 persons – varies greatly as to how used!	*Deep fry* about 3 min (prawns in batter). They toughen if overcooked. In other recipes, add during last 5 min of cooking	*Special occasions*, serve as starters: Prawn cocktail with brown bread and butter. Prawns/shrimps in butter (potted). Prawns, deep fried in breadcrumbs/batter
Scampi (Dublin Bay prawns)	All year in shells or not; raw or cooked. Meat in tail end only. Used as prawns	As for prawns	Serve with tartare sauce, lemon wedges and brown bread and butter
Crab	Best May–Aug. Usually sold ready-boiled. White meat in claws, brown in shell		Serve with salads. Add to soups and stews. Or curry, during last 5 min
Lobster	All year, best March–Oct. Usually sold ready-boiled, should have springy tail. 2 lb/1 kg lobster gives about 12 oz/350 g meat		Use for Lobster Thermidor, Lobster Mayonnaise. Serve with tartare sauce
Mussels	Sept–March. Fresh, bottled, canned, Allow 1 pt/500 ml per person	Rinse well to remove sand. *Poach* or *stew* for 5 min until shells open	Use for moules marinières

Vegetables

Traditionally, vegetables are served to accompany meat, fish and other savoury dishes. But of course they can be a meal in themselves – for example, served with a white sauce (flavoured if you wish), or casseroled, or made into a salad, or a filling for a pie or flan. A vegetable course sometimes follows the roast at a formal meal, or vegetables may be served as an hors d'oeuvre. A platter full of assorted vegetables of contrasting tastes and colours is often more appealing than large amounts of one type; the food value is better balanced, too.

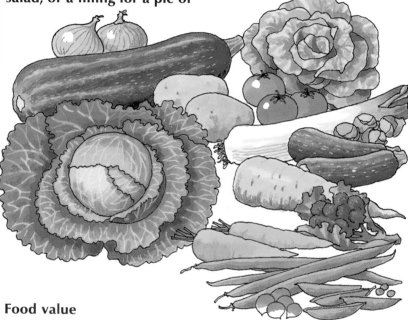

Food value

These notes refer to vegetables in general; more specific points are made under the various vegetable sections which follow. Vegetables are a valuable source of many important nutrients and provide a good deal of essential roughage. Vegetable food values vary according to the variety and age of the vegetable and the length of time which it has been exposed to sunlight. The way that vegetables have been handled and stored during transport also affects their food value, as do your preparation and cooking methods at home.

MAKING THE MOST OF VEGETABLE VITAMINS
1 **Serve** vegetables raw where possible.
2 **Prepare** vegetables just before use (vitamin C rapidly diminishes after peeling and/or shredding).
3 **Do not leave** soaking in water (this further destroys vitamins).
4 **Always plunge** green vegetables into boiling water (this helps to stop further vitamin C losses).
5 **Keep** cooking water to a minimum and use it afterwards for gravies, sauces, casseroles and stocks, etc. Vitamin C and thiamin in particular are destroyed by heat and are soluble in water.
6 **Slightly undercook** rather than overcook (but always be sure to cook potatoes and root vegetables thoroughly).

Buying vegetables

Always make sure that the vegetables you buy are as fresh as possible – not only their flavour, but their food value, will be better. Pre-packed vegetables can look attractive, but loose ones will probably be fresher, particularly if you can still see the soil they came from. Frozen and canned vegetables have a food value comparable to fresh, but bottling destroys some vitamins. Dried vegetables (not pulses) keep indefinitely and so can be useful in the store cupboard for emergencies and to add flavour to other dishes, but they need reconstituting with boiling water according to the directions on the packet, and their nutritional value is not as good as fresh vegetables.

Storage

Always remove at once any wrappers, in particular the polythene kind which tend to collect droplets of condensation inside. This is harmful to your vegetables. Keep vegetables in a cool, dark, dry place. Some, like salads, are best refrigerated, but others should not go in the fridge (potatoes and other root vegetables). See following pages for detailed storage recommendations.

Cooking methods

Vegetables may seem easy to cook, but to get them tasting as delicious as possible requires a certain art. And there are lots of alternatives to the popular British way of boiling!

Boiling

This is indeed suitable for most vegetables, but do not overboil or you will lose shape, flavour and food values. Take a little care and you will always achieve good results.
1 **In general place** only enough water to just cover the vegetables in a pan with well-fitting lid.
2 **Add salt** to taste (a good guide is to add 1 tsp/5 ml to each 1 pt/550 ml water). Do not add salt to pulses until after cooking.
3 **Add** new vegetables and green vegetables to the boiling water. But bring old vegetables and most root vegetables to the boil in cold water.
4 **Then lower** the heat and simmer gently until the vegetables are tender. See charts on following pages for exact times.

Steaming

This little-used method, suitable for most vegetables, gives good results, preserving flavour, shape and food values. You can economize on fuel by steaming a vegetable on top of another dish which is cooking below.
1 **Place** the prepared vegetables directly onto the perforated base of a steamer or in a covered metal colander over a pan of boiling water.
2 **Season** lightly with salt and pepper.
3 **Cook** for the required time – see charts. (Times can vary depending on how fast the water boils.)

Roasting

This method is suitable for root vegetables and potatoes. It is handy when you have the oven on for another dish, and the fat gives the vegetables a delicious flavour.
1 Put the prepared vegetables into a roasting tin containing hot fat (lard, dripping or cooking oil).
2 Cook at Mark 7/425°F/220°C, basting occasionally. See charts for times. You can roast from raw or par-boil to cut time, or roast vegetables round the joint if you like: add the prepared vegetables during the final hour or so of cooking. Consider serving a roast root vegetable as well as potatoes and greens.

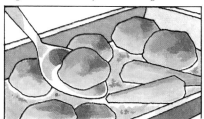

Frying

Frying in shallow fat is suitable mainly for softer vegetables (for example tomatoes, mushrooms, courgettes, aubergines).
1 Prepare the vegetable according to kind (see charts).
2 Heat enough cooking oil (or a mixture of butter and cooking oil) in a frying-pan to come half-way up the sides of the vegetables.
3 Add the vegetables and brown them on one side.
4 Turn them over and brown them on the other side.
5 Reduce the heat and cook the vegetables until they are tender. Harder vegetables can be par-boiled and then fried.

Braising

This tasty, moist way of serving vegetables retains most of their goodness, so long as you make use of the water (see 5 below).
1 Prepare vegetables according to kind and lightly fry in a little butter (or a mixture of butter and cooking oil) until golden brown.
2 Put them into an ovenproof dish and add enough stock to come half-way up the vegetables.
3 Season lightly and add a good-sized knob of butter.
4 Cover and cook at Mark 4/350°F/180°C (see charts for times).
5 Serve with cooking liquid, or use it to make a gravy or sauce (so as not to waste the flavour or food value); or remove the vegetables and boil cooking liquid to reduce and thicken it, and then pour it over the vegetables.

Baking

This is suitable for onions, mushrooms, tomatoes, aubergines or courgettes, and is useful for making the most of your oven when cooking another dish. The butter gives a good rich flavour.
1 Arrange the prepared vegetables in an ovenproof casserole.
2 Brush with melted butter, cover and cook at Mark 5/375°F/190°C until tender (see charts for exact times).
Potatoes are baked without a cover and usually without brushing with melted butter.

Freezing

Only freeze raw when you can be sure of perfect freshness, e.g. home-grown vegetables. However, when a glut results in low prices at the greengrocer, freeze these vegetables as cooked dishes, such as purées (see below). Most vegetables can be frozen raw except for those with a very high water content, such as salad vegetables, tomatoes, white cabbage and potatoes. These must be cooked before freezing. Vegetables can also be puréed and frozen, and this method is good for soups, sauces and baby foods. Prepare and cook the vegetables in the usual way: see charts. Sieve or blend to a smooth purée and pack into rigid covered containers. Potatoes freeze well cooked and mashed. To freeze new potatoes, slightly undercook. To freeze chips, deep fry until tender, but not brown, and drain well.

Blanching

If a vegetable is on the following list, and you know you will be going to eat it within the time it will keep, do not bother to blanch. But rather spend your time blanching those vegetables that need it for long-term storage. To blanch, you plunge vegetables into boiling water for times that vary according to the vegetable type.

Freezer storage times for correctly stored vegetables

Type	Time
Most vegetables	1 year
Cauliflower, leeks, onion, shallots, potatoes (chipped), herbs	6 months
Artichokes, mushrooms (cooked), potatoes (new, whole, boiled), duchesse potatoes, jacket, roast or croquette potatoes, prepared vegetable dishes	3 months
Avocado (purée)	2 months
Mushrooms (raw)	1 month

Most vegetables frozen from fresh keep in better condition and for longer once 'blanched' (see below for explanation and method).

The following vegetables do not need blanching: beetroot, celery, leeks, onions, peppers and tomatoes.

Reasons for blanching

1 To stop the enzymes working that otherwise would spoil the flavour, texture, colour and food value of the vegetables.
2 To kill harmful micro-organisms.
3 To force out air (air trapped inside cell walls expands on cooking, and bursts them so that they leak and give out a scum or froth which although harmless looks and smells unappetizing).

To blanch and freeze

For best results, blanch only 1 lb/450 g vegetables at a time.
1 Wash vegetables thoroughly in cold water.
2 Prepare according to kind, and reject imperfect vegetables.
3 Bring a large saucepan of water to a fast boil. Use 1 gal/4½ litres water for 1 lb/450 g vegetables but remember that the same water can be used several times over.
4 Put a batch of prepared vegetables into a wire basket or muslin bag and completely immerse them in the fast-boiling water.
5 Cover and time from the moment when the water comes back to the boil (over-cooking produces mushy vegetables).
6 Blanch for the exact time, and while blanching, shake the basket or bag so that the vegetables are heated evenly.
7 At the end of the blanching time, drain the vegetables and hold them under ice-cold running water. Cool them for as long as the blanching time – to make sure they are cool right the way through.
8 Drain them well then open-freeze on trays.
9 Pack into polythene bags or into rigid polythene containers with lids in usable quantities.

Vegetable type	Time for blanching
Broad beans (podded), French and runner beans (whole or sliced)	2 min
Broccoli (broken into florets)	3–4 min (depending on size)
Brussels sprouts	3–4 min (depending on size)
Cauliflower (broken into florets)	3 min
Corn-on-the-cob (sweetcorn)	Small: 4 min; medium: 6 min; large: 8 min
Courgettes (thickly sliced)	1 min
Marrow (cut in chunks)	3 min
Parsnips (thickly sliced)	2 min
Peas (podded)	1 min
Swede (cut into chunks)	3 min
Turnips	Whole: 4 min; diced: 2 min

Potatoes

Potatoes are an inexpensive way of making a meal more filling – indeed they can make a meal on their own. To avoid monotony, vary the way you serve them.

Food value

Potatoes contain a high proportion of starch. When eaten in quantity, as in an average diet, they are a major source of vitamin C (particularly new potatoes) and provide some protein and iron. They are also useful sources of thiamin and nicotinic acid, and a good source of B vitamins, and of dietary fibre. Cooking losses (vitamin C in particular) are at a minimum if potatoes are boiled or baked in their skins. Losses are greater if potatoes are fried and greater still if they are boiled after peeling. Greatest losses occur when potatoes are mashed and kept hot. Remember that a large amount of nutrients lie just below the potato's skin; if it is necessary to peel, do it thinly. Instant mashed potato has a similar food value to fresh. Although vitamin C and thiamin are lost in the drying process, the manufacturers usually replace it. Frozen potatoes have comparable food values to fresh. The highest loss of nutrients occurs in potato canning.

Buying potatoes

Most people buy most of their potatoes 'fresh', but do try to make sure they are in fact as fresh as possible. There are many varieties and the most common are listed below. Look for potatoes with a good shape, undamaged, with no disease. Plastic bags of graded and washed potatoes may be less fresh. On average, buy 6–8 oz/175–225 g per person.
Instant and canned potatoes are handy for the store cupboard. Frozen chips are also convenient but are more expensive and often with inferior flavour to fresh.

Main potato types
'New' or Early Crop

In season from May–August. The really fresh potatoes will have the best flavour. Their skins should rub off easily, and the potatoes will be damp to the touch. Only buy in small quantities for immediate use. New potatoes are best served boiled, hot or cold, or in salads. Do not mash them. Larger ones make well-flavoured chips and sauté well. Common varieties are *Home Guard*, *Maris Peer* and *Red Craigs Royal*.

'Old' or Maincrop

In season from September–May. Look for potatoes with a good shape, free from dirt, disease, damage and growth shoots. Once the skins are firmly set, you can economize by buying in larger quantities in large brown paper bags. Store in a cool dark, dry place for up to 3 months. Do not buy green potatoes, which are caused by exposure to light; these can have unpleasant effects. In autumn the flesh of potatoes is waxy but most varieties tend to flouriness after storing. Certain varieties are better suited for particular cooking methods, as follows.
Desirée (red) and *Majestic* are good for general use but use in particular for roasting, chipping and sautéeing.
King Edward (red-white), *Pentland Hawk* and *Pentland Ivory* (white) and *Maris Piper* (white) are also for general use, but are particularly good for boiling, mashing and baking in their jackets.

Ways to prepare and cook new potatoes

Never peel them. Wash and cook them in their skins, or lightly scrape or scrub off skins.

BOILING

1 **Plunge** the cleaned potatoes into enough boiling salted water to just cover them.
2 **Add** a sprig of mint for flavour.
3 **Boil** gently for 15–20 min, depending on their size.
4 **Drain** well.
5 **Serve** tossed in melted butter and sprinkle with chopped parsley, mint, chives or watercress.
Or you can *steam* new potatoes for 20–25 min.

TO MAKE POTATO SALAD

1 **Cook** new potatoes as above.
2 **Remove** their skins and dice them.
3 **While** the potatoes are still warm, mix them with mayonnaise (see p. 46) – enough to coat them.
4 **Add** chopped onion and chopped parsley, or chives, or pepper or paprika pepper.
5 **Serve** with cold meat, or with fish or with salads.

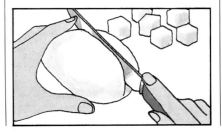

Ways to prepare and cook old potatoes

In general, wash (scrub if necessary) and remove any 'eyes' or blemishes. Cook in their skins or thinly peel using a small sharp knife or potato peeler and cut according to cooking method, see below. Potatoes discolour if peeled and exposed to air. So try and peel them just before cooking. If you do have to peel potatoes in advance, cover them with cold water to keep the air out, but remember that you will be losing vitamin C.

BOILING

1 **Prepare** potatoes as above. Leave small ones whole, cut larger ones into even-sized pieces.
2 **Put** them in a saucepan, barely cover with cold water and add salt to taste.
3 **Bring** them to the boil, cover and boil gently for 20–40 min, depending on their size.
4 **Drain** well.
5 **Serve** with melted butter and chopped parsley.
Or you can *steam* old potatoes whole for 30–40 min, or sliced for 10–12 min.

MASHED

1 **Prepare** (including peeling) and cook potatoes as above for boiled.
2 **Drain**, leaving a little of the cooking water.
3 **Mash** with a wooden spoon, fork, potato masher or electric mixer, adding a good knob of butter, some milk and seasoning for a creamy consistency and a good flavour.
4 **Serve** with meat and vegetable meals, or use mash to top shepherd's pie, fish pie and other savoury dishes.

CHIPS OR FRENCH FRIES

1 Peel the potatoes thinly and cut them into even-sized chips.
2 Rinse them well, drain off the water, and *dry thoroughly* using a clean teacloth (to prevent spitting when lowered into the fat).
3 Deep fry (see p. 65) for 7–10 min until golden brown.
4 Drain well on crumpled kitchen paper.
5 Serve hot sprinkled with salt.
Chips are traditionally served of course with fish, with vinegar or lemon juice too. They also go well with mixed grills, steak, fried eggs, sausages, etc.
VARIATIONS Vary their shape. Cut them into straws (matchsticks), crisps or use shaped cutters to make crinkle-cut or lattice shapes.

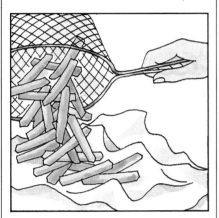

SAUTÉ

1 Thinly peel the potatoes and par-boil for about 10 min.
2 Drain and dry them well.
3 Cut them into thin slices.
4 Heat a little butter or cooking oil in a frying-pan and fry gently on each side, until crisp, brown and cooked through. Shake the pan occasionally to encourage even browning. If you wish, add a little chopped parsley before serving.

ROAST

1 Peel the potatoes thinly and cut them into even-sized pieces (you can leave the small ones whole).
2 Place them in roasting tin containing about 4 oz/100 g hot lard, dripping or cooking oil.
3 Spoon the fat over them thoroughly and cook at Mark 7/425°F/220°C for 40 min–1 hr, depending on size, turning and basting once or twice during cooking. The outside should be crisp and brown and the inside soft.
4 Drain on crumpled kitchen paper before serving with roast meat or other dishes.
VARIATIONS The potatoes can be par-boiled for 10 min; then drained, dried and roasted for 30–40 min. Or you can cook them in roasting tin around the joint for its final hour. For a really crisp outside coating, try par-boiling, draining, drying and rolling potatoes in seasoned flour before roasting.

BAKED (IN THEIR 'JACKETS')

1 Choose even-sized potatoes, scrub them clean, dry them and prick them well all over with a fork, to prevent bursting during cooking.
2 Place them on a tray or directly on shelves of the oven and cook at Mark 7/425°F/220°C for 1–1½ hrs (depending on their size) until soft – or test with small skewer. You can cook them with other dishes at a lower heat, but they will take longer.
3 To serve, make a slit in the top using a sharp knife; then squeeze the potato gently in a cloth to open it slightly. Place a good knob of butter on top and sprinkle over with chopped parsley or chives.
VARIATIONS Thread on skewers for speedier cooking or par-boil for 10 min, drain. dry, prick and bake. Or the cooked potatoes can be halved, their flesh scooped out and mixed with chopped fried onion, bacon, or cheese, butter and seasoning, etc and refilled. Brown under the grill before serving. You can make an alternative filling with cooked flaked fish, chopped parsley, lemon juice and seasoning. Or try topping with sour cream or yoghurt.

Peas and beans

Fresh peas and beans are one of summer's chief delights, vastly superior in flavour to frozen or canned versions.

Food value

Peas and beans are particularly rich in protein and provide more energy and B vitamins than green or root vegetables. Peas and broad beans supply some vitamin C.

Storage

Store peas and beans loose in a cool, dry place for 2–3 days.

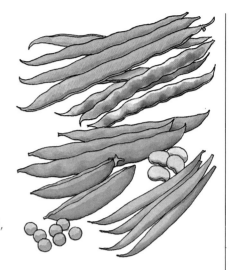

Type and when available	Preparation and cooking	Ideas for serving
Peas May–Oct. Look for smooth, well-filled pods. If pods are wrinkled, the peas inside are probably hard	Allow 8 oz/225 g in pod per person. Remove pods (i.e. shells) and wash the peas. *Boil* with a sprig of mint and 1 tsp/5 ml sugar for 8–10 min (if young); 10–15 min (when larger)	Drain, discard mint and toss in butter. Or serve in onion sauce, using enough to coat the peas thickly. Or serve cold in salads
Broad beans June–July. Young tender beans are best so look for young pods about 10 in/25 cm long	Allow 8–12 oz/225–350 g in pod per person. Remove pods (shell) and wash beans. *Boil* for 10–15 min, or for 20 min for larger (i.e. older) beans. Pods which are only a few in/cm can be cooked and eaten whole	Drain and serve with butter and pepper; or serve with parsley sauce. Or serve cold in salads
Runner beans July–Oct. Look for crisp, firm, smooth beans, which should snap easily and cleanly, unlike tough and stringy beans	Allow 4–8 oz/100–225 g per person. Remove tops, tails and stringy sides, using a small sharp knife. Wash. Slice thickly. *Boil* for 5–15 min depending on age of beans. Remove any scum that rises to the top with a large metal spoon. Or steam for 15–20 min	Drain well and toss in butter. Or serve cold in salads
French beans June–Aug, with smooth skins and no strings. Look for flattish pods which should not be bulging but young and tender, about 5 in/12 cm long	Allow 4–8 oz/100–225 g per person. Snip off tops and tails and wash. *Boil* whole or cut into 2 in/5 cm lengths for 10–15 min. Or *steam* for 15–20 min	As for runner beans, above
Kidney beans June–Nov. Larger than French beans and are not so tender. Colour is purple-green	Allow 4–8 oz/100–225 g per person. Top, tail and pull away stringy sides thinly. Wash. Cut into 2 in/5 cm lengths. *Boil* for 10–15 min. *Steam* for 15–20 min	As for runner beans above

Green vegetables

Most people know that 'greens' are good for them, and this is certainly true. But to preserve maximum goodness and flavour follow carefully the notes below.

Food value

Green vegetables are an excellent source of vitamin C, vitamin A, and they provide some iron and calcium and dietary fibre. You get the most vitamins when these vegetables are eaten raw, and more vitamins from dark outer leaves than the inner. Wilted vegetables have lost a lot of vitamin C and shredding causes further losses. Always prepare just before cooking and do not soak in water.

Storage

Keep green vegetables in a cool, dry, dark, well-ventilated place. Large, tightly packed cabbages and sprouts will keep for 2–3 days. Greens and spring cabbage will keep for 1–2 days. Spinach is best eaten the same day. Cauliflower will keep for 2 days. Use broccoli the same day.

Cooking

Use as little water as possible and always make sure it is boiling before you add the green vegetables.

Type and when in season	Preparation and cooking	Ideas for serving
CABBAGE Available all year. Look for firm ones with crisp leaves. **Spring** cabbage is small with cone-shaped hearts. **Summer** cabbage has large hearts and is firmer. **Winter** cabbage (e.g. Savoy) is like summer, but has curly leaves. **White** cabbage has round solid, tightly packed leaves. Oct–Feb. **Red** cabbage, available from Nov–March, has a purplish bloom. It loses a lot of colour on cooking, and is round, solid and tightly packed	Allow 6–8 oz/175–225 g per person. Remove coarse or damaged leaves and wash well. Cut into wedges or break into leaves, and remove central core and hard stalk. Shred and *boil* in 1 in/2½ cm boiling water for 5–10 min. *Boil* wedges for 10–15 min (red for 15–30 min). *Steam*, shredded for 10 min. *Fry*, shredded for 5–10 min. Red cabbage takes about twice as long to cook as others. Try red cabbage shredded and cooked in a mixture of vinegar and water and brown sugar, chopped onion, cloves and seasoning, for 1½–2½ hrs	Drain well and toss in butter and pepper (try adding nutmeg, too). 'Bubble and squeak' is cooked potatoes and cabbage fried in butter. Stuff cooked whole leaves with mince or a savoury rice mixture to make a parcel, and serve with tomato sauce. Use raw white cabbage finely shredded in coleslaw and other salads. Also for pickling. And as above. Serve spicy red cabbage hot or cold with rich meats such as pork or duck.
GREENS Available all year. They are cabbages picked before the hearts have developed. Spring greens are spring cabbages picked early	As for cabbage above. (Discard any woody stems)	As for cabbage above
CAULIFLOWER Available all year. Look for firm, white, tightly packed heads surrounded by fresh green leaves	A medium size is enough for 4 persons. Trim off coarse, damaged or yellow leaves and wash thoroughly. You can leave the cauliflower whole, but cut a cross in the stalk end; or cut or break into 'florets'. *Boil* or *steam* whole (with stem end down) for 10–20 min, depending on size. *Boil* or *steam* florets for 8–15 min	Drain and serve with butter and pepper. Sprinkle with nutmeg or mace. Or serve with a white or cheese sauce as starter or a main course. Or dip florets in batter and deep fry. Use small florets in salads, either raw or lightly cooked
SPINACH Available all year, but is most tender and at its best from March to April. Look for firm round leaves, a good green colour with little stalks	Spinach 'cooks down', so allow 8 oz/225 g per person. Wash well several times to remove dirt and grit. Trim off thick stalks. Put in a saucepan with only the water that is clinging to the leaves. Heat gently to bring to the *boil*, turning occasionally; then cover and cook gently for 5–10 min, and shake pan occasionally. Or *steam* for 10 min	Drain well, pressing with the back of a spoon in a colander. Mix a good knob of butter or 1–2 tbsp/15–30 ml cream. Top a bed of spinach with poached eggs or cooked fillets of smoked fish and cheese sauce to make Florentine dishes

Root vegetables

An economical way of providing substantial winter meals, the humble root vegetables can be transformed by imaginative cooking.

Food value

Root vegetables contain a high proportion of starch. They are a good source of vitamin A (particularly carrots), supply useful quantities of vitamin C (in particular turnips, swedes and parsnips). Root vegetables also provide dietary fibre.

Storage

Will keep in a cool, dry, dark place for 2–3 weeks.

Preparing leeks (see chart).

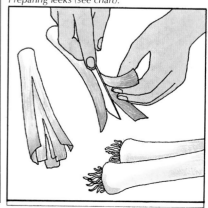

Type and when available	Preparation and cooking	Ideas for serving
Green vegetables (continued)		
BROCCOLI Dec–April. Look for firm, compact florets with fresh green leaves, and few thick stalks (these are usually rather coarse). **White and Purple** types. Purple has a more delicate flavour	Buy 6–8 oz/175–225 g per person. As for cauliflower above. Wash and remove coarse stalks and outer leaves. *Boil* for 10–15 min. *Steam* for 15–20 min	As for cauliflower above. Serve with butter, or with hollandaise sauce
BRUSSELS SPROUTS Sept–March. Look for small tightly packed sprouts with a fresh green colour	Allow 4–6 oz/100–175 g per person. Wash, removing discoloured or loose outer leaves. Trim stalks. *Boil* for 10–15 min, or *steam* for 20–25 min	Drain and serve with butter. Sprouts are good sprinkled over with toasted almonds. Slice thinly for winter salads (raw) and toss in French dressing

Root vegetables

Type and when available	Preparation and cooking	Ideas for serving
CARROTS All the year. *New (young) carrots May–Aug*	Allow 4–6 oz/100–175 g per person. Cut off top, including any leaves and snip off tail. Scrub or scrape lightly with a sharp knife	Drain and toss in butter with seasoning and chopped parsley. Or serve with white or cheese sauce
Old carrots Sept–April	Cut off top and tail and peel thinly. Slice, dice or cut into strips. *Boil* carrots whole, or halved, or sliced or diced for 10–15 min (whole) or 6–10 min in thin slices, diced or in strips. Or *steam*, sliced, for 20–25 min	Use in soups, casseroles, or stews. You can heat cooked carrots in orange juice sweetened with a little brown sugar (good with steamed fish)
PARSNIPS Sept–April	Allow 6–8 oz/175–225 g per person. Cut off tops and tails. Peel, quarter lengthways and then cut out hard cores. Use quartered, sliced, diced or cut into strips. *Boil* for 30–40 min. Or *roast*: par-boil quarters for 5 min then *roast* in hot fat or round joint for the final hour. Or *steam*, sliced for 10 min	Strain, toss in butter and add seasoning. Or serve with white or cheese sauce (use as a filling for vegetable pie or flan). Or use in soups, stews or casseroles or mash with butter and pepper. You can add nutmeg or mace too
SWEDES Sept–May. Large with yellow-orange flesh and a tough skin	Allow 4–6 oz/100–175 g per person. Wash them and peel thickly. Cut into even-sized pieces, or slice or dice. *Boil* for 20–40 min. Or *roast* in chunks in hot fat or with joint for the final 1–1½ hrs; or *par-boil* for 5 min then *roast* for 40–50 min. Or *steam* in chunks for 15–20 min	To serve as a hot vegetable, drain and mash with butter and pepper. You can add nutmeg. Or mix with chopped grilled bacon or grated cheese for good extra flavour. Use in stews or casseroles or serve with onion gravy.

Type and when available	Preparation and cooking	Ideas for serving
TURNIPS All year round. *Young/new turnips April–July.* *Old (or maincrop) Aug–April* and have a stronger flavour	Allow 4–6 oz/100–175 g per person. Wash, remove tops and tails and peel thinly. Young turnips can be left whole. Old turnips can be cut into quarters, sliced or diced. *Boil* for 15–25 min, depending on size and age; or *roast*: *par-boil* for 5 min then *roast* in hot fat or round the joint for the final 45 min. Or *steam*, coarsely diced for 15 min. Or *deep fry* like chipped potatoes	To serve as a hot vegetable, drain and toss in butter with pepper and a squeeze of lemon. Or serve with white sauce. Or with hollandaise sauce – as a starter. Young turnips can be grated raw into salads. Old can be mashed with butter and seasoning. Or use in soups, stews or casseroles
CELERY Sept–Feb. White stalks topped with pale green leaves (yellowing leaves – stale)	Small – allow 1 head per person or large – 3–4 sticks. Trim root, wash and scrub whole, or divide into sticks. Peel away coarse fibres and leaves, cut into 2 in/5 cm lengths or slice thinly. *Boil* or *steam* lengths 15–20 min. *Braise* sticks 50–60 min or small heads (tie each head with string to hold in shape) 1¼–1½ hrs	Raw in salads – short lengths or slices. Sticks with salt, with cheese board – do not trim leaves off inner stalks – attractive. Serve hot with butter. With white cheese or parsley sauce. Add to soups, stews and casseroles
LEEKS Sept–May. Look for good proportion of white stem.	Allow 8–12 oz/225–350 g per person. Remove coarse outer leaves, trim tops and roots. Split down centre to within 2 in/5 cm of base and wash thoroughly to remove dirt and grit. *Boil* whole 15–25 min or sliced 5–10 min. *Braise* whole 1¼–1½ hrs. *Steam*, sliced 15 min	Drain well, serve with butter and pepper. With white or cheese sauce. Soups, stews, casseroles (particularly good with bacon). Raw, finely shredded, in salads; or cooked, cold with French dressing
ONIONS All year round. Look for firm ones with brown papery skin intact. Small – stronger. Large – milder (include Spanish) **Shallots** – July–Jan. Small, strong	Allow 4–6 oz/100–175 g per person. Remove skin and trim off roots to cook whole. To slice or chop, peel back skin towards roots. Hold roots and skin while slicing or chopping. *Boil* whole for 25–35 min. *Steam* whole for 40–45 min, sliced, 15 min. *Bake* – par-boil for 10 min, then *bake* for 15–20 min. *Fry* sliced or rings for 5–10 min	With butter; white, cheese or parsley sauce. Fried – with fried or grilled meat and other savoury dishes. Slice or chop into soups, stews, casseroles and other savoury dishes. Raw, sliced or chopped in salads – particularly with cheese (including sandwiches). Add to potato salad

Salad vegetables

There's more to salads than just tomatoes, lettuce and cucumber! Explore our ideas and give salads a new meaning.

Food value

Most salad vegetables eaten fresh and raw are good sources of vitamin C, vitamin A, and dietary fibre.

Buying salad

In leafy vegetables such as lettuce, look for bright green, crisp and firm leaves, which are not wilting or dry. Avoid leaves which are yellowing or bruised because the food value, flavour and texture will be spoiled. On other vegetables avoid wrinkled skins and bruised flesh. Tomatoes, cucumbers and peppers should have shiny skins and should feel firm. Celery, lettuce and cabbage should have tightly clustered leaves or stalks. To ensure freshness try and buy vegetables which are in season; out-of-season vegetables are usually imported, less fresh – and expensive! On the whole it is better to buy salad vegetables loose; washed and trimmed vegetables in packs look attractive but may not be quite so fresh and bits may have been removed, the outer leaves of a lettuce, for example, which protect and conserve moisture.

Storage

Do not wash or prepare until just before use. Leafy salad vegetables should be wrapped loosely in polythene bags and stored in the fridge or in a cool place. See chart for extra details.

Making salads

All the salad vegetables can be served individually (with or without dressing) or combined. Cabbage, cauliflower, celery, leeks, carrots, mushrooms, peppers and sprouts can also be used for raw salads. Cooked vegetables make good salads served with dressing. You can also use fruit such as apple or avocado or dried fruit such as raisins or sultanas, or orange or grapefruit.

Salad combinations

A green salad, such as lettuce, cabbage and watercress. Tomato and onion, sliced in layers; tomato with cucumber and chives or spring onions; cucumber, raisins and spring onions; cucumber, walnut and radish; apple, celery and beetroot (make a lovely pink salad); sliced celery, sliced onion, sliced or grated carrot; celery and apple with red cabbage and/or walnut; beetroot with orange and sultana; raw mushroom slices with slices of pepper and celery, chopped onion and chopped parsley.

Coleslaw is a combination of shredded white cabbage, grated carrot, finely chopped onion, and seasonings, bound together with mayonnaise or salad cream.

Mixed vegetable salad is a good way of using left-over cooked vegetables, such as carrots, peas, cauliflower, beans and new potatoes. Toss them in French dressing.

Rice or pasta salads Use cooked long grain or brown rice or pasta mixed with cooked vegetables, such as onion, mushroom, celery, peas, beans and/or sweetcorn. Season well. Cooked chopped meat or cooked flaked fish can be added.

Salad Niçoise A mixture of tomatoes, cooked French beans, black olives, garlic, herbs and anchovy fillets, all tossed in a French dressing.

Bean salad can be made from haricot or red kidney beans, cooked, cooled and mixed with chopped raw onion, skinned chopped tomato and crushed garlic; add seasoning and herbs.

Salad dressings

Made and served correctly, these can make a salad more appetizing, and can bring out its flavours. Put on a dressing just before serving or the salad ingredients will go limp and watery. Only use enough to cling to the ingredients; there should be none left in the bottom of the bowl. Pour dressings over the salad and then toss – using two spoons or a spoon and fork.

FRENCH DRESSING (VINAIGRETTE)

Use two parts of salad oil (e.g. olive, corn or sunflower), to one part of vinegar (preferably white wine type).

For example, into a bowl put 2 tbsp/30 ml salad oil, 1 tbsp/15 ml white wine vinegar, a good pinch each of sugar and salt and $\frac{1}{2}$ tsp/ 2.5 ml dry mustard. Beat everything together with a balloon whisk, or a fork; or for a creamier consistency, put into an electric blender for a few seconds.

VARIATIONS Add crushed clove of garlic; or chopped fresh or dried herbs such as parsley, thyme, chives, mint or tarragon; or chopped caper, gherkins or olives; or a good pinch of curry powder; or an onion chopped or grated.

SOUR CREAM/YOGHURT DRESSING

Mix together one carton of sour cream or natural unsweetened yoghurt with 2 tbsp/ 30 ml white wine vinegar, a good pinch sugar, 1 tsp/5 ml salt, a pinch of pepper and 1 tbsp/ 15 ml finely chopped onion.

MAYONNAISE

Ideally, all ingredients should be at room temperature.

1 Put 1 egg yolk into a basin, $\frac{1}{2}$ tsp/2.5 ml each dry mustard, salt and sugar, and a pinch of pepper.

2 Mix well, then add $\frac{1}{4}$ pt/150 ml salad oil, drop by drop at first to prevent curdling, whisking with a balloon whisk or electric mixer or blender until the sauce is thick and smooth. Whisk well between each addition.

3 Gradually add 1 tbsp/15 ml white wine vinegar or lemon juice. If your mayonnaise curdles (separates and goes lumpy) do not panic. Put another egg yolk into another basin and add the curdled mixture gradually, beating or whisking well. For flavouring, you can add chopped chives or parsley, or chopped capers or celery or onion. Always use the same day.

Type and storage hints	Preparation for salads	Other uses
LETTUCE Available all year but at its best from May–Sept. **Cos** is long and crisp with sweet leaves. **Webb** and **Iceberg** are tightly packed and very crisp. **Round** has softer leaves, which can be crisp or curly. Store up to 1 week in fridge, leaving unwashed with roots on if possible.	Never soak, or lettuce will go soggy. Wash, shake off excess water and dry the leaves in a clean tea cloth; or use a special shaker; or whirl round in a wire basket. Inner leaves may not need washing (e.g. Webb and Iceberg). Leave small ones whole and tear large leaves into smaller pieces (to avoid bruising, do not cut)	Braise and serve as a hot vegetable. Use to make soup, when you have a garden glut
CUCUMBER Available from May–Sept. Keeps for 1 week in foil in the fridge	Wash and dry. Leave skin on or peel off thinly, or peel off half in lengthwise strips, or mark with a fork for decorative effect. Slice finely or dice	Use to garnish savoury dishes. Peel, dice and fry gently in butter (in a covered pan) for 10–15 min. Serve with a white sauce. Serve with yoghurt with curry. Use in chilled soups
TOMATOES Available all year but are best from March–Oct. Store for 1 week in fridge or in a cool place, in a container. Or for 2 weeks if under ripe. Keep skinned in foil for 2 days. If skinned and sliced eat the same day	Remove stalk, wash, dry and slice or cut into wedges. To peel tomatoes, plunge the tomato into boiling water for a few seconds, then into cold; or spear the tomato on a fork and hold over a gas flame, turning gently until skin bursts, then peel it off with a knife	Serve as a hot vegetable whole, or halved, and baked, fried or grilled. Use to garnish savoury dishes, cut into slices, wedges or roses. Use skinned and chopped or sliced in soups including Gazpacho, stews and casseroles.

Type and storage hints	Preparation for salads	Other uses
CRESS **Watercress** is available all year. Store in a polythene bag in fridge for 3 days	Separate stalks, trim, wash thoroughly and dry as for lettuce, above	Use to garnish savoury dishes and soup
Mustard-and-cress is available all year. Sold in soil pads in punnets. Stand the whole package in a polythene bag in the fridge to keep for 5 days, but keep the soil moist.	Using scissors, snip off at $\frac{1}{4}$–$\frac{1}{2}$ in/$\frac{1}{2}$–1 cm above the soil. Rinse under running water to separate and remove the black seed cases	Use to garnish savoury dishes
RADISHES Available from April–Oct. Choose small ones, large are often dry. Will keep for 1 week in fridge in a polythene bag	Wash, trim off top and tail. Use whole, sliced or cut into roses: make 4–8 small deep cuts at root end, crossing at centre, and leave in cold water for 1–2 hrs; the cuts will open up to form 'petals'	Serve with cheese at end of meal
SPRING ONIONS Available from March–Sept. Store loose in a polythene bag for 1 week	Trim off root end and the papery outer skin, and trim tops a little. Wash and dry. Use whole if small (mild); or cut into short lengths; or chopped if large (stronger)	Chop and sprinkle over soups, sauces, buttered new potatoes or carrots; or use in savoury flans, pancake fillings, or omelettes, or in potato salad
BEETROOT Available from June–Sept. Sold raw or cooked, which should be moist but not slimy. Remove any tight wrappings and store raw in a cool, dry place for 2–3 weeks; or cooked, whole, and unpeeled, in the fridge for up to 1 week; or keep whole or sliced in vinegar	Peel and grate raw beetroot to serve as a colourful salad ingredient. To cook: trim stalks about 1 in/$2\frac{1}{2}$ cm above the root. Wash, take care not to damage the skin or beetroot will 'bleed' during cooking. Boil for 30 min–1 hr, whole, depending on size. Cool, then the skin will slide off easily. Slice or dice larger ones. Toss in dressing or vinegar	Serve hot with white, parsley or hollandaise sauce. Or as bortsch (beetroot soup). Make chutney (beetroot and onion or apple), or bottle in vinegar (can be spiced)

Mushrooms

Mushrooms deserve a special mention, as they can be used instead of meat in savoury casseroles, pies and so on. They are tasty raw or cooked, hot or cold, and there is no waste.

Food value

They have a high percentage of water, and are rich in B vitamins. With no fat or carbohydrate, they are good for slimming diets. They are available all year, but are cheaper in warmer weather.

Types

Most mushrooms sold in the shops are cultivated, but some people think that wild mushrooms are superior in flavour. Fresh mushrooms should have a firm cap and a fleshy stem. Mushrooms are sold in three grades, depending on the stage of growth.

1 **Button** mushrooms are small with closed cap.
2 **Cup** mushrooms are semi-open, showing a little of the delicate 'gills'.
3 **Open** or flat mushrooms are fully developed, with an open cup and the most mature flavour.

Storage

Store mushrooms in their carton, if any; if sold in a paper bag, put this into a plastic bag, or turn the mushrooms into a sealed container. They will keep for 3 days in the fridge.

Freezing

To freeze whole mushrooms: wipe with a damp cloth, and open freeze on a tray. Pack into polythene bags or a plastic container, seal and freeze to keep for up to 1 month. Use frozen: do not thaw. Mushrooms, sliced and lightly browned in butter, then seasoned with salt and pepper and lemon juice, can also be frozen. They will keep for 3 months.

Preparation

If possible, do not wash mushrooms, and never soak them because they absorb water very easily. Cultivated mushrooms are grown in sterile conditions, and only need a wipe-over with a damp cloth. But very dirty ones can be washed quickly and dried in a clean tea towel. Do not peel, and do not throw away the stems, because of their good flavour. The stems look attractive left attached to cup and button types.
If a recipe specifies removal of stems, save them for stock, or chop them to use in sauces or casseroles.

Cooking

Fry mushrooms or grill them for 2 min on each side if whole, or 3 min if sliced. Mushrooms can be steamed whole, for 7 min; sliced for 5 min; or bake for 15 min. But never overcook them, because they go rubbery, and limp.

Ideas for serving

1 Use all types of mushrooms as a hot vegetable, whole or sliced.
2 Use whole or sliced in soups, casseroles or stews and other savoury dishes.
3 Use in savoury flans, omelettes or as pie or pancake fillings or for stuffings, or sliced on pizza.
4 Cup mushrooms can be stuffed with a breadcrumbs, onion, garlic and bacon mixture, or with a fish mixture.
5 Serve raw button mushrooms in a curry dressing.
6 Make a white sauce with chopped button or cup mushrooms.
7 Use chopped buttons or cups for toasted sandwiches, or on toast.
8 Use button or cup, sliced and lightly fried in butter as a garnish to float on soups.
9 In salads, buttons can be used raw, whole or sliced; cups can be used raw (sliced) or cooked whole or sliced; open can be used cooked and sliced.
10 Serve raw button mushrooms with dips; or make a dip with mushrooms.
11 Use open mushrooms (which need not be perfect) to make chutney. Serve this with cheese or cold meat; it has an excellent flavour.

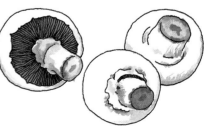

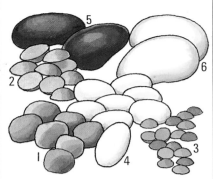

Pulses

Although they feature strongly in vegetarian diets, dried peas, beans, lentils and so on have not been commonly accepted. They deserve a wider use as an inexpensive way to add new flavours to a meal.

Food value

Pulses are a good source of protein and B vitamins.

Buying pulses

They are usually sold in polythene bags, which are preferable to cartons because you can see what you are buying. To ensure freshness, buy from a shop with a good turnover. Pulses which have been kept for a long time are stale and will not soften however long they are cooked. Canned and cooked varieties (kidney and butter beans, mushy peas and pease pudding) are useful as a quick way to make a dish go further, but they are more expensive.

Storage

Keep pulses dry, in their original sealed packets or in stoppered or screw-top jars. They will keep for about 6 months.

Freezing

Cooked vegetables freeze well as they are, or in sauces, casseroles, curries, pease pudding, or soups. Keep for 3–6 months.

Preparation

1 Pick pulses over to remove grit, damaged vegetables and foreign bodies. In general, dried vegetables of this type need soaking before cooking, to soften their skins.

2 Either soak overnight in plenty of cold water, but do not leave for longer (particularly in a warm room) or the vegetables will begin to ferment.

Or place the vegetables in a large bowl and pour plenty of boiling water over them so that they are completely covered. Cover the bowl and soak for about 2 hours.

Or place the vegetables in a large saucepan and cover them well with cold water. Add a pinch of bicarbonate of soda in hard water areas to aid softening. Bring to the boil, remove from the heat, cover and allow to soak for about 2 hours. Drain and discard water.

Cooking

1 Place the soaked, drained vegetables in a large saucepan and cover with fresh cold water. Do not salt as this toughens the skins.

2 Bring to the boil and use a large metal spoon to skim off any foam.

3 Reduce the heat, cover and boil gently until cooked. See chart below for precise times. You must cook pulses thoroughly or they cannot be digested easily. The vegetables must be covered with water during the whole of the cooking time so top up with boiling water if necessary. Adding a pinch of bicarbonate of soda in hard water areas helps cooking. Pressure cookers cut cooking and soaking times for dried vegetables. Pour boiling water over to cover vegetables, cover and leave for 1 hour; then cook at 15 lb/high pressure for about one-third of the normal cooking time.

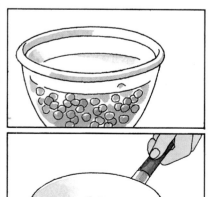

Type	Preparation and serving	Ideas for serving
1 WHOLE PEAS	Soak and cook them for about 1½ hrs	As a hot vegetable; stir in butter and add seasoning. Cook well for 'mushy' peas, and purée. Also use purée for soup (cooked with chopped streaky bacon, onion and herbs)
SPLIT PEAS **2 Yellow or green** (there are no skins on these)	Soak and then cook for about 45 min	Use for soup, as above, or for classic pease pudding
3 Lentils Red is the most common type. Other types are a greenish-brown (these are larger)	No need to soak; cook for 10 min to produce a purée. Soak overnight, then cook for 15 min	As a hot vegetable with butter and added seasoning. Or use for soups, with bacon as a flavouring. Brown lentils keep their shape well and are good for casseroles. Or drain them, cool and coat in French dressing as a salad
BEANS **4 Haricot** are small and white and roundish in shape	Soak, then cook for 1½ hrs	Use for casseroles, and for cassoulet, a classic bean and pork dish from France
5 Red kidney are plump and red skinned	Soak, then cook for 1 hr	Use for chilli con carne, and for casseroles. Or hot or cold in salads
6 Butter beans are larger, a flattish shape and white. They are a British favourite	Soak and cook for 1½ hrs	As a hot vegetable, with butter and pepper. Sprinkle over with chopped parsley, or serve with a parsley sauce. Serve with boiled bacon with butter and pepper added. Use for casseroles (particularly with bacon). Toss in butter and season with pepper as vegetable accompaniment. Sprinkle chopped parsley over. Serve with parsley sauce

Unusual vegetables

Be adventurous and experiment with some of the less usual vegetables now commonly available in our shops. They are easy to cook, once you know how.

Type and when available	Preparation and cooking	Ideas for serving

1 AUBERGINES (EGGPLANT)

July–Oct. Long and oval in shape with a plush, shiny purple skin. Look for an even colour, with firm, smooth and blemish-free flesh. The larger, the better

Allow about 6 oz/175 g per person. Remove the stalk but do not skin. Slice $\frac{1}{4}$ in/$\frac{1}{2}$ cm thick, sprinkle with salt and leave for 30 min, to draw out juice and remove possible bitterness. Then wash and dry. *Fry* or *grill* until golden brown and tender – about 10 min. Or *bake* for 15 min

Use in ratatouille. Or slice and dip in seasoned flour before frying. Or serve with tomato sauce. Or halve lengthways scoop out raw flesh and stuff with mince or a mixture of breadcrumbs, bacon, tomato, onion, cheese and sprinkled with grated cheese

2 COURGETTES

May–Sept. A variety of small marrow. Best 4–6 in/10–15 cm long. Should be firm, and straight with glossy skins

Allow 4 oz/100 g per person. Trim off ends and wash but do not peel. *Boil* small ones whole or thickly sliced for 5–15 min. *Steam* for 15 min. *Fry* sliced or halved lengthwise or sliced thickly for 5–10 min

Serve with butter and lemon juice, and sprinkle over with chopped parsley or tarragon. Courgettes make up a large part of ratatouille. Use them hot or cold in salads. Or serve cold in French dressing. Or stuff as for aubergines

3 PEPPERS (CAPSICUMS OR PIMENTOS)

Available all year, mostly imported. Green, red or yellow, at their best when 3–5 in/8–13 cm in diameter. Mild, piquant flavour, and skin should be bright and glossy but not wrinkled

Wash, and cut off the stalk end, remove inner seed and white membrane, then cut into rings, and chop. To serve whole, *par-boil* for 10 min, stuff and *bake* for 20–30 min. *Fry* chopped pieces or rings or slices for 5–10 min

Stuff whole peppers with a savoury rice mix. Or use them raw in salads. Or lightly fry chopped pieces, slices or rings and add to stews, casseroles or risottos. Use in ratatouille

4 SWEETCORN (CORN-ON-THE-COB)

July–Oct. Should be plump and well formed, golden-yellow in colour, shiny and with stiff green leaves with protruding silky threads. Can buy the kernels, frozen or canned

Allow 1–2 cobs per person. Trim off the leaves and silky threads and wash. *Boil* in unsalted water (salt toughens them) for 12–20 min, depending on size. Do not overcook

Serve the whole cob hot with butter and seasoning as a starter or as a hot vegetable. Use kernels in savoury dishes, e.g. rice, or as a hot vegetable, or in casseroles, sauces or soups, or in flans

5 ASPARAGUS

May–June, homegrown, or from Feb–June, imported. Sold in bunches, should be of even size, with firm tips and green-pink in colour, not longer than 6–7 in/15–18 cm. Asparagus should not be too thick or it may be woody and tough

Allow 8–12 stems per person. Cut off woody end and lightly scrape the white part with a knife, towards the tip. Wash and tie in bundles with tips together. Stand the bunch, tips up, in boiling water to almost reach the tips. *Boil* for 10 min. (You can protect the tips from overcooking with foil)

Drain, untie the bundles and serve hot with melted butter or hollandaise sauce. To eat: hold by the stem and dip each tip in sauce or butter; the stem end is not usually eaten. Serve cold in salads or with vinaigrette or with mayonnaise. Or cooked in savoury flans, etc

6 MARROW

July–Oct. At its best at about 12 in/30 cm long; when it is young with a delicate flavour

Allow 6 oz/175 g per person. Peel off the skin, and cut in half lengthways; remove the seeds and cut into large cubes: *or* cut into thick rings and remove the seeds, *or* cut off the ends of the marrow and remove the seeds with a spoon (to stuff whole). *Boil* chunks for 10–15 min. Or gently *fry* chunks in butter for about 15 min. Or *roast* chunks in hot fat or round the joint for the final 40–50 min. Or *bake* stuffed rings for about 30 min. *Bake* stuffed whole marrow for 1–1$\frac{1}{4}$ hrs

Serve as hot vegetable with butter and pepper. Or with a white or cheese sauce. Stuff the rings or the whole with mince or with a thick white sauce flavoured with bacon and onions, etc

7 GLOBE ARTICHOKE

April–Nov. Flavour is sweet and nutty. Should be green, with tightly-closed fleshy leaves; avoid brown or spreading leaves or purplish centres

Allow 1 per person. Cut off the stem close to its base, and remove outer and dry discoloured leaves. Soak for 15–20 min in cold water to clean well. Then drain thoroughly. *Boil* for 20–40 min, depending on size, until the leaves pull away easily

Drain upside down and serve with hot melted butter or hollandaise sauce; leaves are pulled off one by one and the fleshy bit is dipped in the sauce or butter and eaten. When only the heart is left, remove the hairy 'choke' (the soft flowery part) and eat the heart with a knife and fork. Or serve cold with a vinaigrette dressing

8 JERUSALEM ARTICHOKE

Nov–March. Brown-skinned, they are like small knobbly potatoes. The white flesh has a sweet flavour

Allow 6–8 oz/175–225 g per person. Peel them thinly and immediately plunge into cold water with a squeeze of lemon juice added to prevent discoloration. *Boil* (with another squeeze of lemon juice) for about 20 min until soft

Serve hot with melted butter and garnished with chopped parsley. Or with white, cheese or hollandaise sauce

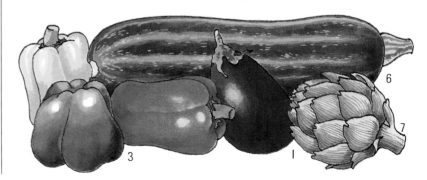

Pasta

Pasta is famous as an Italian speciality, but there are many more types than spaghetti! Water is added to ground wheat starch to make a dough, which is kneaded, formed into different shapes and dried.

Pasta is convenient and economical, needing no preparation and with no wastage. Serve pasta to start a main meal with butter, oil or cream and grated cheese (preferably Parmesan); or as main course with meat or tomato sauce. Many types, such as spaghetti, noodles, macaroni, shells, can be cooked as an alternative to potatoes.

Food value

Mainly carbohydrate, but also provides protein. Wholewheat types provide dietary fibre (see p. 19).

Buying pasta

Pasta is usually bought in packets. Allow 2 oz/50 g or slightly more per person depending whether it is to be served on its own or as part of a dish or meal. There are over 100 different kinds – mainly types of threads and tubes. Colours can vary.

Plain pasta is white; rich yellow pasta contains egg; spinach is added to colour pasta green ('pasta verde') and brown pasta is made from wholewheat including the bran. 'Quick cook' pasta is also available, and if you buy this type of lasagne and cannelloni you can make up these dishes without pre-cooking the pasta.

Storage

Keep in its original packet in a dry cupboard, or in glass jars with lids: pasta can look very pretty in the kitchen. It will keep indefinitely. For storage, cooked pasta should be cooled under running water, and drained, to keep 3 days in the fridge in a covered container.

Freeze only as an ingredient of other dishes, in soup for example, or in made up dishes such as lasagne and cannelloni.

Cooking method

Basic method for pasta, which will double its weight on cooking.

1 Put water in large saucepan. Use 2½ pt/ 1.4 litres to 8 oz/225 g pasta. Bring to the boil and add salt (2 tsp/10 ml to this quantity – too much salt means longer cooking time and can spoil the flavour).

2 Add the pasta gradually. Leave the ends of spaghetti and macaroni sticking out and then curl them round in the pan as the bottom parts soften. Add lasagne pieces one at a time to prevent sticking. Stir in small shapes.

3 Add a knob of butter for a good flavour, and to help prevent pieces from sticking together.

4 Boil (with no lid) until just tender 'al dente' ('to the teeth'), not soggy. Stir occasionally to ensure even cooking. Different types take different lengths of time to cook, but a good guide is 10–15 min (follow directions on pack). Wholewheat pastas need at least 15 min.

5 Drain before serving; no need to rinse.

Serving

Hot pasta should be served straight away with extra butter and grated (preferably Parmesan) cheese or with a sauce such as bolognese (meat) or tomato. To keep hot, place pasta in a covered metal colander over a pan of steaming water. To reheat, plunge a sieve full of pasta in boiling water for about ½ min, and serve immediately. To serve pasta cold, cool under running cold water. Drain well before serving as part of a salad (e.g. with tomatoes, raisins and french dressing).

Dishes with pasta

Macaroni (small types) Mix with cheese sauce to make macaroni cheese (you can add chopped ham, salami and/or tomatoes for variations). Grill for a crispy brown topping before serving. Serve plain with tomato sauce as a snack or starter. Cook with milk and sugar to make a milk pudding.

Noodles (ribbon) Serve plain with meat or fish dishes. Or make into crispy noodles: cook as above for 5 min, drain, run under cold water, dry and deep fry for about 5 min till golden brown; serve with Chinese meals.

Spaghetti (long solid rods) Serve with a meat sauce (see bolognese recipe, p. 57) as Spaghetti bolognese. Serve with tomato sauce, and grated cheese. Serve with meatballs in sauce. Serve plain to go with other dishes.

Lasagne (flat wide leaves) Make lasagne by combining layers of mince flavoured with tomatoes, cheese sauce (see p. 57) and pasta leaves, and cooking in oven.

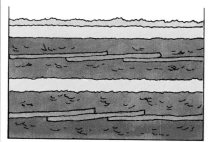

Cannelloni (large tubes) Make cannelloni by filling with mince. Coat with cheese sauce and brown in oven or under grill.

Vermicelli/Small noodles/Alphabet Use to add substance to soups. Add cooked pasta during last few min. Add uncooked pasta during last 10–15 min.

Rice

Rice provides a good alternative to potatoes and it keeps longer. It is easy to cook and can also be made into many sweet and savoury dishes.

Food value

Rice consists mainly of starch and contains about the same amount of protein as potatoes. Brown rice provides dietary fibre (see pp. 18 and 19).

Buying rice

You can buy rice loose, or packeted, or in 'boil-in-bag' packs. Allow about 2 oz/50 g per person, if serving rice in the place of potatoes with a meal, a little less if making up a rice main dish. An average-sized cup holds 8 oz/225 g, enough for 4 people.

White rice

This has the husk and bran removed, and is polished. There are 3 main types:

1 Long grain (often called Patna). Cooking makes grains light and fluffy to go well with or in savoury dishes (especially those with strong flavours, such as curries).

2 Short grain (often called round or pudding rice). This is the cheapest type with short, fatter grains. Cooking makes it soft and creamy, so that it sticks together. Use it for milk puddings and combined with chopped fruit for dishes called condés.

3 Medium grain is a size in between long and short, but is not widely available. This all-purpose type can be used for savoury or sweet dishes, but is mostly used for manufactured breakfast cereals.

Brown rice

Although brown rice is unpolished it is paradoxically more expensive. Only its inedible husk and a small amount of bran has been removed. It is more filling than white rice, with a more chewy texture and a nutty flavour. Available with long or short grains.

'Easy-cook' prefluffed rice is more expensive than other white rice and has been par-boiled to separate the grains and make them fluffier. Follow carefully the directions on the packet, as cooking times, amounts of water, etc, vary.

Flaked rice is broken grains of white rice, and is used to make quick milk puddings.

Ground rice is made from ground broken rice grains and is used for milk puddings.

Rice flour is even more finely ground, and can be used as a proportion of flour in shortbread, cakes and sponges, to give a lighter texture. (1 oz/25 g of rice flour to 4 oz/100 g wheat flour).

Storage

Uncooked: If possible decant into a jar with stopper and keep in a cool dry place.

Cooked: In fridge in covered container for up to 3 days. To reheat, see below.

Frozen: 1 month or 3 months (in cooked dishes).

Left: reheating rice.
Right: separating the grains with a fork.

Cooking method

Rice bought loose should be washed in a sieve under running water to remove white starch powder before cooking.

1 Place 8 oz/225 g (1 cup) long grain rice in saucepan with ¾–1 pt/400–550 ml (2 cups) water. For brown rice, use 1.6 pt/900 ml (3 cups) of water. Add 1 tsp/5 ml salt (and a knob of butter for a good flavour and to help keep grains separate).

2 Bring to the boil, stir once and cover.

3 Reduce heat and simmer for about 10–12 min (or for time given on packet). Brown rice takes much longer, about 40–45 min. Keep the pan covered and to avoid soggy rice do not stir during cooking. When cooked, grains should be tender but not soggy.

4 Remove from heat and separate (i.e. fluff up) grains with fork before serving. Rice should not need draining, having absorbed all the water. Serve hot with meat or curry; or cold flavoured (as below) with salads.

To add flavour, rice can be cooked in stock or watered down tomato juice. Add cooked vegetables (onion, mushroom, celery, pepper) to cooked rice; or cooked meat (chicken, bacon); or fish (canned salmon or tuna, smoked haddock). Cook with your favourite herb or spices. Some will colour the rice: saffron and turmeric, for example, colour rice yellow. Risotto (Italian) and pilau (from the Middle East) are meals in themselves: cooked meat and vegetables are added to the cooked fried rice.

FRIED RICE

Fry cooked rice quickly in a little cooking oil for about 3 min, stirring gently throughout. Good with Chinese dishes and with mixed fried vegetables served with chicken or fish.

REHEATING RICE

Bring ½ in/1 cm lightly salted water to boil in saucepan. Add rice. Cover, reduce heat and simmer gently for 3–5 min
or in metal colander (covered) over pan of simmering water for 5–10 min.
or in oven in covered dish with a little water or knob of butter – about 10 min at Mark 4/ 350°F/180°C.

Soups

Very versatile, soups can offer a meal in themselves, or simply be served as a starter. For economy, you can make soups from bones, cheap cuts of meat or low-cost vegetables, or even use up left-overs.

Soup types

Soups can be made from meat, vegetables or fish. Even fruit (e.g. pears in cider, blended and chilled) can be made into refreshing summer soups. Clear soups, such as consommé made from well-flavoured stocks, can be served to whet the appetite. Broths are more filling, made from stock with pieces of vegetable, meat, chicken, and rice or barley. Some soups, such as fish chowder, and those made from winter root vegetables, can be very thick and filling. For creamed soups (e.g. cream of chicken, cream of mushroom) add cream (see below) for a rich smooth texture.

Soups can be served hot or cold e.g. Vichyssoise (leek and potato) or Gazpacho (tomato-based). Ready-made soups can be bought in cans, or dehydrated (add water and cook according to directions) in packets. You can improve them by adding milk, top of the milk, or cream plus extra vegetables, or make

packet soups go further with your own stock. These soups can also be used to thicken and flavour casseroles and stews, and concentrated canned soups can make the basis of a sauce. Some soup powders, convenient to keep available in your store cupboard, can simply be added to a cup of hot water.

Food value

This depends on the soup ingredients. Fresh soups made with milk, meat or fish, or with cheese (sprinkled on top) or vegetables can make a nourishing meal. Soups preserve the goodness of vegetables, which might otherwise be lost with the cooking water. Bought soups are nutritionally of less value.

Storage

Most soups keep in the fridge for 1–2 days. Cover them to prevent

evaporation and flavours affecting other foods. However soups from fish stock should be made and used the same day.

Freezing

Most soups can be frozen, depending on their ingredients, but do not add cream, egg yolks or garnishes until reheating. Soups keep for 3 months, stock for 6 months.

Making soup

The basis of good tasty soups is a well-flavoured *stock*. You can buy stock cubes but fresh stock can easily be home-made, using up left-overs or bits of food normally thrown away. Stock cubes are a good standby, but they can often overpower the flavour of other fresh ingredients.

To make stock

1 **Place** in a large saucepan: raw or cooked meat bones (broken up small); or raw or cooked poultry carcass; or fish heads, skin, bones and tail; or vegetables (chopped) or the clean peelings of vegetables such as celery, carrots, turnip, parsnip, leek, mushroom (but not green vegetables).
2 **Add** a chopped onion, bouquet garni (see p.53), salt, 6 peppercorns and cover completely with water.
3 **Bring** to the boil and skim off any scum with large flat spoon.
4 **Cover,** reduce heat and simmer gently for 5–6 hrs (meat), 3 hrs (poultry), 20 min (fish), 1½ hrs (vegetables).
5 **Strain,** cool and then remove any solidified surplus fat.
Pressure cookers save time and fuel and take much of the smell out of stock-making (see p. 84).

Thickening soups

Purée cooked vegetables in sieve or blender to make soups thicker (potatoes are particularly effective).
White sauce can be the basis of a soup with added vegetable purée, chopped meat and vegetables, etc.
Milk makes a slightly creamier soup and goes well with puréed vegetables.
Cream: add a little of the hot soup to the cream, then stir this into the main soup. Use for vegetables and meat, e.g. cream of tomato, mushroom, onion, asparagus or chicken. Add just before serving and do not reboil (to avoid curdling).

Egg yolks can be mixed with a little milk or cream and stirred into the soup just before serving. To avoid curdling do not boil.
Flour or cornflour can be mixed with a little cold water, milk or stock to make a smooth, runny paste. Stir into the soup and bring to the boil.
Beurre manié is a mixture of equal amounts of butter and flour. Put a small piece into the soup and whisk as you bring to the boil. Repeat until you achieve the desired thickness.

MIXED VEGETABLE SOUP
A basic method for 4 people:
1 **Prepare** and slice or chop 1 lb/450 g mixed vegetables such as carrots, turnips, cabbage, swedes, onions, celery, leeks or tomatoes.
2 **In a large** saucepan, heat ½ oz/15 g butter and 1 tbsp/15 ml cooking oil.
3 **Fry** 2 chopped rashers of streaky bacon until just coloured.
4 **Add** the vegetables and fry gently for another 5 min – do not brown.
5 **Stir** in 2 pints/1.1 litres stock and season with salt and pepper.
6 **Bring** to the boil.
7 **Cover,** reduce heat and simmer gently until vegetables are tender, 1–1½ hrs.
VARIATIONS Add fresh or dried herbs, or crushed garlic, or for final 20 min of cooking add long grain rice, or pasta.

CREAM OF VEGETABLE SOUP
Follow steps **1–7** above.
8 **Blend or sieve,** reheat and stir in ¼–½ pint/150–300 ml cream (single, or double for a richer creamier soup). Add just before serving and do not boil or soup will curdle.

GARNISHES
Garnishes improve flavour and appearance, and are particularly effective for paler, white soups, for example, potato. You can use: chopped parsley or other chopped fresh herbs; croûtons (small cubes of fried or toasted bread); paprika pepper; grated cheese or Parmesan cheese sprinkled on top; or a swirl of cream or natural (unsweetened) yoghurt. For a substantial snack meal, serve soup with toast, or hot crusty (French) bread, or garlic bread, or with cheese or sandwiches. To serve with thin soups (e.g. French onion): toast one side of a thick slice of crusty bread; put cheese on other side and grill till bubbling; then float this on soup, cheese side up. You can add dumplings to thicker soups.

> **TIP**
> To make croûtons, cut bread slices into small cubes and fry until golden brown. Drain well. Or toast whole slices of bread and then cut into cubes.

Herbs, spices and other flavourings

Making food tasty is an art acquired by every good cook, and methods vary with each individual. Herbs and spices were originally used to preserve food and even to make it digestible and palatable enough to eat. Today, thankfully, we generally no longer need their preservative powers but herbs and spices are still used to flavour and improve taste.

Food value

Many herbs aid the digestion of rich foods, for example, sage and thyme, and some flavourings, like pepper, can also stimulate the appetite.

Using herbs

Herbs are available fresh or dried, or you can grow your own; they take up little space in a window box or in pots on a sill. Fresh herbs generally give a better flavour, but dried herbs are perfectly acceptable. Use twice as much fresh herbs as dried in recipes. To dry your own herbs: wash and shake off excess water; spread herbs out on a tray or plate and dry in a warm place (such as an airing cupboard); or tie in bunches (separating the herbs to avoid cross flavouring) and hang in an airy place. When dry and brittle, store as below. When buying dried herbs, purchase small amounts from a shop with a speedy turnover.

Storage

Dried herbs should be kept in an airtight glass or china container in a dark place. Racks are attractive but light spoils the herbs and fades their colour (the same applies to spices). Use dried herbs within 6 months. Fresh herbs will keep well in the fridge in an airtight glass jar for several weeks. Pack parsley and chives down tightly.

Freezing

Frozen fresh herbs cannot be used as a garnish but can be added to soups, stews, casseroles, stuffings, etc. Freeze in washed, dried bunches of individual herbs, or bouquet garni (see below). Wrap and store in polythene bags or in small parcels of foil. Use within 6 months. Use frozen, there is no need to thaw.

Main types of herbs

Bay leaves (1)

Bay leaves are used fresh from the tree or as whole dried leaves. Dried ground leaves have weaker flavour. The flavour is strong and spicy. Use for stock, stews, soups or casseroles; to infuse in milk to flavour savoury sauces, sweet creams and custard; in bouquet garni; and in marinades. Always remove them before serving.

Marjoram (2)

Available fresh or dried (more pungent). Use sparingly – flavour is slightly bitter and spicy. Use in soups, stews (particularly pork), pizza, rissoles, stuffing, omelette, and on roast pork.

Basil (3)

Available fresh or dried (good flavour). Sweet, pungent; use sparingly since cooking improves flavour. Use in tomato dishes, salads, vegetables, and with lamb and lamb's liver.

Oregano (4)

Available dried. Strong herb with flavour distinctive of Italian dishes. Use in tomato dishes, pizza, lasagne, bolognese sauce; and in salads, salad dressing and marinades.

Tarragon (5)

Available fresh or dried (flavour not so good). Strong. Use in egg, chicken and fish dishes, in salads, marinades, hollandaise sauce, and to flavour wine vinegar for salad dressings.

Bouquet garni

A bundle of sweet herbs, usually parsley, thyme and bay leaf. Use fresh, or buy dried in ready-made bags. Use for stocks, soups, stews, casseroles, and *always* remove before serving!

Mixed herbs

A combination of dried herbs: parsley, sage, thyme, tarragon, oregano or marjoram, sold in packets and jars. Use as for bouquet garni, above.

Parsley (6)

This has a tangy sweet flavour, and a good strong green colour. Available plain or curly-leaved (curly is better for garnishing). An important ingredient in bouquet garni. Use chopped to make parsley sauce, parsley butter and in salads. Use sprigs or chopped parsley to garnish savoury dishes, or plain boiled root vegetables. Use chopped in salads.
To chop: rinse and dry. Using a large sharp knife and a board, hold tip of knife down firmly with one hand and raise and lower handle in other hand, passing back and forth over parsley pile. Dried parsley is also available, but the flavour is most inferior to fresh, and the colour is lost.

Mint (7)

A main summer herb, used in cooking water for vegetables (especially new potatoes and peas). Mint sauce (see p. 57) is served with lamb; or use mint jelly, or mint butter. Use mint in salads, dressings, fresh fruit dishes, fruit drinks and cups, and to flavour tea. Does not blend well with other herbs. Dried mint is not so flavoursome. Chop as for parsley, above.

Nos. refer to illustration overleaf

TIP
To speedily chop parsley or mint, put them in a cup or small bowl and use scissors. Or snip parsley directly onto food to garnish.

Chives (8)
Hollow grass-like leaves with a mild flavour like onions but more delicate. Use fresh: dried chives have little flavour. Mix into sauces, or onto baked or mashed potato, or in scrambled eggs or omelettes or into cream or cottage cheese. Use as a garnish, chopped onto egg dishes, or in salads, soups, or in potato salad. Also use in sandwiches, with egg or cheese. Chop with a knife or easier still, snip with scissors.

Rosemary (9)
Available fresh or dried, but is better fresh. Its strong taste can overpower other herbs: it is sweet, pungent and aromatic. Use for roast lamb, or on grilled lamb chops with garlic; for casseroles, sauces for lamb and poultry, marinades, dressings; for fish, shellfish, veal and dishes flavoured with wine and/or garlic.

Sage (10)
Available fresh or dried (good flavour). Its powerful, almost bitter, flavour goes well with pork. Serve sage and onion stuffing with poultry, pork and duck. Sage is also used in herb-flavoured sausages. Put whole fresh leaves onto joints for roasting or add to salads, marinades or to egg dishes.

Thyme (11)
Available fresh or dried (good flavour). The flavour is powerful, slightly sharp and easily overpowers more delicate flavours so use carefully. Lemon thyme is less strong with a lemony tang. Use in stuffings for roast chicken, for stocks, soups and for vegetables (particularly tomatoes, potatoes and courgettes); and for fish, meat and poultry. Good for casseroles with wine. Often mixed with marjoram or rosemary, and an essential ingredient of bouquet garni.

Spices

Spices come from the seeds of plants grown in hot climates. They are available whole or ground. Use a pestle and mortar to grind your own. Store as for herbs and use within 1 year (after this they may taste musty).

Cinnamon (12)
This comes whole as bark in thin sticks, looking like rolls of dried paper, or ground, which is stronger. Fragrant, slightly sweet, spicy flavour but quickly loses its aroma, so buy a little at a time. Use whole for spicing hot drinks (e.g. mulled wine, or punch) or for fresh or stewed fruit. Add to pickling liquids. Use ground for baking and sweet dishes, or sprinkle onto milk puddings or custards. Use in fruit pies, crumbles, fruit sponge puddings, Christmas puddings, and in cakes and gingerbread. Use in savoury dishes such as ham, pork or stuffed cabbage. Add a pinch with a little sugar to hot milk for a pleasing bedtime drink.

Nutmeg (13)
Available whole for grating. It loses its flavour quickly, so grate straight onto food or use a special nutmeg mill (it is very hard). Its sweet, very spicy taste is strong when freshly grated. Use for milk puddings, in custards, in cakes, biscuits, sauces for fish, to flavour meat or chicken; or in a meat loaf, beef stews, casseroles or pies. Sprinkle onto soups. Use to season vegetables after cooking, such as carrots, cauliflower, spinach or potatoes, and to flavour fruit punches and mulled wine.

Cloves (14)
Available dried as whole, unopened flowers, or ground. They have a strong aroma with a spicy taste. Whole cloves should be plump and oily, and not easily broken. Use whole for pickling, or to stud joints of bacon or pork; or in fruit punches, mulled wine, stewed pears, or in apple pie. Infuse in milk for bread sauce, and to make marinades for meat or fish. Use ground in cakes and puddings (e.g. Christmas pudding), in mincemeat, baking and in milk puddings.

Ginger (15)
This comes fresh or dried as a whole root in irregularly shaped pieces which need cooking to develop their flavour. Ground dried ginger is also available. It has a strong easily recognized aroma, with a sweet hot flavour. An essential ingredient in curry powder. Sprinkle ground ginger on melon; use in meat stews, casseroles, poultry, vegetable soups or cheese dishes; in chutneys, pickles, stewed fruit and puddings, cakes, gingerbread or biscuits. Whole ginger is used in marinades, chutney and curries.

Mixed spice
A dried ground blend of spices: cloves, cinnamon and allspice. Use for stewed fruits, puddings, pies and cakes (sponge and fruit); and in biscuits and punches. A good substitute for separate spices.

Allspice (16)
This comes as whole dried berries or ground. A mildly spicy, biting taste, like a mixture of cloves, cinnamon and nutmeg. Used in pickling spice and mixed spice. Use whole for marinades, curry, pickles and chutney; whole or ground to flavour fish, beef, lamb or ham dishes, and for pea soup; ground to flavour vegetables (e.g. carrots), cakes, biscuits, milk puddings, chocolate puddings and fruit pies.

Pickling spice
A mixture of dried spices. Buy it or mix your own from mustard seed, coriander, allspice, chillies, whole ginger, peppercorns and mace, tied in a piece of muslin. Use for preserving (onions, herrings) and in chutneys and pickles.

Curry powder
This can be mixed at home or bought as a yellowish powder. It usually consists of a mixture of pepper, chilli, cardamon, cayenne, coriander, cumin, fenugreek, ginger, mustard seed, turmeric, mace and clove! Hotness varies with different blends. Use for eggs, fish, poultry, meat, vegetables or soups.

Curry paste is curry powder mixed to a thick paste with clarified butter, oil or vinegar.

Condiments

Pepper
Available as whole peppercorns or ground. Green fresh pepper is sold in bottles or cans to flavour meat or poultry. Black pepper is picked green and dried. White pepper is the ripened berry (with skin and fleshy part removed), dried to become less aromatic and less strong. Both black and white pepper is better when freshly milled: use for general seasoning. (White is best for white sauces, and where the speckled effect of black is not desirable).

Mustard
Available as whole seeds, ground or mixed. It comes from the ground black (for aroma) and white (for pungency) seeds of the mustard plant. In paste form it is ready-mixed with water but the dry powder is stronger. Whole seeds are used for pickling. Mustard is the traditional accompaniment to beef, bacon and sausages. Also use with cheese dishes including Welsh rarebit; and for salad dressing and sauces. Speciality mustards are available from many different countries: French and German types are generally milder and are mixed with vinegar to become more acidic.

To mix dry mustard Add *cold* water drop by drop to make a smooth paste. Allow to stand for 10–15 min to develop its hot taste.

Salt
Salt is an essential mineral (see p. 19). It is used as a condiment; and also as a preservative. Kitchen salt is rock salt, pumped from salt beds. Available in blocks or in crystals of varying coarseness (coarse kinds are best to use with a mill). Table salt is rock salt finely ground and specially treated with added magnesium carbonate to remain free-flowing. Sea salt, made by evaporating sea water, has a good flavour and an attractive appearance but is not suitable for use in a mill. Savoury salts can be made or bought: table salt is crushed with garlic, celery seeds and/or onion.

Other flavourings

Onion
This has a pungent distinctive smell and flavour. Strength varies with size and type (see p. 45). The red type is stronger than the more delicate white. Use raw sliced into salads, in sandwiches (with cheese) or on toast. Use to add basic flavour in soups, stews, casseroles, sauces and mince dishes, or chopped as a garnish (raw or fried). Dried onion (flakes) may be used instead of sliced or chopped onions in cooked dishes but the flavour is not so good.

Garlic
Bought as whole bulbs which look like small onions with white, pink or mauve skin. These separate into 'cloves'. Choose hard bulbs: the cloves should not have shrunk away from their paper-like sheath. Also available dried (less strong) as powder, granules or salt. It has a powerful often obtrusive (and lingering!) flavour, and has antiseptic properties. For a milder flavour, cut a clove in half and rub round inside of cooking dish or rub direct onto joint, then discard. For good stronger flavour, roughly chop a peeled clove and then crush with salt, using flat side of knife on board or plate. The garlic is ready for use when the white flesh and juice turns clear. You can use a garlic press but this is difficult to clean. Use to flavour meat, fish or vegetable dishes; or crushed in salad dressings or garlic butter.

Lemon
Use finely grated lemon rind or 'zest', or peel wafer-thin slivers, or rub skin with sugar lump (to use in sweet dishes), or use a 'lemon zester'. Use the sour juice in salad dressings instead of vinegar. Serve slices, wedges or juice to flavour fish. Use chopped peel in cakes or as flavouring and garnish with fruit dishes; or in lemon sauce. Lemon peel is a good addition to bouquet garni, lemon juice and peel flavours lemon curd and lemon meringue pie.

Lemon zester

TIP
Before grating lemons (or oranges) dip grater into cold water so that the peel slips off easily.

Vinegar
Cider, wine or beer are fermented to produce a weak acid solution, which is vinegar. It is used in cooking, preserving, pickling, marinading or sprinkled straight on food (e.g. fish and chips). Malt vinegar, made from beer, is cheapest for everyday use on food. It is dark, with a strong flavour, but it can mask other flavours. Use for pickling and chutney. White and red wine vinegars are good for salad dressing, mayonnaise and sauces (including mint). Cider vinegar is pale in colour with a strong smell of apples. Use in marinades for pork or where a recipe specifies. Distilled vinegar is clear and strong and mainly used for pickling. Flavoured vinegars can contain herbs, spices or fruit, and are sold mainly in health food shops. Tarragon vinegar, for example, is particularly good for salad dressing and marinades.

Vanilla
The dark brown dried pods of a climbing orchid. Available as essence, good and strong (you only need a few drops at a time) but often only synthetic inferior versions can be found. Essence will flavour cakes and their cream fillings, chocolate dishes, custards and ice-cream. Pods have better flavour and aroma. Use pods (1–2) to flavour caster sugar (leave them in the sugar jar). Can be re-used: warm them in milk for puddings, creams, custards, etc, then wash and dry them for next time of use.

Wine
Wine gives a distinctive taste to cooking. (The alcohol vaporizes early in cooking.) Use red wine for beef, e.g. Boeuf bourguignonne and lamb, white for cooking chicken, and pork.

Beer
Beer, for example, brown ale can be used for beef and onion stews or carbonade.

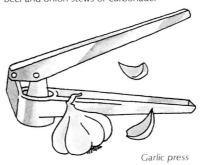
Garlic press

TIP
When you only need a small amount of lemon juice, make a hole in a lemon with a clean skewer, and squeeze out what you want. Wrap the lemon in cling film and keep in fridge for re-use.

Anchovy essence
This thick pink bottled sauce is made from boned anchovies pounded with vinegar, pepper and spices. Piquant and very salty, so use with care. Use in white sauces for fish and eggs, or in mayonnaise, meat pies or casseroles.

Worcestershire sauce
Made from vinegar with anchovies, tamarinds and many other ingredients. Use it in salad dressings, mayonnaise, omelettes, scrambled eggs, batter mix, gravies, sauces, soups and pâtés, for casseroles and meat loaves, and as a classic ingredient for barbecue sauce.

Soy sauce
A thin dark brown bottled sauce made from soya bean extract, salt, sugar and caramel. Add liberally in Oriental cooking. Also use with meat, poultry, fish or shellfish, in cooking or on the plate; its salty flavour brings out the taste of the other ingredients.

Tabasco
A thin, red and very hot bottled sauce made from peppers and vinegar. So use only a drop or two in mayonnaise, coleslaw, salads, prawn cocktail sauce, tomato dishes, meat loaves, marinades, sauces and gravies.

Bovril
A commercial meat extract, and a valuable source of iron. Use in soups, casseroles, gravies or mixed with hot water to make a drink.

Marmite
A commercial yeast extract which is very strong and salty and a valuable source of B vitamins. Spread thinly in sandwiches or on bread or biscuits. Use sparingly in scones and savoury biscuits.

Stock cubes
These can be diluted with water and used for speed and convenience where stock is needed in a recipe; but the flavour is not as individual as if you make your own stock (see p. 52). Afterwards add salt with care as they are fairly salty, and avoid using them too often as they tend to make dishes taste the same.

Sauces

A good sauce will set off – or even improve – the flavour and appearance of other foods, often adding that extra touch that turns an ordinary meal into a delicious delight.

Food value

This will depend on the ingredients used in the sauce. Sauces with meat, eggs, cheese and milk provide body-building protein.

Sauce consistencies

These vary from thin to thick as follows.

Pouring: for general use as sauce to moisten food and add flavour.

Coating: a thicker sauce to cling in a layer around food.

Binding: used to hold food together before frying for dishes such as croquettes or fish cakes.

To thicken a sauce:

You can use flour, cornflour (pure starch from corn) or arrowroot (starch from plant root), 1 tbsp/15 ml white flour has same thickening power as ¾ tbsp/12 ml cornflour or arrowroot; or use custard powder; or eggs; or vegetable or fruit purées.

Sauces made with flour, cornflour or custard powder need thorough cooking for a good flavour. Arrowroot is cooked as soon as it thickens, and unlike flour and cornflour is not suitable for thick sauces.

Storage

Once made, sauces are generally best served as soon as possible. To prevent lumps, keep them warm rather than allowing them to cool, and then reheating. To keep sauce warm pour into a warmed jug or bowl and stand this in a pan of hot water (or stand the saucepan in a larger saucepan of hot water). Place a sheet of dampened greaseproof paper on the surface of the sauce to stop a skin forming (which can also cause lumps). Before serving, remove the paper and stir the sauce well.

Freezing

Some sauces freeze well (see opposite) and it is worth keeping a supply of these (e.g. tomato, bolognese). Pour sauce into rigid polythene or foil container, cool, cover and freeze. Or cool and pour into polythene bag. You can line a small box or storage container to form even shapes to save space in your freezer. Freeze and seal (remove box if used).

Making sauces

Allow ¼ pt/150 ml of a sauce per person.

THE 'ROUX' METHOD

This makes a plain white sauce which is the basis for many savoury sauces and other dishes. It will freeze; reheat from frozen, stirring gently.

1 Melt 1½ oz/40 g butter or margarine in a small saucepan.

2 Stir in 1½ oz/40 g flour with a wooden spoon. Cook gently for about 2 min, stirring well. The 'roux' should bubble (you cook longer for a browner sauce).

3 Remove from heat and a little at a time stir in 1 pt/550 ml milk (or enough to produce desired thickness). Stir well all the time to prevent lumps.

4 Return pan to hob and bring to the boil, stirring well, so that the sauce thickens.

5 Cook gently for another 3 min, stirring well to avoid sticking and burning.

6 Season to taste with salt and pepper.

This makes a pouring sauce: for a coating sauce use 2 oz/50 g each butter and flour; for a binding sauce use 3–4 oz/75–100 g each butter and flour.

THE 'BLENDING' METHOD

This is used for most sweet sauces, and is usually made with cornflour, arrowroot or custard powder. They will freeze.

1 In a basin blend 3 tbsp/45 ml cornflour with a little milk (from measured 1 pt/550 ml) to make a smooth paste.

2 Bring the rest of the milk to the boil with a knob of butter.

3 Pour onto the paste, stirring well with a wooden spoon.

4 Pour sauce back into saucepan and bring to the boil, stirring well to prevent lumps, until thickened.

5 Cook gently, stirring well to avoid sticking for another 3 min.

6 Add salt and pepper for a savoury sauce or sugar for a sweet sauce.

This makes a pouring sauce: for a coating sauce use 4½ tbsp/65 ml cornflour. This method is not suitable for a binding sauce.

The roux method, stages 2 and 3.

Sauce	Method	Serve with
Cheese	Stir in 6 oz/175 g grated cheese and a good pinch of dry mustard. Do not re-boil as cheese may toughen and become stringy	Vegetables: cauliflower, broccoli, leeks or celery. Fish, pasta or eggs. For 'au gratin' dishes: cover food with sauce, sprinkle with breadcrumbs or grated cheese and brown under grill
Mushroom	Stir in 4 oz/100 g lightly fried mushrooms (small whole ones, or sliced, or chopped)	Fish, meat or poultry
Mustard	Mix together 1 tbsp/15 ml dry mustard with 1 tbsp/15 ml vinegar. Stir into sauce	Fish
Onion	Boil 2 onions in lightly salted water and chop. Stir into sauce	Lamb or chicken, sausages
Parsley	Stir in 4 tbsp/60 ml chopped parsley	Fish, boiled/bacon or vegetables
Caper	Stir in 2–3 tbsp/30–45 ml capers and 2 tsp/10 ml vinegar	Lamb, herrings
Egg (Do not freeze)	Stir in 2 chopped, hard-boiled eggs and 1 tbsp/15 ml chopped parsley or chives	Fish or poultry
Béchamel (well-flavoured white sauce)	Put milk in saucepan with small piece each onion, carrot, celery; a bayleaf, 6 peppercorns. Bring slowly to boil. Remove from heat, cover and 'infuse' (allow to stand) for 15–30 min. Strain and use as normal. Vary as for white sauce above.	Vegetables, meat or fish

Savoury white sauces

Make up a basic white sauce to a coating consistency, using roux method. All the sauces above can be used for filling savoury flans, vol-au-vents (pastry cases) or pancakes. Or use as toppings for snacks on toast: simply spread on toast and brown under grill. These sauces will freeze except where indicated.

Other savoury sauces

Gravy, see p. 27. Freezes well.
MINT SAUCE
Serve with roast lamb. Do not freeze.
1 Wash small bunch of mint and finely chop leaves on a board with 2–3 tsp/10–15 ml sugar.
2 Put chopped mint into small bowl/jug/ sauceboat and stir in 1 tbsp/15 ml boiling water (or vegetable cooking water).
3 Add vinegar to taste – about 1–2 tbsp/ 15–30 ml.
4 Allow, if possible, to stand for about 1 hr before serving.
APPLE SAUCE
Serve with roast pork, duckling or pork sausages. Freezes well.
1 Peel, core and slice 8 oz/225 g cooking apples.

2 Place in saucepan with 2–3 tbsp/30–45 ml water and bring to the boil.
3 Cook gently without lid until pulpy (about 10 min).
4 Mash well with wooden spoon with ½ oz/ 15 g butter and a little sugar, or use a blender.
BREAD SAUCE
(Serve with roast chicken or turkey or sausages.) Freezes well.
1 Put ½ pt/300 ml milk in saucepan with 1 sliced onion, 3 cloves, 3 peppercorns and a bayleaf.
2 Heat without boiling for about 10 min to flavour milk.
3 Strain, then to the milk add 2 oz/50 g breadcrumbs and 1 oz/25 g butter.
4 Season and cook gently over low heat for about 10 min. Serve hot.
TOMATO SAUCE
Serve with fish, chops, pasta and rice dishes, or vegetables. Freezes well.
1 Gently fry 2 chopped rashers of streaky bacon with 1 chopped onion in 1 oz/25 g butter for 5 min without browning.
2 Stir in 1½ tbsp/25 ml flour, then add 1 lb/ 450 g skinned and chopped tomatoes, crushed clove garlic, bay leaf, 1 tsp/5 ml mixed herbs and 1 tsp/5 ml sugar.

3 Season and bring to the boil, stirring well.
4 Cover and cook gently for about 35 min.
5 Sieve or blend, reheat and adjust seasoning if necessary.
NOTE For a better colour add some tomato purée, or use 14 oz/396 g can tomatoes instead of fresh ones.
HOLLANDAISE
Serve with fish, in particular salmon, and vegetables, in particular broccoli and asparagus. Do not freeze.
1 Put into a small saucepan 2 tbsp/30 ml each white wine vinegar and water, and add a few peppercorns.
2 Boil rapidly until reduced to about 1 tbsp/ 15 ml.
3 Strain into a bowl and whisk in 2 egg yolks.
4 Sit the bowl on top of pan of gently simmering water.
5 Whisk the egg mixture, slowly adding 4 oz/ 100 g butter in small pieces. Add 1 at a time, allowing mixture to thicken slightly before adding the next.
6 Season with salt and pepper, when all the butter has been added and the sauce is thick.
NOTE Should the sauce curdle because of overheating, put another egg yolk into a fresh bowl and gradually whisk in the curdled mixture.
BOLOGNESE SAUCE
This is an Italian meat sauce served with spaghetti. Freezes well.
1 Heat 1 tbsp/15 ml cooking oil in a pan and lightly fry 2 chopped rashers of streaky bacon, a chopped onion and a crushed garlic clove for about 5 min.
2 Turn heat up and add 8 oz/225 g minced beef and 3 oz/75 g chopped chicken livers. Brown well and stir in small can (8 oz/225 g) Italian tomatoes, ¼ pt/150 ml red wine, 1 tbsp/ 15 ml tomato purée, 1 tsp/5 ml oregano and seasoning.
3 Bring to the boil, cover, reduce heat and cook gently for about 30 min until sauce is thick.

Sweet sauces
SWEET WHITE SAUCE
Serve with sponge or fruit puddings or crumbles. It will freeze.
Make a white roux sauce by blending method adding sugar to taste.
VARIATIONS Stir in 1–2 tbsp/15–30 ml brandy or rum (serve with rich fruit pudding such as Christmas); or 1 tbsp/15 ml orange or lemon juice and some grated rind (serve with light sponge puddings); or 1 tsp/5 ml mixed spice or nutmeg (serve with light fruit puddings).
JAM SAUCE
Serve hot with sponge puddings, or cold with ice-cream. Do not freeze.
1 Heat 4 tbsp/60 ml jam with ¼ pt/150 ml water in a saucepan.
2 Mix 2 tsp/10 ml arrowroot with a little cold water to make a smooth runny paste and stir into the jam.
3 Bring to the boil. The sauce is ready when it turns clear.
4 Add few drops of lemon juice.
CHOCOLATE SAUCE
Serve with sponge puddings, ice-cream or profiteroles (cream-filled balls made from choux pastry). Freezes well.
1 Put 2 oz/50 g plain chocolate in a bowl with 4 tbsp/60 ml golden syrup and ½ oz/15 g butter.
2 Place bowl on top of a saucepan of simmering water.
3 When melted beat well with wooden spoon until sauce is glossy and smooth.
LEMON/ORANGE SAUCE
Serve hot or cold with sponge puddings, crumbles, ice-cream, meringues or soufflés. Do not freeze.
1 Blend, in a saucepan, ½ oz/15 g cornflour with ½ pt/300 ml water.
2 Bring to the boil, stirring well.
3 Add 2 tbsp/30 ml sugar, 1 oz/25 g butter and grated rind and juice of a lemon or orange, and 1 egg yolk.
4 Reheat, stirring, without boiling.
NOTE To make other fruit sauces – use canned fruit (purée fruit and use juice instead of water), or use puréed fresh fruit.
CUSTARD SAUCE
Serve hot with pies and puddings; cold with jelly, fruit. Do not freeze.
1 Blend 1½ tbsp/25 ml custard powder and 2 tbsp/30 ml sugar with a little of ½ pt/300 ml milk.
2 Boil the rest of the milk and pour onto the custard mixture.
3 Return to saucepan and bring to the boil, stirring well until thick.

TIP
If your sauces go lumpy, don't despair. Either whisk the sauce briskly in the pan, or sieve to remove lumps or put in blender.

Milk

Milk, our first food, is important all through our lives.

Food value

Cow's milk has been called the 'most complete' of all foods. Milk contains high-quality protein, and vitamins A and B, and its good calcium content helps to build and maintain strong bones and teeth, but it lacks iron and vitamin C. Milk is an inexpensive source of most nutrients, and especially valuable for children and teenagers, expectant and nursing mothers, the sick and elderly.

Buying milk

Most homes get daily deliveries of milk from their milkman, but 'running out of milk' is a common crisis for larger families. To avoid it, keep supplies of UHT, dried or evaporated milk, see our chart opposite.

Cream

Cream consists of the fat of the milk plus a small proportion of the other milk constituents and water.

Freezing

Single cream does not freeze and no types will whip satisfactorily on thawing. Cakes and puddings decorated with cream will freeze satisfactorily, and small cream piped rosettes can be frozen separately to add to cakes and puddings (a good way to use up small amounts of left-over cream).

Sour milk

Fresh milk contains bacteria and under warm conditions they multiply rapidly leading to that familiar sour smell and taste. Finally the milk 'clots' and separates into curds (solids) and whey (a watery liquid).

Instead of automatically discarding sour milk, use up for cooking recipes where bicarbonate of soda is an ingredient – for example, scones, cakes and puddings. If milk has separated, use the watery whey and discard the curds (or add seasoning and chopped herbs and serve as home-made curd cheese).

Yoghurt

Yoghurt is made from skimmed milk, which is pasteurized, and then 'inoculated' with special bacteria under controlled temperatures and times. Types: *Fat free* has less than 0.5% milk fat; *low fat* has no more than 1.5% milk fat. Whole or real fruits in sugar syrup, or fruit juice syrups, are simply added for *fruit-flavoured*.

Storage

The live bacteria present in all yoghurt remain dormant at low temperatures. But at room temperatures or higher, they become active and produce more acid. When the acid content becomes too high, the bacteria are killed, the flavour is spoilt and the yoghurt separates. So always store in the fridge, and follow carefully the 'use by' or 'sell by' date stamps on the cartons. Always buy from a refrigerated cabinet.

Uses

As a dessert on its own. Or for adding to other puddings. Unsweetened yoghurt can be used in recipes in place of soured cream, and can be added to savoury dishes such as soups or casseroles just before serving to give a special flavour without increasing fat content to any great extent. Serve unsweetened natural yoghurt as a side dish with hot spicy curries (e.g. yoghurt and peeled, sliced or diced cucumber) or as a salad dish, with apples and celery.

To make yoghurt

You can buy yoghurt-making kits or follow this simple method for making extra yoghurt at home.

Use equipment that has been thoroughly washed and rinsed.
1 Heat 1 pt/550 ml sterilized or UHT (long life) milk to 110°F/43°C. Alternatively use pasteurized milk, bring to the boil, then cool to 110°F/43°C.
2 Mix in 1 tbsp/15 ml natural, unsweetened, live yoghurt (i.e. must not be pasteurized).
3 Cover and leave undisturbed at same temperature for 8 hrs, in an airing cupboard, for example, until 'clots' form and the yoghurt sets. Chill. You can then add chopped fresh fruit, dried fruit, chopped nuts, etc.

TIP
You can increase the volume of whipped cream by folding in the whisked white of an egg, but this is not suitable for piping.

TIP
If you see milk about to boil over, simply turn off the gas or quickly remove from heat and put down with sharp tap to stop it rising over the top edge of pan. To prevent milk boiling over, stand a pie funnel in the saucepan.

Milk types	Methods of processing	Use for	Storage
Pasteurized, sold in bottles as 'silver top', and in cartons	A mild heat treatment kills harmful bacteria, e.g. TB. Flavour not affected Cream rises to form the familiar 'top of the milk'	Drinks (on its own or as milk shakes, or added to tea, coffee, chocolate, etc), cereals, puddings, sauces, batters, bread, cakes, etc. 'Top-of-the-milk' can be used instead of cream (will not whip). Or poured off to leave milk for a low fat diet.	Do not leave milk bottles on step for more than 1 hr – sunlight destroys its vitamins. Wipe outside of bottles and store in fridge for 2–3 days, moving old milk in a set pattern to make room for new. Never add old milk to new. Keep milk covered and away from strong smelling foods, as it absorbs odours
Homogenized, sold in bottles as 'red top' and in cartons	Milk is forced through small holes to make the fat globules smaller and distribute them evenly, and permanently so that there is no top cream layer. The milk is then pasteurized. Marginally more expensive than pasteurized	As above, but no 'top-of-the-milk'. The choice between pasteurized and homogenized is a question of personal preference	As above
Channel Isles and South Devon. Sold in bottles as 'gold top	Pasteurized, but high fat content gives rich creamy flavour and colour. More expensive	As above, but with extra thick and creamy 'top'	As above
Sterilized, sold in bottles	Homogenized milk is bottled and heated to high temperatures for up to half an hour to make it sterile. Has distinctive 'cooked' or 'boiled' flavour	As above, providing flavour is acceptable. Makes good milk puddings, but cannot be used for junket	Unopened bottles keep for several weeks in fridge, or for 1 week out of fridge. Opened bottles: store as for pasteurized
UHT (Ultra-High Temperature), popularly known as Long Life and sold in foil-lined cartons	Homogenized and treated to very high temperatures to sterilize the milk and make it keep	As for sterilized, above. Useful for catering, camping and emergency supplies, yoghurt making	Unopened packets keep for several months out of fridge; once opened store as for pasteurized
Dried milk, sold in packets, jars or cartons, usually 'low-fat'	Milk's high water content is evaporated to leave powder or granules. 'Low-fat' is made from skimmed milk, with loss of vitamins A and D	Mix carefully according to directions and then use as for pasteurized above, providing flavour is acceptable. Good for emergency supplies, camping, etc. Add to cooked dishes (e.g. soups, casseroles, sauces) to improve their food value, being a rich source of calcium and protein. Low-fat types are useful for low-fat diet	Once mixed, store as for pasteurized. Store powder in airtight jar or tin for up to 3 months in cool dry place away from strong smells which it will absorb
Evaporated, sold in cans	Heated to a low temperature to reduce some of the milk's water content then canned, sealed and sterilized	Thicker than fresh milk so add water according to directions on the can. Use as fresh milk in tea, coffee, etc, or in recipes, providing flavour is acceptable. Or use undiluted to pour on puddings. Good for reserve supplies. Can be whipped (see tip, p. 60)	Unrefrigerated unopened cans keep for 1 year. Once opened, store as for fresh milk in or out of can
Condensed, sold in cans	Even more water is evaporated and sugar is added	Add water according to directions on can and then use for sweet sauces and puddings. Or use undiluted to pour on fruit, etc.	Unopened cans, as above. When opened store as for fresh milk in or out of can. After opening milk will thicken and darken in colour

To whip cream

Use double, whipping or two parts double to one part single.

1 Chill cream and use cool clean bowl, and whisk. Use a fork for small amounts, a balloon whisk, or use a rotary whisk or small electric mixer on a low speed (with a deep bowl).

2 Proceed gently watching the consistency all the time; take care, because cream can thicken very quickly, especially in a warm room or if not perfectly fresh. When it just forms soft peaks, it holds the maximum amount of air.

3 Stop whipping at this stage, otherwise cream can start to curdle and then go buttery. Cream that is too thick does not pipe evenly, and does not fold well into mousses, fools, etc so spoiling the final consistency.

CHANTILLY CREAM

This is ideal for filling cakes, decorating trifles, flans, jellies and creamy desserts.

1 Put ½ pt/300 ml double cream, ½ tsp/2.5 ml vanilla essence and 1 tbsp/15 ml sieved icing sugar into chilled mixing bowl.

2 Whisk carefully until cream will hold soft peaks; do not over whisk. You can add rum, brandy or sherry if you wish.

TIP
Always rinse a milk saucepan out with water before using to make cleaning easier (better still, use a non-stick pan which you keep for milk and sauces).

Cream type and fat content	Method of processing	Use for	Storage
Single, sold in bottles or cartons sealed with foil. 18% fat	Homogenized, pasteurized and cooled	Pouring into coffee and over cereals and puddings including fresh or stewed fruit. Stir into soups, casseroles and sauces just before serving. Will not whip	Keeps in fridge for 2–3 days in summer, 3–4 days in winter
Whipping, sold in bottles or cartons. 35% fat	Pasteurized but not homogenized	Whip (see method p. 59) and use for piping to decorate cakes and desserts; in fillings for cakes and pastries	As for single above
Double, sold in bottles or cartons. 48% fat	Slightly homogenized then pasteurized	Use for richer pouring (see single) or for whipping. Allow to float on coffee, or stir in a swirl into soup before serving. Can be whipped	As for single above
Double-thick, sold in bottles or cartons. 48% fat	Heavily homogenized then pasteurized	Serve in spoonfuls with puddings. Will not whip	As for single above
Double Extended Life, sold in vacuum-sealed bottles. 48% fat	Heated, cooled, homogenized, bottled, vacuum sealed and then heated again	Serve in spoonfuls with puddings. Will lightly whip	Can be kept 2–3 weeks in fridge unopened. After opening, keeps as single
Sterilized, sold in cans. Available as half cream, 12% fat, or cream, 23%	Homogenized, canned, sealed, heated, cooled	Has a slight caramel flavour. Use half cream for pouring, and full cream for spooning. Will not whip	Unopened, keeps for 2 years. Opened keeps as for single
UHT single, sold in foil-lined cartons. 18% fat	Homogenized, heated and cooled	Use for pouring. Will not whip. Handy for picnics and camping holidays	Keeps for 6 weeks unopened. When opened, keeps as for single
Clotted, sold in cartons and bottles. 55% fat	Heated, cooled, then cream crust is skimmed off	Thick cream with its own distinctive flavour and yellow colour. Use with scones and jam for cream teas, or for pastries, or cake fillings or for puddings	Store in fridge for 2–3 days in summer. and 3–4 days in winter
Sour cream, sold in cartons. 18% fat	Single cream is turned sour by the action of bacteria. To sour cream, add 1 tbsp/15 ml lemon juice to $\frac{1}{4}$ pt/ 150 ml single cream. Cover and leave in warm place for about 15 min	Use for making scones, and where specified in cakes recipes. Stir into casseroles or soups just before serving. Serve with baked potatoes and chopped chives	Follow sell-by/use-by date on carton

TIP
Chilled evaporated milk can be lightly whipped. But for a better result boil the can for about 15 min in a pan of water, taking care that it remains completely covered for the whole time. Then chill for several hours before opening and whisking.

Cheese

Cheese is the oldest way we know of preserving and concentrating the goodness of milk. As a change from meat or fish use cheese, cooked for main meals. Or serve 'raw' for snacks or light meals, or in place of (or as well as!) puddings.

Food value
This varies according to the cheese, depending on type and make-up of milk used. Cheese is a good source of high-quality protein and, in the case of hard cheeses, of fat. Cheese also contains calcium, added salt, vitamin A and riboflavin.

Cheese types
Hard cheese
Made from milk, soured or ripened with a 'starter' culture of bacteria and coagulated by adding rennet; then the mixture is cut or broken to allow the whey to separate from the curd, which is scalded or heated so it shrinks and releases yet more whey. As the curd settles or shrinks, the final drops of whey are drained off, and salt is added as a preservative and to bring out the flavour. The curd is pressed in moulds for varying times and removed as whole cheese, which is ripened or matured at correct temperatures and humidity.

Cottage cheese
Made from pasteurized and skimmed fat-free milk. The curd is cut up into small cubes and slowly heated to develop the right texture. The whey is drained off, and the curd washed several times and

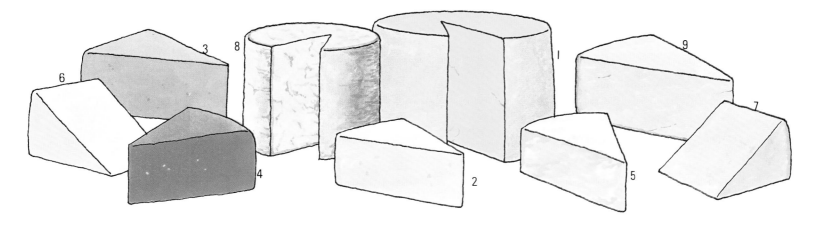

cooled, to give the familiar crumbly appearance of this soft white cheese. Salt and single cream are added and the cheese is packed into cartons.

Curd cheese

Has a clean acid flavour with a slightly granular, soft-spreading texture. A 'starter' culture develops acidity and coagulates the milk. Traditionally, the curd is hung in a cloth for 2–3 days to drain and is scraped into a clean cloth every day. Salt is added and when the cheese is firm enough, it is packed.

Soft cheese

Sold as a variety of small cheeses. The curd is carefully scooped into hoops and left to drain for several days without pressure, being turned occasionally and salted. It has a high moisture content and ripens quickly. The flavour is mellow and slightly acid with a soft-spreading texture.

TIP
Save time later on by grating quantities of cheese at one go, and then keeping spare supplies in screw-top jar in fridge. Cheese which has become too old and hard for serving on its own can usually be used up for grating.

British hard cheeses

	Type	Appearance	Texture and taste	Hints for using
Hard-pressed	**1 Cheddar** This most famous of British cheeses is also made in Canada, New Zealand and Holland	Colours range from pale to deep yellows	Close texture with clean taste that can be mild, medium or strong	Good for snacks, e.g. with pickle or raw onions, and sandwiches. Add a slice to cooked hamburgers and place under hot grill to melt cheese. Useful cheese for cooking, grates well
	2 Derby	Yellow honey colour	Open buttery texture, clean tangy taste. *Sage Derby* has added chopped sage leaves	Serve on its own or as part of cheese board. Good with fruit and cider
	3 Double Gloucester	Orange-red	Open buttery texture with delicate creamy taste	Serve on its own or as part of cheese board. Good with beer, or with fresh fruit salad and cream
	4 Leicester	Orange-red	Open texture, buttery mild mellow taste	Serve on its own or as part of cheese board. Especially good for Welsh rarebit (see below)
Lightly pressed	**5 Caerphilly**	White	Close texture, clean, mild, slightly salty taste	Serve on its own or as part of cheese board. Good with celery and bread and butter
	6 Lancashire	White	Soft crumbly texture, clean mild taste	Serve on its own or as part of cheese board. Good for cheese on toast. Or crumble to make a topping for soups, stews or casseroles
	7 Wensleydale	White, or blue-veined	Fairly close texture, clean, mild slightly salty taste	Serve on its own or as part of cheese board. Or with apple pie
	8 Stilton	White, or blue-veined	Soft, close texture. White is mild and crumbly. Blue vein is rich, mellow and creamy	Serve on its own or as part of cheese board at end of meal, traditionally with port
	9 Cheshire	White, or red	Crumbly texture, mild, mellow and slightly salted	Serve on its own or as part of cheese board. Useful cheese for cooking

Cream cheese
Soft cheese, made with cream rather than milk. It has a soft, rich, mildly acid flavour, with a buttery consistency and is usually sold in cartons or foil wrappers.

Processed cheese
Cheddar-type hard cheese ground to pulp or melted with milk, then pasteurized, cooled, moulded and packed.

Cheese spreads
Made from cheese, butter and preservatives combined into a soft-spreading bland mixture.

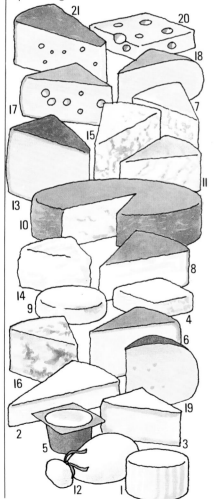

Continental cheeses			
Type	Appearance	Texture and taste	Hints for serving
FRENCH			
1 Boursin	Creamy white. Small cylinders	High cream content, with a buttery texture, very soft. Available plain, or mixed with herbs and garlic or covered with pepper	Serve at end of meal or as a snack
2 Brie	Outer crust is downy white, usually mottled with patches of reddish-brown. Soft inside is cream-coloured. Usually sold in wedges cut from flat round cheese. Inside should be flowing and bulging out of crust	Creamy, rich flavour. The crust is edible	Does not keep well: eat on day of purchase or soon after. Serve at end of meals, or with tossed salad for lunch
3 Camembert	Off-white downy 'mouldy' crust. Creamy yellow inside. At peak inside will bulge out from beneath crust in a solid, soft mass. Small flat disc shapes	Should feel springy when whole cheese is pressed gently. Mild with rich creamy tang	Will not keep well. Serve at end of meal, or with tossed salad for lunch
4 Demi-sel	Small white square, usually wrapped in foil. No rind	Smooth creamy texture. Mild flavour with slight sour hint. Fresh and unripened	Serve as a snack or spread on sandwiches, on biscuits, etc
5 Petit Suisse	Pure white, small cylinders. Usually sold in plastic container or wrapped in paper	Fresh, unripened. High fat content. Rindless, soft and creamy. Flavour mild with slight sour tinge	Does not keep well: eat as soon as possible after purchase. Serve as dessert, sprinkled with sugar, with strawberries, etc
6 Port Salut	Semi-soft, pressed discs. Thin orange rind with creamy yellow inside	Flavour is mild, buttery, creamy, smooth. Matured	Serve as snack, or at end of meal
7 Roquefort	Creamy white and blue-veined, made from ewe's milk. Cylindrical with thin (almost transparent) crust	Strong taste; rich, pungent and salty, leaving sharp sensation on tongue and lingering after-taste	Serve at end of meal
8 St. Paulin (similar to Port Salut)	Small wheel shape. Thin orange-coloured washed rind	Semi-soft texture. Flavour varies with brand and age, but is usually mild, bland and buttery	Serve at end of meal or as snack
ITALIAN			
9 Bel Paese	Pale cream sold in disc shapes	Soft texture with consistency of firm butter. Mild flavour. Ripened. One of Italy's best soft cheeses	Serve at end of meal as a snack, or with fruit
10 Gorgonzola	Famous blue-veined cheese. Made in large cylindrical shape	Softer and creamier than Stilton and Roquefort. Matured. Strong, rich, creamy; pungent-tasting with strong aroma	Serve at end of meal with fruit (apple and pears in particular) or in sandwiches with apple
11 Dolcelatte	Blue-veined	Milder with more delicate flavour than Gorgonzola	Serve as for Gorgonzola
12 Mozarella	Pure white with soft plastic casing. Made in various shapes	Moist and smooth with close texture. Unripened. Mild flavour; delicate, creamy, slightly sweet	Does not keep well. Use in cooking, melted over hamburgers, pizzas, for toasted sandwiches, and for lasagne

Type	Appearance	Texture and taste	Hints for serving
Italian (continued) **13 Parmesan**	Straw-yellow with hard brownish rind, often with a black protective layer. Also sold ready grated	Matured for a very long time. Texture is hard, brittle and flaky. Flavour is sharp, piquant and distinctive	Keeps almost indefinitely. This is the famous grating cheese and in particular use for savoury sauces, omelettes, sprinkled over pasta dishes or in soups, especially Minestrone, or in pizzas
14 Ricotta	Pure white. Made from whey drained from a cheese curd. Comes in various shapes	Fresh unripened. Texture is fine and slightly moist. Flavour is bland and sweetish. Dry Ricotta is cured and salted to make a grating cheese	Will not keep long. Serve as a dessert, sprinkled with sugar with fruit; for lunch or a snack, or as a cheese dip
DANISH **15 Danish Blue/ Danablu**	Thin yellow-white surface is slightly greasy. Inside is creamy white with blue veining	Texture is soft with creamy consistency. Spreads and slices well. Taste is stronger than Mycella (see below). Sharp, distinctive and piquant – often very salty	Serve as a dessert with grapes or walnuts, or in salads
16 Mycella	Brownish-white rind is dry and slightly greasy. Inside is soft white-cream, marbled with evenly spaced blue-green veins	Flavour is rich and creamy, less salty than other blue cheeses and mildly aromatic	Serve as a dessert or as hors d'oeuvre with grapes
17 Samsoe Denmark's most popular cheese	Rind is dry and yellow (sometimes wax-coated). Yellow-white inside has regularly shaped holes (pea to cherry size)	Texture is firm, supple. Bland, buttery, with mild, slightly sweet, nutty flavour. Matured	Good all-purpose cheese, use grated or sliced
DUTCH **18 Gouda**	Small wheels with rounded sides and flat tops and bottoms. Waxed red or yellow rind. The inside is straw-yellow with small uneven holes	Firm to touch. Mild, creamy, buttery, taste. Spiced Gouda has added cumin seed – tangy, with firmer texture. Dutch Mature Gouda is longer matured with darker, dry rind. A pronounced after-taste, cloying to the palate. Smoked and salt-free types are also available	Serve sliced or cubed with salad or a snack, or use in cooking for sauces, etc
19 Edam	The whole cheese is a shiny red ball with flattened top and bottom. This coating of paraffin wax has thin natural rind beneath. The inside is pale yellow	Firm and supple, with less fat content than Gouda, so slightly harder. A matured cheese, with mild bland taste. Can be spiced with cumin seed for tang	Serve as a snack, or sliced with salad, or in sandwiches
SWISS **20 Emmenthal**	Hard rind, rich yellow to brown; inside ivory to light yellow. Hard, cooked, pressed cheese specially treated to produce characteristic holes or 'eyes' over surface	Ripened. Firm, supple, easy to cut. Mild, smooth, mellow taste, nut-like and slightly sweet	Serve cubed in salads or as a cocktail snack. Grated on toasted snacks or on fish, chicken, egg or vegetable dishes. Use for fondue
21 Gruyere	Similar to Emmenthal but smaller and stronger. Colour is light yellow to amber; holes are small	Hard, cooked, pressed. Hard rind, supple interior. Ripened. Taste varies with age, but is similar to Emmenthal, although sharper, more acid and salty. The higher fat content makes it richer and creamier	Serve at end of meal, or use for fondue or quiche or on soups, or for veal escalopes

Buying cheese

Specialist food shops will sell you pieces cut from a whole cheese, which is the best way to buy many cheeses. But for everyday, cheese is sold pre-packed in plastic. Cottage, curd and cream cheeses can be bought loose by weight, but are often packed in cartons. Imported soft cheeses are wrapped in foil and may be sold in boxes, or as individual portions, which are a good way of experimenting with a new kind. Avoid hard cheeses that are dry, cracked, sweaty or oily. Cheeses sweat when they get too warm, and the flavour is spoilt. Soft cheeses from abroad, such as Brie and Camembert, should feel soft but not rubbery when lightly pressed.

Storage

Buy cheeses in small quantities for serving on their own, as cheese does not usually keep well. Store hard cheese wrapped in foil or polythene (to prevent drying) in the door of the fridge, or in a polythene box or covered cheese dish in cupboard. Refrigerated cheese should always be allowed to reach room temperature before serving. This takes about an hour. Most cheeses can be frozen, but hard cheeses may crumble after thawing, and soft cheeses will not ripen after freezing. Grated cheese freezes well.

Serving cheese

The cheese board can take the place of, precede, or follow, the dessert. Buy small quantities of several different types, and arrange on wooden platter with cheese knife. Serve with butter and biscuits (a selection of water, salted or sweet plain such as digestive) and/or bread (rolls, French, wholemeal or rye). Salad vegetables such as radishes, celery or watercress make a pleasant accompaniment, as does fresh fruit, in particular grapes and/or apples.

CHEESE FLAN

1 Pour into 8 in/20 cm flan ring lined with shortcrust pastry, a mixture of 3 beaten eggs (size 2 or 3), ½ pt/300 ml milk, 3 oz/75 g grated cheese and salt and pepper.
2 Bake at Mark 4/350°F/180°C for 35 min or until filling is set.
3 Serve hot or cold.

FLAN VARIATIONS To the mixture you can add chopped fried onion or mushrooms, or green peppers or arrange sliced tomatoes in flan before adding egg mixture.

CHEESE-ON-TOAST

Popular quick snack. Toast bread on one side. Then place sliced cheese on untoasted side and put back under grill until bubbling and brown. You can add tomatoes and/or chopped onion, and serve with grilled bacon.

WELSH RAREBIT

1 Place in small pan (for each person) 2 tbsp/30 ml brown ale, ½ oz/15 g butter, 4 oz/100 g grated cheese (Cheddar, or Leicester for particularly good flavour). Add ½ tsp/2.5 ml dry mustard and salt and pepper.
2 Heat gently until creamy.
3 Pour over toast slices then place under hot grill until hot and bubbling.
VARIATION Top with a poached egg.

CHEESE SOUFFLÉ

1 Melt 1 oz/25 g butter in a saucepan and stir in 1 oz/25 g plain flour.
2 Cook for 2–3 min then take off heat.
3 Gradually stir in ¼ pt/150 ml milk and bring to the boil, stirring well.
4 Add 3 oz/75 g grated cheese but do not re-boil.
5 Cool slightly before stirring in 3 egg yolks, one at a time.
6 Whisk 3 egg whites until stiff and fold into the sauce, using a metal spoon.
7 Pour mixture into a buttered 2-pt/1.1-litre soufflé dish and bake at Mark 4/350°F/180°C for about 30 min until well risen and brown. Serve immediately or it will collapse. (Good with dressed salad).

> **TIP**
> When adding cheese to sauces (see p. 57) leave until last and do not overcook as the cheese becomes stringy and tough.

Fats

Some fat is essential for successful, flavoursome cooking. Learn to understand the uses and advantages of the many different types.

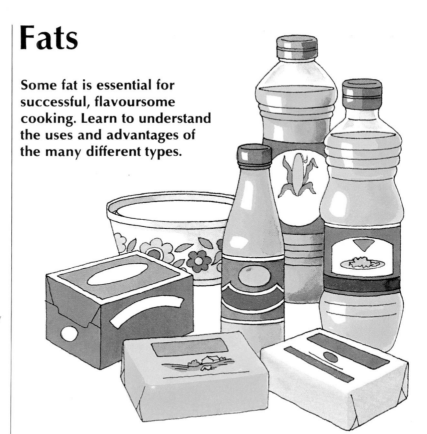

Food value

Fats provide energy in a concentrated form and people doing physical work or exercise need more of them. They help to keep the body warm and form a protective layer around internal organs such as the heart, liver and kidneys. Fats stop you getting hungry too soon after your last meal because they take longer to digest than other foods. The taste of many foods is improved by fats as, for example, when butter is added to boiled vegetables, or to bread. Indeed many dishes would be tasteless if fats were left out – fats act as a solvent for other flavours. Nevertheless, as you will be aware, many nutrition experts believe that modern diets contain too much fat, and you might like to bear this in mind when planning family menus and choosing cooking methods.

> **SAFETY TIP**
> If pan catches fire, DO NOT move it and DO NOT pour water on it. Turn off heat, and smother flames with pan lid, plate or tea towel wrung out in cold water.

Fat type	Use for	And to make
Butter The butter types below do not in fact often appear on the packs, which are usually only labelled 'salted', 'slightly salted' or 'unsalted'		
'Sweet cream', the most popular type, is made from fresh cream from New Zealand, Great Britain and Eire. It takes 18 pt/12 litres of milk to make 1 lb/450 g butter! Salted, and yellow in colour. Usually sold in parchment or gold-foil wrappers. **'Lactic' or 'ripe'** comes from Denmark, Holland and other European countries. It is made from fresh soured cream, with a full flavour and very fine texture. Whiter and softer than sweet butter. Slightly salted and usually sold in silver foil. **Unsalted butter:** can be 'sweet cream' or 'lactic', but has no added salt, and is more expensive	**Spreading** on bread and sandwiches, scones, buns, rolls, toast, muffins, crumpets: as a base for spreading jam/honey. In sandwiches, butter makes a damp-proof layer for protecting bread from moist fillings, also adds its own distinct taste and texture. **Frying** but burns easily, and is better mixed with an equal quantity of cooking oil; gives good flavour. **Glazing and garnishing** vegetables to improve their taste, appearance and texture; also used to garnish meat and fish **Greasing** cake tins, pudding basins, etc **Melting** over unusual delicate vegetables (e.g. asparagus) to enhance their luxury	**Cakes,** to improve the flavour and keeping qualities, and to give a fine even crumb texture. **Pastry,** to give short texture, a crisp crust and a pleasing flavour and colour **Shortbread:** as above. **Biscuits,** to bake them golden brown, and make them crisp and light. **Puddings,** to enrich 'bread and butter', 'crumbles' and 'Charlottes'. **Sauces,** to make them richer **Butter cream** for filling cakes. **Brandy butter** for Christmas pudding. **Puff pastry** gives a more delicate flavour and texture

Storage

Most fats and oils do not store well. After a time they smell slightly 'off' and finally go rancid. So keep fats cool, stored in the fridge in their original wrappers away from strongly flavoured foods which can taint them. Keep oils in a cool dark cupboard. In very cold weather, oils may thicken, but this does not spoil them.

Type	Keeps for
Butter	2 weeks
Margarine	2–3 months
Cooking fats	1 year
Suet (freshly grated with a little flour)	1 week
Packet suet	6 months (once opened, 4 months)
Oils	3 months

Deep fat frying

1 Choose oil if possible, because it can be heated to a high temperature without burning.
2 Use a heavy-based, deep saucepan or a special deep-fat fryer, with wire basket (see p. 14). Fat must be not less than 2 in/50 mm deep but should not come more than half-way up the pan.
3 Test the temperature, using a thermometer 375°F/190°C is good for deep frying. A cube of bread should brown in about 1 min.
4 Lower food into the fat and lift it out, using the basket or a perforated spoon. (Battered foods may stick if lowered into fat in the basket so place basket in fat and gently drop food into this).
5 Always make sure food is dry before putting into fat, to cut down on bubbling.
6 Don't put in too much at one time, or the temperature falls, and the food becomes greasy.
7 Drain and dry food on crumpled kitchen paper before serving.
8 Allow oil to cool when you have finished frying and strain into clean jar or bottle, or back into cleaned pan (cover with lid). Provided it has not burned, the same fat can be used several times over and new added as required. But always remove cooked bits and sediment, which will burn when next used for frying and can also cause oil to decompose.

Fat type	Use for	And to make
Margarine Made from vegetable oils plus milk solids and vitamins. The *soft* type is sold in tubs, and is pale yellow. This makes a good substitute for butter and is more expensive than hard margarine which is bright yellow and often a blend (sold in packets). Low-calorie types also available	**Spreading** (soft types spread easily even when cold). **Frying, glazing** as above but without such a good flavour. **Greasing** cake tins, pudding etc	**Cakes, pastry, shortbread, biscuits, puddings and sauces.** Soft types cream more readily (good for cakes and pastry) than the hard type which is good for puff pastry
Lard Made from pork fat, with a white, firm texture and pronounced flavour. The fat has been 'rendered down' (i.e. heated to melt, and then strained)	**Greasing** cake tins/pudding bowls, etc. **Frying**, either shallow or deep. **Roasting**	**Pastry:** lard makes the shortest pastry. Mix with other fats (margarine or butter) to give a short, rich result
Dripping Commercial dripping is 'clarified' fat (usually from beef) and is more expensive than lard, with good flavour. Clarifying removes pieces of food and gravy from the dripping from your own joint: place dripping in the pan, cover with cold water and boil for 3 min. Strain and cool. Then lift up solidified fat and scrape particles off the bottom	**Spreading**, to make dripping toast (sprinkle with a little salt). **Frying** (but evaporate water first by heating in pan until bubbling stops). **Roasting**, but use the same type as the meat to be roasted. **Yorkshire pudding**, to give flavour of the meat	**Cakes and pastry** (clarified)
Suet Buy shredded in packets (mixed with starch to keep grains separate) or in one piece from a butcher. To prepare butcher's suet for pastry: remove any skin and grate or chop finely. Dredge with flour to prevent sticking together		**Suet crust pastry** for savoury or sweet puddings **Christmas pudding**
Vegetable fats/shortenings These are soft but firm white fats made from vegetable oils, with no distinct flavour. 'Whipped-up' versions make lighter cakes and pastries	**Greasing** cake tins, pudding bowls, etc	**Pastry** (good for shortening). **Cakes** (good for creaming). **Puddings, shortbread and biscuits** but with less flavour than butter or margarine
Cooking oils In general these are fats from vegetables, nuts, cereals and seeds, or frequently from blends of several of these	*In general:* **Frying,** shallow or deep. **Marinading** meat or fish, with vinegar, spices and herbs. **Greasing:** brushes easily onto grill racks, cake tins and food. **Roasting**	*In general:* **Cakes:** best to use recipes developed for oils, or use 1 tbsp/15 ml to replace 2 oz/50 g other fat in recipe. **Pastry:** as above. **Salad dressings,** with vinegar, seasoning, mustard powder, garlic, herbs, etc. **Mayonnaise**

MAIN OIL TYPES		
Olive oil pressed from olives, expensive but with good flavour. Oils from Spain and Greece have stronger taste, French oil is more delicate	Not suitable for frying: has low smoking point. Otherwise as above	See general note above, and particularly good for salad dressings and mayonnaise
Corn oil Bland flavour	As above but well suited for deep fat frying	As for olive oil
Sunflower oil Pleasant taste	See general note above	As for olive oil
Peanut or ground nut oil, sometimes called Arachide, which is its French name. Light and bland	See general note above	As for olive oil
Soya Relatively cheap, but has strong flavour	See general note above	See general note, but not suitable for salads or mayonnaise

Sugars

There are many different kinds of sugar, each one suited to a particular need. Sugar (sucrose) is obtained from cane, grown in hot climates, and beet, grown in temperate climates. Sugar also occurs naturally in most other fruit and vegetables.

Food value

Sugar is a source of concentrated energy, easily and quickly used by the body. It is an essential for many cooking methods, and prolongs the freshness of baked foods and confectionery. Being a particularly acceptable form of pure carbohydrate, sugar is pleasant and easy to eat. Too much sugar can lead to overweight and dental decay.

Storage

Keep granulated and caster types indefinitely in bags or airtight containers in a dry place. Leave icing sugar tightly wrapped in its cardboard container, to keep for up to 6 months (once opened it is liable to become lumpy). Store brown and demerara in an airtight container for one year or more, but it may go lumpy.

Buying sugar

Generally, weight for weight, all refined sugars are equally sweet. But the finer the sugar, the quicker it dissolves, and the sweeter it seems (a good example is icing sugar).

Using sugar to decorate

GLAZING

Sprinkle icing or brown sugar over fruit dishes or custards and heat under fierce grill to caramelize sugar.
Or mix 2 tbsp/30 ml sugar (caster or granulated) with 2 tbsp/30 ml water and bring to the boil. Brush onto buns and other yeast mixtures as soon as they come out of oven. Use to glaze gingerbread too.
Or gently warm some golden syrup or honey and brush over buns and other yeast mixtures.

SIFTED ICING SUGAR

Sift icing sugar on top of baked, cooled plain or sandwich cakes. You can gently draw in diagonal lines with the point of a skewer or knife to make a pretty lattice pattern. You can dust biscuits (e.g. Viennese) with sugar too.

GLACÉ ICING

Use for sponges and Victoria sandwich and small cakes.
1 **Sift** 4–6 oz/100–175 g icing sugar into bowl.
2 **Gradually stir** in 1–2 tbsp/15–30 ml warm water. Mixture should be thick enough to coat back of spoon.
3 **Adjust** consistency by adding more water or sugar.
4 **Add** colouring if liked, or artificial flavourings, or cocoa, or coffee; or lemon or orange juice instead of the water.
5 **Use** straight away. Spread with palette knife, dipped in jug of hot water.
6 **Add,** if liked, any of the following: vermicelli (chocolate), candied fruits, chopped/whole nuts, crystallized cherries, angelica, coconut, grated chocolate.

Sugar types	Use for
Granulated Medium-sized white crystals; cheapest type available	General sweetening including cooking. Caramel, in sweets or for 'crème caramel'
Caster Pure, white and free-flowing, with fine, small crystals	Sprinkling on cakes, and fruit pies to decorate, Sprinkling on cereals and fruit to sweeten (dissolves more quickly than granulated). In cakes, gives a finer texture than granulated. Caramel and meringue. Glazing (see above)
Icing Crystals are ground to a fine smooth powder	Sprinkling on cakes and puddings to decorate. Icing to decorate cakes and biscuits including buttercream for filling and decorating. Sweet-making. Meringue (for extra fine result). Glazing cakes and buns
Preserving Large crystals of white sugar	Jam, marmalade, jelly, preserving fruit (in syrup) and pickles. Large crystals dissolve slowly and do not settle at bottom of pan: jam needs less stirring to prevent burning
Cube Selected granulated sugar, moistened and moulded	Hot drinks: very easy and convenient to measure and dissolves more quickly than granulated
Soft brown Finely grained less refined sugars; available from golden beige to dark brown	Sweetening, and to add a distinct flavour. Coffee. Fruit cakes and fruit puddings. Crispy topping on creamy custard-type dishes (crème brûlée (sprinkle over top and crisp under grill)
Demerara Coarse crystals of fully refined sugar mingled with molasses to give distinct flavour	Sweetening coffee. Sprinkle on breakfast cereals, in particular porridge. Sprinkling on fruit. Some fruit cakes, though too coarse for most cake-making. Sprinkling on fruit cakes and puddings to decorate
Coffee crystals White or brown (and even multi-coloured), take longer to dissolve	Developed especially for coffee: as crystals dissolve, so coffee becomes gradually sweeter
Golden syrup Made from selected liquids after refined sugar has been crystallized	Spreading on bread, toast, etc. Sauces, cakes, puddings (as an ingredient or as a topping, including treacle tarts and puddings). Glazing cakes and buns (yeast) to decorate: melt and brush over
Treacle Dark brown liquid with rich flavour	Strong flavouring. Cakes and puddings, particularly fruit types, and treacle tarts and sponge puddings. Spreading on bread, toast, etc. Sweets, in particular toffees
Glucose Powder or liquid	Sweetening drinks (powder); sweets and icings (liquid)
Honey Colour, consistency and flavour varies with area. Only natural source of sweetness on this list, and needs no refining	Spreading on bread, toast, etc. Topping for sponge puddings. Filling in cakes (Victoria sandwich). Sweeten tea, porridge, etc, for distinctive flavour and in cakes and puddings, sweetening fruit.
Maple syrup Very sweet, made from sap of maple tree. Use sparingly	Spreading on bread, etc. Pouring on pancakes and waffles
Artificial (synthetic) sweeteners Are available in liquid, powder or tablets	Use for sweetening only: they have no other properties of sugar. Slimming – no energy value

COLOURED SUGAR

This can be made to sprinkle over cakes and cold sweets. Put some caster sugar on plate with a few drops of artificial colouring. Work into sugar with fingers (a messy job). Spread on a tray to dry in a warm place. Store in jar.

BUTTER CREAM

Use for filling sponge cakes or for decorating (topped with grated chocolate, sweets, chocolate vermicelli, etc).
Beat together 3 oz/75 g butter or soft margarine and 8 oz/225 g sifted icing sugar and 2 tbsp/30 ml milk. For variation, try adding cocoa powder blended with a little hot water, or coffee essence; or orange or lemon juice and grated rind.

Using sugar in cooking

Uses	For
Essential ingredient	Sweets and icing, cake making
Sweetening	Improving palatability of many foods and drinks – fruit dishes in particular
Preserving	Canned and bottled fruits, jams, jellies, marmalade, chutneys, pickles
Setting ('gel formation')	Jams, jellies and marmalade.
Lightening (enables creamed fats to trap air; keeps flour soft so that it can expand – see 'raising agents').	Cakes.
Stabilizing egg whites to retain largest possible amounts of air.	Meringues, soufflés
Feeding dried yeast	Bread

Sugar can also add flavour and colour in the form of caramel (burnt sugar).

TIP
Rub lumps of sugar over rind of orange or lemon until well coloured. Crush, dry on tray in warm place and store in jar. Use to flavour puddings and sauces.

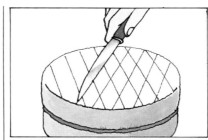
Making a lattice pattern in sifted icing sugar.

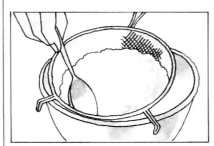
Glacé icing: sift icing sugar into a bowl.

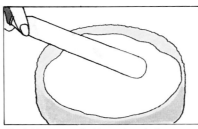
Glacé icing: spread with a palette knife.

Spreading butter cream icing.

TIP
When weighing syrup or treacle, dust scales with flour and syrup will slide off easily. You can do the same for measuring spoonfuls, or heat the spoon over a gas flame, wearing an oven glove.

Raising agents

In cookery this is the technical term for what we add to cakes and other baked goods to make them 'rise'.

Rising gives a lighter, more open texture which is more pleasant to eat and easier to digest. The raising agent can be a gas itself, for example air, or can produce gases, as do yeast, baking powder and bicarbonate of soda. Either way, the result is bubbles of gas in a mixture which will also contain bubbles of steam from the liquid present. The heat of the oven expands the gas and steam bubbles and stretches the flour which is then set by further heat.

Types of raising agent

Air
This can be introduced in a number of different ways.

1 Sieving flour so that the air is trapped between the flour grains. Used for pastry, batters and sponges.
2 Beating the mixture. Used for batters, such as Yorkshire pudding and pancakes.
3 Raising the flour above the bowl when rubbing in fat. Used for shortcrust pastry, scones or cake-making.
4 Creaming together fat and sugar. Used for cake-making.
5 Whisking eggs, either whole or just the whites. Used for cakes, soufflés and meringues.
6 Folding pastry into layers. Used for flaky and for puff pastries.
It is not possible to measure amounts of air in a mixture so the main test is appearance: a whisked sponge cake mixture should look thick and creamy. The fat and sugar for a cake should look light coloured and soft; egg whites should stand in peaks; and whole whisked eggs should look thick and creamy.

Yeast
Yeast is made up of living cells which need food and moisture to produce gas (carbon dioxide). It is used for bread-making and is usually added to the liquid (dried yeast also needs sugar) and then added to the flour. Kneading the dough distributes the yeast evenly. See also bread-making, p. 25.

Chemical raising agents
1 Bicarbonate of soda can be used by itself (e.g. for gingerbread) and sieved into the mixture with the flour. When liquid is added and the mixture is heated, carbon dioxide gas is formed. Or the bicarbonate of soda can be added with acid (e.g. cream of tartar or with sour milk as for scones) to which it reacts to form gas. Store in an airtight tin for 2–3 months.
2 Baking powder is a mixture of one part bicarbonate of soda to two parts cream of tartar. When water is added the bicarbonate of soda reacts with the cream of tartar to form carbon dioxide gas. Use for gingerbread, scones and plain cake mixtures and store in an airtight tin for 2–3 months.

Pastry

Pastry-making is one of the most individual of cooking arts. People will get different results even with the same ingredients and methods, but if you carefully follow the instructions below, you should get good results.

To make pastry you need:

1 Flour (see p. 22). Use plain flour, 'weak' (ordinary) for shortcrust and suet, 'strong' for flaky and puff. You can use a mixture of half wholewheat and half self-raising for shortcrust. Use self-raising, or plain plus baking powder, for suetcrust. It is usually better to sift flour, although with good quality flours it is not essential. Try sifting if your pastry is not so successful.

2 Fat Use butter, hard margarine, vegetable fat, lard, mixture of butter and lard, or suet according to the type of pastry. Fat should be soft enough to rub in easily but not too soft. The type of fat determines the flavour, too, and is a personal taste. Soft margarine is not suitable. Remove fats from fridge about 2 hrs before using.

3 Salt improves the flavour and helps the flour to give a good structure to the pastry.

4 Water Only use just enough to achieve the correct consistency. Too much can produce tough pastry; too little makes the pastry difficult to roll out.

5 Baking powder is used only in suetcrust.

6 Lemon juice is used for richer puff pastry to counteract the richness and help elasticity.

Simple rules for pastry-making

1 Keep everything cool and this includes the ingredients, the equipment and your hands. Only choux and hot water crust require any heat during preparation; so in general use cold water for mixing. A marble slab is useful for rolling pastry.

2 Handle the pastry as little as possible, using fingertips only (or a wire pastry blender) for rubbing in fat.

3 Rest the pastry in a cool place before using (and even between rollings). This particularly applies to richer flaky and puff but shortcrust also improves with a short rest before baking.

4 Roll as lightly and as little as possible, using short strokes of the rolling-pin, all one way, turning the pastry at right angles. Do not stretch the pastry when rolling or when putting into tin or over pie as it will only shrink back during cooking and spoil the shape. Do not turn the pastry over and avoid using too much flour on the board when rolling out.

It is better to roll out a little larger than the required size and then trim: trimmings can be re-rolled and used for decoration.

Decorating pastry

Cut pastry into thin strips and use plain or twisted for lattice effect on fruit or jam tart; or make pastry leaves for savoury pies. To attach decorations, moisten them with water. Glaze by brushing pastry lid with milk or beaten egg, for savoury or sweet pies. Take care to brush evenly as pools of liquid will make the pastry soggy. Dredge with caster sugar for sweet pies.

General methods

SHORTCRUST

A basic, everyday pastry which becomes melt-in-the-mouth magic in the hands of a good cook. 'Short' pastry should be light and should crumble easily when cooked. Use half the amount of fat to flour. The fat is rubbed in, coating each flour grain with fat to keep grains separate. Use for savoury and sweet pies, or for flans, tarts, tartlets or pasties.

1 Sift 8 oz/225 g plain flour with a good pinch of salt.

2 Weigh 2 oz/50 g hard margarine and 2 oz/50 g lard and cut into small pieces.

3 Use fingertips only to rub fats into the flour, until the mixture looks like fine breadcrumbs.

4 Sprinkle 2–3 tbsp/30–45 ml cold water over mixture and stir in with a round-bladed knife (e.g. palette knife). The mixture should now bind together and leave the sides of the bowl clean.

5 Knead lightly until the pastry is smooth and free from cracks.

6 Roll out to shape required to a thickness of about ⅛ in/3 mm. Roll only once, although trimmings can be rolled again to make decorations for pies, etc.

7 Glaze if wished and bake at Mark 7/425°F/220°C until well browned.
MAKES top and bottom crust for 7 in/18 cm pie; or an 8 in/21 cm flan; or the top for a 2-pt/1.1-litre pie dish.

FLAN PASTRY
Sweeter and richer than shortcrust, with two-thirds of rubbed in fat to flour. Use this for sweet flans and for tartlets.

1 Sift 8 oz/225 g plain flour with a good pinch salt.

2 Cut 3 oz/75 g hard margarine and 3 oz/75 g lard into small pieces.

3 Use your fingertips to rub the fat into the flour: mixture should resemble fine breadcrumbs.

4 Stir in 1 tbsp/15 ml caster sugar.

5 Stir in 2 beaten egg yolks (size 4) until the mixture begins to stick together, then use your hands to knead the mixture until it becomes a light, smooth but firm dough.

6 Roll out and use as required.

7 Bake at Mark 6/400°F/200°C.
MAKES 8 in/21 cm flan in a dish or ring.

TIP
When a recipe specifies 8 oz/225 g shortcrust pastry it usually means a mixture made with 8 oz/225 g flour and 4 oz/100 g fat.

FLAKY PASTRY

This should consist of light, delicate, crisp, but crumbly flakes. Use it for savoury and sweet pies, sausage rolls, or vol-au-vents. Flaky, rough puff and puff pastries must all rise in layers. The fat is therefore added in pieces, and by repeated folding and rolling, the layers of dough become covered by layers of fat.

1 Sift 8 oz/225 g plain (or strong plain) flour with a good pinch of salt.

2 Soften 6 oz/175 g butter, margarine or a mixture of butter and lard – use a palette knife to soften or work the butter on a plate. Divide into four.

3 Rub one-quarter of the fat into the flour, using fingertips, so that the mixture resembles fine breadcrumbs.

4 Mix to a soft elastic dough with about 8 tbsp/120 ml cold water, using round-bladed (palette) knife.

5 Roll the pastry on a lightly floured surface into a rectangle, with its length three times its width, making sure the edges are straight.

6 Cut another quarter of fat into small flakes and dot these over the top of two-thirds of the pastry.

7 Fold the unbuttered third over on top of the buttered middle section, then fold the remaining buttered third over on top of it.

8 Seal the edges by pressing with rolling-pin and turn pastry so that folded edges are to the sides.

9 Roll out again and repeat twice steps **6–8**, adding fat each time.

10 Leave to rest, wrapped in greasproof or polythene bag in fridge for 30 min.

11 Roll out to a thickness of $\frac{1}{8}$ in/3 mm on a lightly floured surface and use as required.

12 Bake at Mark 7/425°F/220°C.
MAKES two 7 in/18 cm pie tops.

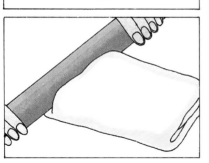

PUFF

This uses equal quantities of flour and fat for a richer, crisper, more flaky pastry which rises more evenly. It takes a long time and a lot of trouble to make and is better made the day before using so that it can cool and become firm before shaping and baking. But the results are truly impressive! Use for savoury pies, vol-au-vents, bouchées (tiny vol-au-vents) and sausage rolls; and for cream horns, cream slices and fruit pies.

1 Soften 8 oz/225 g unsalted butter on a plate with a palette knife and shape this into flattish square.

2 Sift 8 oz/225 g plain (or strong plain) flour with a good pinch of salt.

3 Mix to a firm dough with about 8 tbsp/120 ml cold water and a squeeze of lemon juice.

4 Knead well on a lightly floured surface.

5 Roll the pastry out into a rectangle, making sure the edges are straight and the corners square.

6 Place the fat square on one end of the pastry and fold over the other end to enclose the fat.

7 Seal down the edges by pressing with a rolling-pin.

8 Roll out into a rectangle, with the length three times the width.

9 Fold into thirds, as for flaky.

10 Seal edges again, using the rolling-pin.

11 Rest the pastry in the fridge in wrapped greaseproof or in a polythene bag for 15 min.

12 Repeat steps **8–11** five more times.

13 Shape the pastry as required, but roll out thinner than other types: it rises much better.

14 Bake at Mark 8/450°F/230°C.

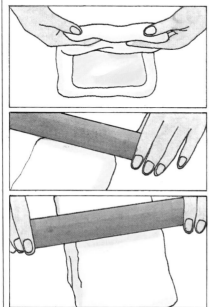

SUET CRUST

This is simple to make, using suet fat and self-raising flour. Use it for savoury and sweet puddings, in particular for traditional steak and kidney pudding. Or for dumplings, or for roly-poly, either savoury with mince, or sweet with jam.

1 Sift 8 oz/225 g self-raising flour (or 8 oz/225 g plain flour with 2 tsp/10 ml baking powder) with 1 tsp/5 ml salt.

2 Stir in 3 oz/75 g shredded suet.

3 Mix with about 7 tbsp/105 ml cold water to make a soft, elastic (but not sticky) dough, using round-bladed knife.

TO MAKE A PUDDING

1 Roll out two-thirds of the dough to $\frac{1}{4}$ in/$\frac{1}{2}$ cm thick and line a lightly greased 2-pint/1.1-litre basin (fold into four and then gently unfold in basin).

2 Spoon in filling (can be sweet or savoury).

3 Roll out the remaining dough into a circle to make the lid.

4 Dampen the edges of the dough in the basin with water.

5 Place the circle on top and press the edges together firmly to seal.

6 Trim off the excess pastry.

7 Cover with greased foil or a double layer of greased greaseproof paper, and tie this on with string. Make a deep pleat in the cover to allow the pudding to rise during cooking.

8 Place in a large pan and pour round boiling water to come half-way up the sides of the basin.

9 Bring to the boil, cover, reduce heat and steam gently for $2\frac{1}{2}$–3 hrs (fruit, cooked or raw) or 5–6 hrs (uncooked meat filling).

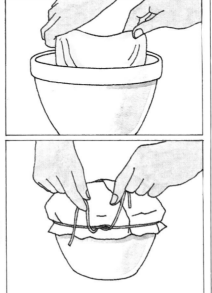

CHOUX

A light piped pastry casing with a hollow centre, which is usually filled with cream for rich desserts. Use for éclairs, profiteroles and cream buns. Alternatively choux can be filled with a savoury mix. Aigrettes are small balls of flavoured (for example, cheese) choux pastry.

1 Sift 5 oz/150 g plain flour with a good pinch of salt.

2 Place $\frac{1}{2}$ pt/300 ml water and 4 oz/100 g butter in a saucepan and heat gently until butter melts. Then increase heat and bring to the boil.

3 Remove pan from heat and quickly tip in all the flour. Beat well until the paste is smooth and leaves the sides of the pan clean. But do not over beat as this results in a fatty mixture.

4 Cool slightly and gradually beat in 4 beaten eggs (size 3 or 4), adding them a little at a time, and continuing to beat well until the mixture is smooth and glossy.

5 Cover the pan and allow the paste to cool.

6 Put the choux paste into a piping bag with a large nozzle and pipe out desired shapes.

7 Bake at Mark 6/400°F/200°C for 10 min then reduce heat to Mark 4/350°F/180°C for about 25 min until crisp, golden and puffed. Try not to open oven door during cooking.

8 Remove from oven and split éclairs, etc open to release steam and allow pastry to dry inside

HOT WATER CRUST

This is moulded while warm. An especially strong and crusty pastry casing to stand up to moulding and to hold a large amount of filling. Use for deep savoury 'raised' pies, usually made with raw meat fillings, which are seasoned and moistened with a little stock (for example, veal and ham; or pork).

1 Sift 12 oz/350 g plain flour with 1 tsp/5 ml salt and make a well in the centre.

2 Place 4 oz/100 g lard in a saucepan with ¼ pt/150 ml milk and water (half and half). Heat gently until the lard melts then bring to the boil.

3 Pour into flour and beat with wooden spoon to form a soft dough.

4 Knead until smooth.

5 To shape: roll out two-thirds of the pastry and use to line a greased pie mould standing on a baking sheet or use a cake tin or loaf tin. Keep remaining pastry covered.

6 Fill and cover with rolled-out remaining pastry. Trim and then pinch joins together to form a fluted edge.

7 Brush lid with beaten egg.

8 Cook at Mark 6/400°F/200°C for 20 min then at Mark 3/325°F/160°C for 1–2½ hrs. MAKES one pie, 3-pt/1.4-litre capacity.

BISCUIT CRUST

A biscuit and butter mixture, which is used for sweet flans and cheesecake. It is very easy and quick to make.

1 Lightly grease a shallow 8 in/21 cm flan dish, sandwich cake tin or a flan ring standing on a baking sheet.

2 Crush 6 oz/175 g biscuits, which can be wheatmeal, plain, gingernuts or mixed broken biscuits: use a rolling-pin or an electric blender.

3 Mix in 3 oz/75 g gently melted butter, stirring well.

4 Put into a flan dish and press firmly round and down with the back of a metal spoon to line the dish.

5 Chill until hard before filling with cheesecake mixture, fruit and cream/custard, etc.

LINING A FLAN CASE

It is easiest to use a plain or fluted flan ring on a baking sheet; or a loose-bottomed sandwich tin on a baking sheet.

1 Roll out the pastry (shortcrust) into a circle about 2 in/5 cm larger than the flan ring.

2 Lift pastry on the rolling-pin and lower into the greased ring.

3 Ease pastry into tin, pressing gently into corners, and leaving no air between pastry and tin. Try not to stretch the pastry.

4 Cut off excess by drawing sharp knife along the top edge. Or you can use scissors and leave a little pastry above the rim to allow for shrinking during cooking. Or on a fluted ring roll your rolling-pin over the top to trim off the excess pastry.

> **TIP**
> When using a flan dish or a sandwich cake tin, line it with foil for easy removal. When the flan or cheesecake is filled and cold, simply pull up from tin and peel away foil. Or fold over foil top ready for freezing.

To remove a baked flan Slide flan and ring onto a serving plate then gently lift off ring. With a loose-bottomed tin, sit flan on top of an upturned mug or jar and then ease off side ring, and slide flan off base onto serving dish.

'BAKING BLIND'

A technique used for shortcrust flans and tarts which are to be filled; or if a pastry case is being made in advance.

1 Roll out the pastry and line a greased flan dish or ring. Metal ones are best, for maximum heat conduction. And always place tin on a baking sheet, again to ensure good heat conduction.

2 Cut out a circle of greaseproof paper, slightly larger than the case. Grease one side and place greased side down on the pastry (or you can use a fat wrapper).

3 Half-fill with uncooked dried beans, rice or pasta (cool and keep in jar especially for this purpose; use over and over again.) Alternatively, you can make a special collection of small pebbles to use for this.

4 Bake at Mark 6/400°F/200°C for 10–15 min, carefully remove paper and all the beans, etc and put back into oven again for 5 min. When small tarts are baked blind, there is no need to line as above; simply line greased tins with pastry and prick them well with a fork.

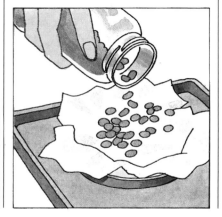

TO MAKE PASTRY PIES (IN A DEEP DISH)

1 Roll out pastry to about 2 in/5 cm larger than dish.

2 Cut round pastry to trim off about 1 in/2½ cm.

3 Brush rim of dish with water and place strip of pastry on. Seal and trim at join.

4 Fill pie (filling should be cold).

5 Brush pastry edge with water.

6 Lift rest of pastry on rolling-pin and carefully place on pie dish.

7 Press lightly onto pastry strip around edges to seal.

8 Trim off excess pastry with a knife; or use scissors which are better because you can leave a little pastry overhanging to allow for shrinkage or decoration.

To seal and decorate edges, simply pinch round with finger and thumb pressing against index finger of other hand; or to thicken the edge, first 'knock up' from underneath with back of knife, and then make shallow cuts all round to flute edges; see diagrams for other ideas. Cut small slit in the centre of the pastry to allow steam to escape.

Storage

Shortcrust can be stored as a dry mix in a plastic bag or sealed jar for up to 3 months in the fridge.

Shortcrust, flaky and puff, made up, and wrapped in foil or cling film, can be kept for 2–3 days in the fridge.

Shortcrust, baked blind, and stored in an airtight tin, will keep for up to 10 days.

Choux, suet, and hot water crust must be used as soon as made. The time for keeping cooked pastry dishes depends on the filling (shortcrust keeps longer).

Freezing

Frozen uncooked shortcrust, flaky and puff will keep for 4 months. Unbaked pies and flans will keep for 3 months; baked will keep for 4–6 months.

Remember to allow time for defrosting uncooked pastry, otherwise you do not save much time. It may be more worthwhile to freeze flaky and puff, because they take longer to prepare than shortcrust.

Biscuits

There are many methods of making biscuits. Here we have chosen three popular types.

Storage

Will keep in an airtight tin for about 2 weeks, but do not ice or dredge with sugar to store. Soft types can be interleaved with waxed paper (you can use the waxed paper from inside cereal cartons).

Freezing

Most biscuits can be frozen raw or baked for up to 6 months. Shortbread will freeze, baked, for 3–4 months.

SHORTBREAD

1 Cream 4 oz/100 g butter or margarine and 2 oz/50 g caster sugar until light, pale and fluffy.

2 Sift in 5 oz/150 g plain flour and 1 oz/25 g fine semolina and carefully mix into the creamed mixture.

3 Gradually draw the mixture together and knead lightly until smooth.

4 Press the mixture gently into a buttered and floured 7 in/18 cm sandwich tin, prick all over with a fork and sprinkle with a little extra caster sugar.

5 Leave in the fridge for about 15 min, then bake at Mark 3/375°F/170°C until a pale golden brown (about 30 min).

6 When cooked leave in tin for 5 min, then turn out, cut into 8 triangles while still soft and cool on a cake rack.

FLAPJACKS

1 Put into a saucepan 4 oz/100 g butter or margarine, 4 oz/100 g soft brown sugar, 3 oz/75 g golden syrup and heat gently, stirring, until melted.

2 Add 8 oz/225 g rolled oats and mix well.

3 Spread the mixture into a greased shallow tin, 8 in × 12 in/20 cm × 30 cm. Smooth the top with a knife.

4 Bake at Mark 4/350°F/180°C for about 20 min or until golden brown.

5 Leave in the tin, cool for 5 min and cut into 24 squares or bars. Cool before removing from the tin.

EASY BISCUITS

1 Sift together 8 oz/225 g plain flour with 1 tsp/5 ml baking powder.

2 Rub in 4 oz/100 g butter or margarine (use your fingertips) until the mixture looks like fine breadcrumbs.

3 Stir in 6 oz/175 g caster sugar, 1 beaten egg (size 3 or 4) and 1 tsp/5 ml vanilla essence; mix to a smooth dough.

4 Knead lightly on a floured surface.

5 Wrap and chill in the fridge for about 15 min.

6 Shape into a long roll about 2 in/5 cm in diameter.

7 Use a sharp knife to cut into about 40 ½ in/1 cm thick slices and place on lightly greased baking trays.

8 Bake at Mark 5/375°F/190°C for 10 min, until golden in colour.

9 When cooked, leave the biscuits on the trays for 3 min then lift onto a wire rack to cool.

VARIATIONS Replace the vanilla with 2 tsp/10 ml ground ginger or mixed spice (add this with the flour); or add 1–2 oz/25–50 g chopped cherries, or nuts, or grated plain chocolate.

Batters

Learn how to beat up a basic batter and you can make a large selection of sweet and savoury dishes.

Pouring batter

This basic method is used for pancakes, Yorkshire pudding, sweet baked batter pudding or Toad-in-the-Hole.

Method

1 Sift 4 oz/100 g plain flour with a pinch of salt into a large basin.

2 Make a well in the centre and break in 1 egg (size 3 or 4).

3 Using wooden spoon or (better) a balloon whisk, gradually beat in ½ pt/300 ml milk until mixture is smooth (or use ½ milk, ½ water). Batter does not *improve* with standing but can be made up and left to stand if convenient.

PANCAKES

Good at any time and are traditionally served on Shrove Tuesday.

1 Make up pouring batter as above, to give 8–10 7 in/18 cm pancakes. Transfer to a jug for easy pouring; or leave in bowl and use a ladle or cup.

2 Heat a little lard or cooking oil in a heavy frying-pan (non-stick is preferable) until really hot. Pour off any excess – it should merely coat the base.

3 Remove pan from heat and pour in a little batter – just enough to coat base of pan thinly when quickly swirled round.

4 Place on moderate heat and cook until small bubbles appear on surface and underside is golden brown.

5 Turn pancake over, using spatula or palette knife (the more ambitious can toss or flip!) and lightly brown second side.

6 Turn out onto plate or greaseproof paper.

Pancake ideas

Serve sweet sprinkled with caster sugar, rolled up, with lemon wedges; or with honey and cinnamon; or filled with jam and cream; or with stewed fruit, such as apple and clove; or filled with mashed banana; or filled with ice-cream (serve at once) topped with jam sauce or maple syrup; or filled with fruit pie filling; or with drained canned fruit and whipped cream; or with butter cream flavoured with grated orange and/or lemon rind and sherry or liqueur. Crêpes suzette are pancakes folded and heated in a sauce prepared from fresh orange juice, sugar, Cointreau and brandy (flamed).

Serve savoury with melted butter, salt and pepper; or filled with thick white sauce flavoured with one or some of the following: cheese, ham, onion, green or red pepper, bacon, mushroom, mixture of cooked vegetables, flaked cooked fish, canned salmon or tuna, or cooked chicken; top with a sauce, e.g. tomato. Or fill with a mince mixture or with mushrooms fried in butter with garlic, plus tomato purée; or with flaked canned salmon mixed with sour cream and a little cayenne pepper. Top with a white cheese sauce, for example.

To store batter

Keep in covered container in fridge for 2–3 days.

To store pancakes

Cool, stack, wrap in polythene bag or cling film, and keep in fridge for up to 1 week. It is best to interleave the pancakes with pieces of greaseproof paper.

To freeze pancakes

Cool, interleave with greaseproof paper and wrap in foil. Unfilled keep for 6 months, filled keep for 3 months.

YORKSHIRE PUDDING

Traditionally served with roast beef.
1 **Make up** pouring batter as before.
2 **Put** 1 oz/25 g lard or dripping (or hot fat from the roast) into baking tin, about 8 in/21 cm square. (Must be a tin: other flameproof materials do not get hot enough).
3 **Heat** in hot oven, Mark 7/425°F/220°C for 2–3 min until very hot.
4 **Quickly pour** in the batter. While pouring, place tin on drop-down oven door (if available) or put tin on low heat on hotplate. Then return tin to top shelf of oven for 30–35 min until well risen and crisp.
This quantity will also make 12 individual puddings. Dot fat in patty tin, then proceed as above, but cook for only 15–20 min.

TOAD-IN-THE-HOLE

1 **Arrange** 1 lb/450 g pork sausages in baking tin about 10 in/25 cm square.
2 **Cook** at Mark 7/425°F/220°C for 10 min.
3 **Meanwhile make up** pouring batter.
4 **Pour** into tin over sausages and return to oven for 30–35 min.

SWEET BATTER PUDDING

1 **Make up** pouring batter as before and mix with 1 lb/450 g peeled and sliced cooking apples, or drained canned fruit, adding a pinch of mixed spice and sugar to taste.
2 **Cook** as for Yorkshire.
3 **Sprinkle** with sugar to serve.
Plain pouring batter cooked as for Yorkshire above, can be served with jam, honey or golden or maple syrup for a filling pudding.

Coating batter

This basic mixture is used for frying fritters, pieces of fish or meat, sausages and vegetables (for example try courgette or aubergine slices). Follow same directions as for pouring, but use half the amount of liquid (i.e. ¼ pt/150 ml milk, or milk and water mixed).

APPLE FRITTERS

1 **Peel** and core 3 or 4 cooking apples and cut into rings about ¼ in/½ cm thick.
2 **Dip in** coating batter and deep fry (see p. 65) until golden brown. You can shallow fry but the result is not so even.
3 **Drain** on crumpled kitchen paper and sprinkle with caster sugar.
4 **Serve** immediately.
VARIATIONS Try bananas, peeled and halved lengthways; or canned pineapple rings or apricot halves; or mix the caster sugar with a little ground cloves or cinnamon.
For savoury fritters, use luncheon meat slices; or corned beef slices; or sausages; or vegetable slices.
For corn fritters: fold 11 oz/312 g tin drained sweetcorn kernels in batter mix, and fry spoonfuls in hot fat till golden, turning once.

Cakes

Everybody loves a slice of cake to turn tea time or elevenses into a treat. Richer cakes can be served instead of puddings. And making cakes is fun, a good way to introduce children to cooking.

Food value

The food value of pastries, cakes and batter recipes, such as pancakes, is mainly the provision of carbohydrates (from the flour and sugar) and fat. Some protein is obtained from flour and any eggs or milk in the recipe. Vitamins A and D are also present if butter or margarine is used.

Baking cakes

Try not to open the door of the oven during cooking; if you must, do it as gently as possible.

To test if a cake is cooked

You can press the top of large cakes lightly with your finger tip: they should be spongy, and should give only very slightly. Your finger should leave no impression because the cake should spring back again. For fruit cakes, insert a warm skewer or knitting needle: if it comes out clean the cake is cooked. Small cakes are cooked when well risen, golden brown and firm to the touch; small cakes and sandwiches should be shrinking away from the sides of the tin.

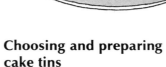

> **TIP**
> Instead of greaseproof paper you can use the waxed paper from inside cereal packets for lining cake tins.

Choosing and preparing cake tins

Use shallow tins for sponges and sandwiches; and deep tins for fruit cakes. Non-stick versions save time (see below). Special shapes are available for special occasions: e.g. hearts and numbers.
Grease all cake tins lightly, even if non-stick. Brush over with cooking oil or rub with a butter or margarine wrapper. Tins without a non-stick coating should be also dredged with flour as an added prevention to sticking. Sprinkle a little flour into the greased tin, shake it around to give a fine coating and tip out excess. For fatless sponges, use half flour and half caster sugar mixed together, which will also give a crisper finish to other cakes.
Line cake and sandwich tins with greased greaseproof paper. Lining the base only is sufficient for Victoria sandwich but for richer mixtures and fruit cakes, the whole tin should be lined with a double layer of paper to prevent the outside from browning too much and from drying. For extra rich fruit cakes (such as wedding and Christmas cakes), which require very long cooking, tie a double layer of brown paper round the sides too.

Storage

Always store cakes in an airtight tin. Small cakes, sponges and sandwiches will keep up to 3 days; gingerbread will keep 1–2 weeks; rich fruit cakes wrapped in greaseproof, then foil, will keep 6 months or more (do not put foil next to the cake as acid in the fruit makes tiny holes).

Freezing

Baked cakes can be stored frozen for 4–6 months; uncooked mixtures (but not whisked sponge) for 2 months; fruit cakes (see note under storage) for 1 year.

To make cakes you need:

1 Flour, see p. 22. Use self-raising for plain cakes, and to give an even texture for sponges. However, self-raising is not suitable for rich fruit cakes as it makes them rise too much, and then they usually sink in the middle. This type of cake requires plain flour with added baking powder.

In general use a 'weak' (ordinary) flour as the gluten in 'strong' flours makes heavy cakes. Always sift your flour to make cakes lighter, and the flour easier to combine with other ingredients. If you wish, wholemeal or wheatmeal flours can be added as a proportion to many recipes, but do not use for rich cakes, or delicate (e.g. whisked) mixtures. These flours usually need extra raising agents and more moisture.

Cornflour, arrowroot and soya flour can be added as a proportion of wheat flour (1 oz/25 g in every 8 oz/225 g of flour mix). They contain no gluten and so help to 'weaken' the flour mix, to produce lighter cakes (especially good for sponges).

2 Sugar, see p. 66. Caster sugar is generally best for cake-making, because it dissolves more readily to give a finer cake. Syrup, honey and treacle can also be used and give a closer, moister texture, which is particularly good for chocolate cakes and gingerbread. Brown sugars add extra flavour to fruit cakes. Granulated sugar is only used for the rubbed-in method (see below).

3 Fat, see p. 64. Butter gives a good flavour, and is particularly suitable for rich cakes. Margarine is more economical. All types are suitable. Soft tub margarine creams more easily for creamed mixtures and is also good for 'all-in-one' recipes.

Lard should be used alone only in cakes with a lot of flavouring or spices, because it has a pronounced flavour, as has dripping. Flavourless vegetable fat can also be used for cakes. To use oil, you should follow specially-developed recipes to ensure the right proportions; oil makes good gingerbread.

4 Eggs Size 3 is usually suitable. Always have eggs at room temperature for cake-making – do not use straight from the fridge.

5 Liquid Moisture gives off steam, which lightens a cake. Milk or water is usually used. Sour milk can be used in cakes which include bicarbonate of soda, to give a better rise.

6 Raising agents, see p. 67.

TIP
Freeze large cakes cut into slices so that you do not have to thaw and use the whole cake at one go.

Basic ways to make cakes

There are literally hundreds of different cake recipes, but most kinds can be mixed using one of the following basic methods.

Creaming

All ingredients should be at room temperature, so take fat, eggs and milk out of fridge the night before or early in the day. For example:

VICTORIA SANDWICH
1 Cream 4 oz/100 g butter or margarine with 4 oz/100 g caster sugar. Beat with a wooden spoon or with an electric beater until the mixture is light, fluffy, creamy and pale.
2 Beat together 2 eggs (size 3 or 4) and add to the mixture a little at a time, beating well after each addition to avoid curdling (separating).
3 Gradually fold in 4 oz/100 g sifted self-raising flour, using a metal spoon to slice through the mixture gently. The mixture should drop easily from the spoon given a sharp tap but should be too thick to pour. If it seems too stiff, add a little milk.
4 Divide the mixture between two 7 in/18 cm prepared sandwich tins, and level each with a knife.
5 Bake on the same shelf in the centre of the oven, Mark 5/375°F/190°C for 20 min or until golden and well risen. The cakes should be firm to the touch and shrink away from the sides of the tins.
6 Turn out and cool on a cake rack.
7 When cool, sandwich together with jam and sprinkle caster sugar over the top.
SANDWICH CAKE VARIATIONS For a chocolate version, replace 3–4 tbsp/45–60 ml flour with the same amount of sifted cocoa; for coffee cake, add 2–3 tsp/10–15 ml coffee essence or 1 tbsp/15 ml instant coffee mixed with a little hot water, at stage 2. Or flavour with almond or vanilla essence.
ALTERNATIVE FILLINGS Sandwich cakes together with butter cream as well as or instead of jam. You can flavour the butter cream with grated orange or lemon rind, or cocoa, or coffee. Or add almond or vanilla flavouring. Use the same mixture and method to make small cakes in paper cases or patty tins, but cook for about 15 min only.

Creaming.

Rubbing in

Used when there is half as much fat as flour.
CHERRY CAKE
1 Sift 8 oz/225 g self-raising flour with a pinch of salt.
2 Rub in 4 oz/100 g butter or margarine, using your fingertips, until the mixture looks like fine breadcrumbs.
3 Stir in 4 oz/100 g caster or granulated sugar and 4 oz/100 g glacé cherries which have been washed, dried and halved.
4 Make a hollow in the centre and pour in a mixture of 1 beaten egg (size 3) and 1 tsp/5 ml vanilla essence and 6 tbsp/90 ml milk. Mix with a wooden spoon to make a soft consistency which will drop off when the spoon is tapped on the bowl. Add a little more milk if necessary.
5 Put the mixture into a prepared 6 in/15 cm cake tin, and level the top with a knife.
6 Bake on the middle shelf of the oven at Mark 4/350°F/180°C for about 1¼ hrs (the cake should be golden, well risen and firm to touch).
7 Turn out of the tin and cool on a wire rack.
VARIATIONS To make a plain cake, leave out the cherries; or to make a light fruit cake stir in 4 oz/100 g mixed fruit at stage 3; or use 1 oz/25 g caraway seeds for a seed cake.

Rubbing in.

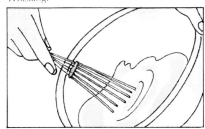
Whisking.

Melting.

Whisking

Used for sponges. It is usually a mixture with no fat, but with a high proportion of eggs and sugar. For example:

SWISS ROLL
1 Stand bowl over pan of hot water. (But this is not necessary if using an electric mixer.)
2 Break 3 eggs (size 3 or 4) into the bowl together with 3 oz/75 g caster sugar. Whisk until light and creamy; the mixture should leave trail when you lift up the whisk.
3 Remove the bowl from the pan and fold in 3 oz/75 g sifted plain flour, using a metal spoon.
4 Pour into a lined, greased Swiss roll tin, 11 × 7 in/28 × 18 cm.
5 Bake on the middle shelf of the oven at Mark 6/400°F/200°C for 6–8 min; the sponge should be golden-coloured, firm and well risen.
6 Turn the sponge onto a sheet of greaseproof paper covered with caster sugar.
7 Trim off its edges and spread it with warmed jam.
8 Roll up while still warm (use the paper to make the job easier).
9 Cool on a wire rack then dust with caster sugar once again.
VARIATIONS For a chocolate Swiss roll, replace 1–2 tbsp/15–30 ml flour with cocoa. To make a sponge cake, grease and flour two 7 in/18 cm sandwich tins, divide mixture between the two and bake at Mark 5/375°F/190°C for 20–25 min. Turn out, cool and fill.

Melting

The method used for cakes containing heated syrup or treacle. For example:

GINGERBREAD
1 Sift 8 oz/225 g plain flour with 1 tsp/5 ml bicarbonate of soda, 2 tsp/10 ml ground ginger, 1 tsp/5 ml mixed spice and a pinch of salt.
2 Heat in a saucepan 4 oz/100 g butter or margarine with 4 oz/100 g soft brown sugar, 4 tbsp/60 ml golden syrup, 3 tbsp/45 ml black treacle and ¼ pt/150 ml milk until melted but not boiling.
3 Pour this into the dry ingredients along with one beaten egg. Mix with a wooden spoon until smooth.
4 Pour into a greased, lined cake tin, 7 in/18 cm square.
5 Bake at Mark 3/325°F/160°C for 1–1¼ hrs.
6 Leave in the tin for 5 min then turn onto a wire rack to cool. Keeps in an airtight tin for 1–2 weeks.

VARIATIONS For a fruit gingerbread, add 4 oz/100 g dried fruit (such as a mixture of sultanas and mixed peel).

Fruit

Perhaps the most attractive and appealing of all foods, fruit is delicious on its own or cooked into a wide variety of dishes.

Food value

You get the most goodness out of fruit which is eaten raw. Citrus fruits are particularly rich in vitamin C which is also found in strawberries, black and red currants, and raspberries. Vitamin A comes in apricot, peaches, oranges, bananas and rosehips. Unripe fruit contains starch, which on ripening turns to sugar. There is useful roughage in all fruits, especially in the skin and in the seeds.

Frozen fruits still contain most of the vitamins, and dried fruit is a good source of B vitamins. Some A and C are obtained from canned and bottled fruit, particularly from the juice, but some have been destroyed, and even more will be if the fruit is further cooked.

Buying fruit

Look for unblemished firm fruit, and for economy buy fresh fruits which are in season. You can also buy fruit which has been frozen, canned, bottled, dried or vacuum-packed. When buying dried fruit look for cellophane-wrapped or loose types so that you can check that it does not have a dry surface indicating that it is stale and old.

Storage

Keep fruit in a *cool*, dry place with plenty of air circulating round it. Place large fruits in a bowl or container and keep dry because wet fruit deteriorates very quickly. When eating fruits complete with skin, always wash them first because of the insecticides used during growing, but do not wash until just before using. To avoid bruising, always handle as gently as possible. Keep soft fruits in the fridge in a punnet or container, and cover them to prevent fruit smells (for example, strawberries) transferring to other foods (such as milk, or eggs). Do not put bananas in the fridge. Soft fruit will only keep 1–2 days and is usually sold very ripe so it is better to eat the day it is bought. Storage times for hard fruit varies with ripeness; most fruits can be ripened at home. Vacuum packs will keep unopened for 3 months.

Freezing

Buy fruit ready frozen or freeze your own at home, but aim to pick and freeze as quickly as possible. Fruit for freezing must be of excellent quality, fully ripe and free from blemishes and bruises. You can use the following freezing methods:

1 Freeflow, for when you want the fruit to stay separate. 'Open' freeze on trays then pack into polythene bags or plastic containers; with this method you use small quantities at a time, and the fruit stays a good shape. Will keep for 2–12 months (time varies with the type of fruit).

2 Dry with sugar used for soft juicy fruit, whole or sliced. The juice from the fruit combines with the added sugar to make a natural syrup. Keeps for 8–12 months.

3 In sugar syrup, a good method for non-juicy fruits and for those which discolour during preparation and storage, e.g. apple, pear, peach, rhubarb. Will keep for 8–12 months.

4 Puréed, recommended for well-ripened or even slightly damaged fruit, and takes up less space in the freezer. You can use the puréed fruit for mousses, ice-cream or fools. Soft fruits are usually puréed and frozen raw; hard fruits are lightly cooked first, then sieved or blended, and sweetened (if liked). Keeps for 3–12 months.

Cooking methods

Stewing
FOR FRESH FRUIT
Use 3–4 oz/75–100 g sugar and ¼ pt/150 ml water (soft fruits) or ½ pt/300 ml (hard fruits) for each lb/450 g fruit.

1 Prepare fruit according to kind (see chart).
2 Gently heat together the water and sugar in a saucepan until dissolved.
3 Add the fruit and simmer gently (to avoid spoiling the shape) until soft.
Berries, soft fruit, apple slices take 10–15 min.
Apples and pears (quartered) and plums take 15–25 min.
Cooking pears take 20–50 min (hard ones take 2 hrs at least).
4 Serve hot with custard sauce or milk pudding or cold with cream or ice-cream.
If you wish, you can lift out the fruit after cooking and boil the syrup to thicken it.

FOR DRIED FRUIT
1 Wash 1 lb/450 g fruit – one kind, or a mixture of prunes, apricots, peaches, apples and/or pears.
2 Soak fruit in 1 pt/550 ml water for 12 hrs or overnight *or* pour over 1 pt/550 ml boiling water, cover and allow to stand for about 2 hrs.
3 Put fruit with water used for soaking into a saucepan and simmer gently until tender, at least 30 min or more.
If you wish you can remove the fruit and boil the syrup to thicken.

Baking
APPLES
1 Choose medium-sized cooking apples – wash, dry and carefully slit the skin of each apple round its middle.
2 Remove cores (you can use an apple corer) and place apples, whole, in an ovenproof dish.
3 Fill each apple with soft brown or demerara sugar and top with a knob of butter.
4 Pour round 3–4 tbsp/45–60 ml water and cook at Mark 6/400°F/200°C until tender, 45 min–1 hr.
5 Serve with custard.
VARIATIONS Fill with honey or golden syrup, sultanas and chopped nuts; or with mixed dried fruit and brown sugar with a pinch of mixed spice, cinnamon or ginger in each apple; or with mincemeat; or peel the upper half of the apple and then cook as above, then 15 min before the end of the cooking, top the apples with a meringue mixture (see p. 80).

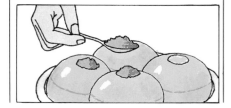

Type and when available (Nos. refer to illustration)	To prepare and use raw	To prepare and use cooked
APPLES Available in an abundance of varieties and colours **Cookers** Large, firm, acid-tasting and pulp easily on cooking. Available all year, e.g. *Bramley's Seedling* (**1**), *Grenadier* (**2**) **Eaters** vary in size and colour, from yellow/russet to deep red. Available all year, home-grown July–Nov, with imported varieties for the rest of the year **Homegrown** *Cox's Orange Pippin* (**3**) Best flavour. Palish green with orange-red flush. *Laxton's Superb* (**4**) Similar to Cox, but slightly sweeter. *Worcester Pearmain* (**5**) Rich red with pale green streaks, juicy, sweet. *Egremont Russet* (**6**) Crisp and nutty. **Imported** *Golden Delicious* (**7**) Pale green with delicate flavour. *Granny Smith* (**8**) similar to Golden Delicious	For dessert wash and dry just before eating to serve with cheese. Peel (if wished), core and chop or slice for savoury salads (dip in lemon juice to prevent browning) and fruit salad; or to garnish meat or game or sausages; or as sandwich fillings (with cheese and/or sultanas)	Whole: core and *bake*. Peel, core and slice: then *stew*, or use for pies or puddings. Jam, chutney. Apple sauce. In stuffings for pork or mackerel Peel (if wished), core and slice or cut into rings, and *fry* in oil/butter mixture and serve with pork, game, sausages, mackerel or herring. For *fritters* Peel, core, cut into rings and dip in coating batter. *Stewed* Use for pies, puddings, pancake fillings or fools. Use in stuffing

BANANAS
1 **Peel** and halve lengthwise.
2 **Sprinkle** with lemon juice and cook at Mark 5/375°F/190°C for about 20 min.
Serve warm or chilled with warmed honey or golden or maple syrup and cream.

PEARS
1 **Peel** 4 stewing pears, halve them lengthways and remove their cores.
2 **Place** them in an ovenproof dish and pour round ¼ pt/150 ml water and sprinkle sugar over to taste.
3 **Cover** and cook at Mark 3/325°F/160°C for 2–3 hrs until tender.
Serve hot or chilled with custard or cream or chocolate sauce or ice-cream.

To purée fruit
Rub through a nylon sieve; do not use metal as this can affect the colour and the taste of the fruit; or use an electric blender. Use ripe soft fruit, stewed fruit (sweetened or unsweetened), or canned or bottled fruit.

FRUIT FOOL
Mix together equal quantities of cooled fruit purée and whipped cream. Or you can use half whipped cream and half custard. Pour into individual glasses and decorate with grated chocolate or chopped nuts. For extra flavour you can add lemon and/or orange rind, or vanilla essence.

FRUIT SALAD
Prepare a mixture of fruits (see chart) such as apple, pear, banana, orange, grapes, according to kind. Toss them in lemon juice. Then add a syrup made with ½ pt/300 ml water and 3–4 oz/75–100 g sugar, heated together until dissolved, and cooled before adding; *or* a mixture of syrup and fresh orange juice; *or* a mixture of syrup or orange juice and cider; *or* a can of fruit, including its syrup, such as apricot halves, peach slices or pineapple chunks. Serve with cream.

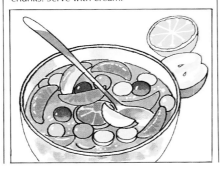

Type and when available	To prepare and use raw	To prepare and use cooked
PEARS Home-grown, Oct–Feb; imported, all year **Dessert** *Conference* (**9**) Irregular tapered shape, green-russet skin, can be eaten when crisp or ripened at home. (Can be used for cooking, too.) *Comice* (**10**) have a better flavour, with a tough skin but are sweet and juicy underneath. *Williams* (**11**) have yellow skins. **Cooking** pears are the smaller, tougher, green types	Wash and dry just before eating to serve as a dessert. Peel and core then halve, or quarter, or slice or chop for savoury salads or fruit salads: or serve with Parma ham or salami and mango chutney and soft cheese, as an hors d'oeuvre	*Baked* (whole and peeled only or peeled, halved or quartered, and cored) – try baking or stewing in red wine or cider. Serve hot or cold. *Stewed* pears can be used for pies, puddings, fools or pancake fillings. Or use for bottling and chutney
BANANAS (12) Available all year and are the fruit of a tropical tree. *Jamaica* bananas are long and large; cream-coloured flesh and little flavour. *Canary* bananas are smaller with pinker flesh, and stronger flavour	As a dessert: or in fruit salad, dipped in lemon juice and served with custard or cream; or set in jelly, or as milk shakes; or a sandwich filling, mashed with lemon juice; or sliced with lemon juice to accompany curry	*Baked* – see below. Or halve lengthwise (skin on) and *grill* cut side till golden. Serve with syrup and cream. Or *fry* slices to accompany chicken (Maryland). *Fritters* Peel, cut into four, dip in coating batter and deep fry
ORANGES Imported all year round. **Sweet** *Jaffas* (**13**) Large, with thick, rough and deep orange skin. Sweet and juicy. From Israel. *Ovals* (**14**) Small, oval, golden yellow. From Cyprus. *Navels* (**15**) have a characteristic growth at one end, with thin skins. Seedless, sweet and juicy; from Spain, Israel, Morocco and Brazil. *Blood* (**16**) oranges (from Spain) have red flecks in their flesh and the skin has a red tinge. **Bitter** *Seville* (**17**) Jan and Feb. Thin skin; juicy and sour	For dessert, peel skin off, divide into segments. Or remove pith and inner skins and use in fruit salad, gateaux, etc. Skinned segments can garnish duck and cold desserts or use whole slices. Juice makes drinks and sauces.	Rind (grated) and juice *flavours* cakes, puddings and their fillings, sweet and savoury sauces, icings, mousse, stuffings and sweet or-savoury pancake fillings Use for marmalade or for sauces (use flesh and juice) to serve with duck
LEMONS (18) Available all year. Yellow skin and juicy, acid flesh. Usually a thick skin means less juice. *Genoa* type is the most common	Slices and wedges are used to garnish fish dishes and veal. Juice is used for drinks, and jam-making (a good source of pectin)	Juice and grated rind is used to *flavour* cakes, puddings and fillings; sweet and savoury sauces; or stuffings. Or for lemon meringue pie, lemon curd and marmalade

Type and when available (Nos. refer to illustration)	To prepare and use raw	To prepare and use cooked
GRAPEFRUIT (1) Available all year. Smooth, thick yellow skin, acid flesh, yellow or pinkish, with large pips or seedless. Slightly sweeter types are available	As appetizer or for breakfast, halved and sprinkled with brown sugar and/or ground ginger. Use skinned segments in fruit or savoury salads. Use juice for drinks	Marmalade. *Grill* and serve as appetizer
LIME (2) Available all year, especially Feb–July, has a small lemon shape with yellow skin when ripe, and a sharp flavour	As for lemons (except as a garnish for fish and veal)	
TANGERINES (3) Oct–Feb. Similar to a small orange. Thin skin is easily removed; sweet flavour. *Clementine* (4) not so sweet, with a closer rind. *Mandarin* (5) a flatter shape, thin skin and very sweet flesh. *Satsuma* (6), a seedless mandarin	As dessert or in fruit salads and other desserts, puddings	Marmalade
APRICOTS (7) May–Aug and Dec–Feb. A stone fruit with velvety, yellow-orange skin and flesh. Soft and juicy when ripe	Wash and dry before serving whole or halved and stoned, as dessert or in fruit salads	*Stewed* in pies, puddings with custard or cream. Good with almonds. Jam, bottling

Type and when available	To prepare and use raw	To prepare and use cooked
PEACHES (8) June–Oct. Round fleshy fruit with a large stone, yellow-orange skin and flesh. Home-grown or South African or Italian. Ripe when soft at stalk end	As a dessert (wash and dry before serving), in fruit salad. Skin should come off easily. If not dip in hot water for a few seconds then plunge into cold. Raw or cooked, use chopped in savoury salads. Bottle (with brandy). Pickle, or use for fool or for condé	*Stew*, skinned and halved or quartered and use for pies, puddings and flans, or serve with cream, ice-cream or custard sauce
NECTARINES (9) Aug–Sept and Dec–May; like peaches but skin is shiny and smooth. Only a few are home-grown	As for peaches	As for peaches
RHUBARB (10) A vegetable with sour stalks. Jan–March – forced rhubarb with pink tender stalks. March–July – firmer rhubarb, thick and green with a pink-red tinge, and more acid. The leaves are poisonous		*To prepare*, wash, trim ends and cut into short lengths. *Stew* and serve with custard or use in pies, puddings or crumbles. (Add toppings to raw or stewed fruit.) Good stewed with ginger and served with crystallized ginger. Use for chutney, pickle and jam. Rhubarb fool
PLUMS Aug–Oct. **Dessert** (can be used for cooking, too). *Victoria* (11) Juicy, with yellow-red skin. *Czar* (12) Dark blue skin with golden flesh. **For cooking only** *Santa Rosa* (13) Small and acid with purple skin. *Golden King* (14) Green-yellow and acid. A white bloom is a sign of freshness	Wash and dry. Use whole, or halved and stoned, in in fruit salad	*Stewed* whole or halved and stoned, serve with custard. Or use in pies, puddings, crumbles, fools. Good stewed with walnuts. Jam and bottling
DAMSONS (15) Aug–Oct. A small plum, with purple skin and yellow flesh. Sour unless very ripe (firm – not hard). A white bloom is a sign of freshness		*Stew* whole or halved and stoned as plums. Jams and chutneys
GREENGAGES (16) July–Sept. A small green-yellow, round plum with good flavour and a white bloom	Wash and dry before serving if ripe, as dessert	*Stew* whole, or halved and stoned. *Bake* in pies, puddings. Jam

Type and when available	To prepare and use raw	To prepare and use cooked
GRAPES (17) Available all year as a small green, white or black juicy fruit sold in bunches with small seeds. Also small green seedless. Usually imported, but home-grown are supposedly better. Fresh grapes should have a bloom	Wash and dry before serving. Whole (seedless) or halved and seeds removed in fruit salad. Serve with cheese at end of meal	
MELON Best and cheapest June–Sept, but available all year. Has a thick skin, with watery flesh, hollow centre and a layer of flat pips. When ripe, the flat end (not the stalk) should feel soft. *Honeydew* **(18)** Oval with pale green-white skin, or dark green and ridged. The flesh is green-yellow. The most plentiful and the least expensive. *Canteloupe* **(19)** Round with dark green-ridged skin, and pink-yellow flesh, slightly scented. *Charentais* **(20)** Small (each serves only 1–2 persons), with yellow-green skin, and yellow scented flesh with a distinctive flavour; expensive. *Water melon* **(21)** Large round or oval in shape, smooth green skin, and pink-red flesh with large seeds embedded in it. Usually sold in thick slices	Halves or wedges with pips removed, as appetizer, can be sprinkled with ginger. Or with skin removed and cubed in fruit or savoury salads. Remove flesh from large melon, halve and fill with fruit salad. Good with orange and/or grapefruit segments (peeled) as starter or dessert	
PINEAPPLE (22) Available all year. A tropical fruit, expensive, with cylindrical shape with pointed leaves at top. The hard skin is dark orange, with 'eyes', and the firm juicy flesh is cream to dark yellow	Remove skin and cut into slices horizontally. Cut out core to leave rings. Serve raw as dessert with cream, in rings or cubes (rings cut into pieces): or in a fruit salad	*Stewed*, cold with cream, or for gateaux, or for mousse. Make *fritters* with rings. Use in pork curry. Or brush rings with butter and grill to serve with gammon. Make pineapple upside-down pudding
AVOCADO PEARS (23) Available all year. A pear-shaped fruit with a green to purple-brown skin which is non-edible, tough and shiny (often rough). The flesh is soft, oily and pale green, with a buttery texture and a large stone. Flavour is mild and fragrant	Halve lengthways and remove stone. Fill hollow with vinaigrette; or with cream cheese and onion; or with chopped ham, cooked onions, garlic and tomatoes – or with mayonnaise and prawns. Use peeled and chopped in salads and sauces, or mashed or puréed as a dip. Also in sweet dishes and in fool (with gooseberry)	Soup

Type and when available *(Nos. refer to illustration)*	To prepare and use raw	To prepare and use cooked
STRAWBERRIES (1) A popular soft red fruit. The juicy flesh has a round central 'hull' and small pips embedded in its outer surface. Home-grown, May–July and Sept–Oct. Imported at other times but flavour is not so good	Pull out stalk with hull, and wash and dry. Use whole in fruit salad and other cold desserts, such as gateaux, trifle, etc. Purée as fool or as mousse, or for milk shakes. Strawberry shortbread. On their own with cream or ice-cream	Jam
RASPBERRIES (2) A soft, juicy red fruit with central hull, and a sweet, slightly acid flavour. June–Sept	Pull out hull and wash and dry. Use in pies and puddings. On their own with cream or ice-cream. Raw in fruit salad and other cold desserts	Jam, or *stewed* in pies and puddings
LOGANBERRIES (3) Similar to raspberries but larger with a hard central hull, and a dark red-purple in colour. June–Sept	As for raspberry above	
BLACKBERRIES (4) Similar to raspberries but dark red-black in colour. Wild, or cultivated which are larger and more juicy and have a different flavour. July–Oct	As for raspberry above	Makes good jam and jelly. Or cook with apple, and use in pies, or serve with custard or cream
GOOSEBERRIES (5) May–June. Many varieties, round or elongated, smooth or hairy. **Cooking** types are green and sour, with firm flesh, and many pips/seeds. **Dessert** types (usually larger) are green to yellow-white, or russet and are soft and pulpy, with a sweet flavour and large seeds. July–Sept	Wash and remove stalk and snip off top and tail with scissors. Serve as a dessert, or in fruit salads	*Stewed* in pies and puddings. Jam, fool or as a sauce for mackerel. *Stewed* and served with custard
BILBERRIES (6) (wimberries, whortle berries) Smaller than blackcurrants, dark blue-mauve with small seeds, and a distinct flavour. Grown wild in England and Wales. June–Aug	Very sour and usually need a lot of sugar	*Cook* in (or lightly stew first) pies, puddings

Type and when available	To prepare and use raw	To prepare and use cooked
CRANBERRIES (7) Dark red or crimson berries usually from America, and smaller than a cherry. Hard yellow flesh with small seeds. Oct–Feb (imported), and July–Aug (home-grown)	Too sour	For pies and puddings. Use for sauce (turkey and pork). Use for jelly
BLACK CURRANTS (8) Small round fruits grown in clusters, and black when ripe with a rich flavour All currants are available June–Aug (home-grown)	*To prepare,* remove stalks and snip off top and tail with scissors. Too sour to eat raw	Use (raw or stewed) in pies and puddings (good with apple) and other fruit desserts. Use for jam or jelly. Juice for milk shake
RED CURRANTS (9) Similar but are bright red	Slightly sweeter – as above	
WHITE CURRANTS (10) Less common, with an almost transparent skin	Sweet. Eat raw in cold desserts or as above (but not for jam, jelly or milk shake)	
CHERRIES Small, round fruit with stone. Can be home-grown or expensive early types are imported. **Dessert (11)** types are bright red, black or yellow. Best-known are White and Black Hearts. May–Aug. **Cooking (12)** types July–Aug, e.g. Morello, black	Wash and dry and serve for dessert. Or remove stalk, halve and stone (or use special tool which pushes out the stone while fruit stays whole), for fruit salad and other cold desserts	Use (raw or stewed) in pies or puddings. *Stewed,* in thickened syrup, for Black Forest Gateaux. Jam, or for bottling
POMEGRANATES (13) The size of an orange with a hard russet-coloured skin, and a red flesh containing a mass of seeds. Sept–Jan	Remove skin with knife, break into pieces and suck juicy flesh from the seeds. Use the juice in drinks and fruit salad	
DATES (14) Fresh types are not widely available, but are in season Oct–Feb. The fruit of the date palm tree, oval with brown firm sweet flesh and a long cylindrical stone. They come whole 'on stem' or stoned and pressed into shapes for cakes, etc. Solid dried, in packets or boxes	Serve as traditional Christmas fruit	Use in cakes, puddings, fruit loaves, e.g. date and walnut
FIGS (15) Imported in large numbers. They are juicy with small seeds. *Green* figs have green skins and yellow-green flesh. *Purple* figs have purple skin and red-purple flesh. Sept–Dec. Dried types also available	Serve fresh figs as dessert or as a starter with ham. Use dried figs in dried fruit salad	

Puddings

'What's for pudding?' goes up the familiar cry at the end of the first course. Although puddings may seem to have gone out of fashion in recent times, everybody still loves them.

Pudding or dessert?

What's the difference? On the whole the words are interchangeable, but many people use 'pudding' to describe the more filling and heavier of the ideas below (like sponges and crumbles) and 'dessert' for the lighter mousses, meringues and so on. Try and choose a pudding that gives a good balance to your meal. There is often an element of contrast in successful pudding selection. For example, a hot pudding makes a good sequel to a cold first course, and vice-versa. And if you have a light first course a heavier type of pudding goes down well. If you use pastry in your first course, avoid it for your pudding. In the same way, don't follow a fried first course with a fried pudding, such as fritters or pancakes. And of course the heavier hot puddings go down particularly well in winter, and the lighter, chilled type are refreshing on a warm day.

Cooking methods

STEAMED SPONGE PUDDING

Not 'stodgy' if you follow this method.

1 **Lightly grease** a 1½ pt/900 ml pudding basin and put a small round of greased greaseproof paper in its bottom.

2 **Put** a quantity of Victoria sandwich mix (see p. 73) into the basin and cover with a double layer of greased greaseproof paper (or foil) and tie firmly with string. Make a wide pleat in the top to allow for the pudding to rise.

3 **Steam** for 1½–2 hrs: place in a large saucepan with boiling water to come half-way up the sides of the basin. Sit basin on wooden pot stand or old saucer. Or use steamer. Cover and keep water boiling gently; top up if necessary with boiling water.

4 **Serve** with custard or jam sauce.
VARIATIONS As for Victoria sandwich; put 2 tbsp/30 ml jam or golden syrup or stewed fruit pie filling in the basin then top with the mixture; or add spices or 2–3 tbsp/30–45 ml dried fruit; or flavour with the grated rind of an orange and/or a lemon. Alternatively, makes 6–8 individual puddings, which will require 30–45 min cooking. Freezes well, cooked or uncooked.

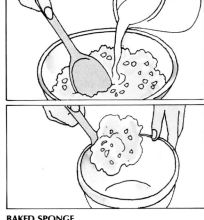

BAKED SPONGE

A basic recipe with many possibilities.

1 **Lightly grease** a 1½ pt/900 ml pie dish and fill with Victoria sandwich mixture (see p. 73).

2 **Bake** at Mark 4/350°F/180°C for 30–40 min until well risen and golden brown.

3 **Serve** with custard or jam sauce.
VARIATIONS As for Victoria sandwich; or put 3 tbsp/45 ml jam, or golden syrup in the bottom and top with the mixture; or use mincemeat, or fruit purée, or pie filling; or add 4 oz/100 g dried fruit with the flour; or flavour the sponge with grated rind of orange and/or lemon. You can also use the same mixture to make 6–8 individual puddings in which case cook for 20 min. Freezes well, cooked or uncooked.

SUET PUDDINGS

Correctly made, these are light and delicious – but you need to start them cooking early!

1 **Lightly grease** a 1½ pt/900 ml pudding basin and line it with suetcrust pastry (see p. 69).

2 **Fill** with stewed fruit, drained canned fruit or pie filling.

3 **Top** with pastry, cover and steam (see p. 69), for 2–2½ hrs.
OR

1 **Sift** 6 oz/175 g self-raising flour with a pinch of salt.

2 **Mix in** 3 oz/75 g shredded suet and 2 oz/50 g caster sugar.

3 **Add** enough milk to make a soft mixture which drops easily off the spoon.

4 **Put** into a greased 1½ pt/900 ml pudding basin.

5 **Cover** as for steamed sponge pudding and steam for 1½–2 hrs.

6 **Serve** hot with jam or fruit sauce.
VARIATIONS Put 2 tbsp/30 ml jam or golden syrup, or stewed fruit, or pie filling in the bottom of the basin then top with the suet mixture, and steam as above.

CRUMBLE TOPPING

Crumbles are always family favourites.

1 **Prepare** fruit (apples, rhubarb, plums, black currants, or gooseberries) according to kind and arrange in an ovenproof dish with 4 oz/100 g caster sugar.

2 **Sift** 6 oz/175 g plain flour and use your fingertips to rub in 3 oz/75 g butter or margarine, until the mixture looks like fine breadcrumbs.

3 **Stir** in 3 oz/75 g caster sugar and sprinkle this mixture over the fruit.

4 **Bake** at Mark 6/400°F/200°C for about 35 min.

5 **Serve** with custard sauce or cream.
VARIATIONS Use fruit already stewed or a can of fruit pie filling, and cook for 25 min. Or flavour the crumble mix with grated orange or lemon rind; or with 1 tsp/15 ml mixed spice, cinnamon, nutmeg or ginger (sifted in the flour). Or replace the caster sugar in the topping with soft brown or demerara sugar. Fruit crumbles freeze well cooked or uncooked. Or you can freeze a handy supply of topping on its own.

COBBLER

Makes a scone-like topping which is a good alternative to crumbles. Use this mixture as for crumble above.

1 **Sift** 8 oz/225 g self-raising flour with a pinch of salt.

2 **Rub** in 2 oz/50 g butter or margarine until the mixture looks like fine breadcrumbs.

3 **Stir** in 1½ oz/40 g caster sugar.

4 **Make** a hollow in the centre and pour in enough milk to make a soft dough.

5 **Knead** lightly on a floured surface then roll out to ½ in/1 cm thick. Cut out small shapes (e.g. rounds) using a floured cutter or a sharp knife.

6 **Overlap** shapes on top of the filling in a greased ovenproof dish.

7 **Brush** the shapes with milk and bake at Mark 7/425°F/220°C for about 15 min until the topping is golden brown.

8 **Serve** with custard sauce or cream.
Freeze topping separately, uncooked.

FRUIT PIES

This classic English pudding can have a top crust only or a bottom and top crust. Use shortcrust pastry for either; or flaky or puff can be used for top crust only. 8 oz/225 g of shortcrust makes a top and bottom crust for an 8 in/21 cm pie plate. Half this quantity of flaky and puff makes the top crust only. See pp. 68 and 69.
Fillings Use raw fruit, peeled and thinly sliced (apples) or halved (plums, etc), mixed with sugar to taste; or use stewed fruit, sweetened to taste; or use a can of pie filling. Serve with custard sauce or cream.
VARIATIONS Apple, rhubarb or a mixture of the two; black currants, or apple and black currants; blackberries, raspberries or apple and either of these; cherries; gooseberries; plums (you can use tinned); apricots (you can use tinned). Fruit pies freeze best uncooked.

TARTS

A delicious change from pies.

Egg custard

1 **Line** a flan ring with shortcrust pastry (see p. 68).

2 **Fill** with egg custard mix (see p. 80) and sprinkle with grated nutmeg.

3 **Bake** at Mark 7/425°F/220°C for 10 min, then reduce to Mark 4/350°F/180°C for about 20 min: custard should be just set.

4 **Serve** cold.
Do not freeze.

Treacle or mincemeat

1 **Line** a pie plate with shortcrust pastry.

2 **Spread** with a mixture of golden syrup and breadcrumbs (stiff enough to spread thickly) or mincemeat. Leave edges free. Add a 'lattice' pastry topping if you wish (see p. 68).

3 **Bake** at Mark 7/425°F/220°C for about 20 min until golden brown.
Freezes well, cooked or uncooked.

Bakewell

1 **Line** a flan ring with shortcrust or flaky pastry.

2 **Spread** inside base with jam.

3 **Fill** with Victoria sandwich mix (see p. 73). but halve the quantities) but fold in 3 oz/75 g each ground almonds and cake crumbs with the flour.

4 **Bake** at Mark 7/425°F/220°C for 15 min then reduce to Mark 4/350°F/180°C for 25 min and firm and golden brown.

5 **Serve** hot or cold, dusted with icing sugar, with cream or custard; or top with glacé icing to serve as a cake.
Freeze cooked or uncooked.

MILK PUDDINGS

A cooked mixture of cereal, milk, sugar and flavourings. Not at all boring, if correctly cooked! Do not freeze them.

Rice pudding

1 **Put** 1½ oz/40 g washed short grain rice and 2 tbsp/30 ml caster sugar into a buttered 1½ pt/900 ml ovenproof dish.

2 **Pour** on 1 pt/550 ml of milk and grate some nutmeg over the top (or use ready grated nutmeg). Dot with butter.

3 **Bake** at Mark 2/300°F/150°C for 2½ hrs (stir two or three times during first hour, to make the pudding creamy).
VARIATIONS Add 2–3 tbsp/30–45 ml dried fruit such as sultanas; or add 1 tsp/5 ml mixed spice, nutmeg or cinnamon; or serve cold with drained canned fruit as fruit condé.

Tapioca, Sago

Cook these the same way as rice.

Semolina

1 **Heat** 1 pt/550 ml milk in a saucepan and sprinkle on 4 tbsp/60 ml semolina.

2 **Bring** to the boil, stirring well. When thick, cook for a further 3 min, stirring all the time.

3 **Take** off the heat and stir in 2 tbsp/30 ml caster sugar.

4 **Pour** into a lightly buttered ovenproof dish (1½ pt/900 ml), and bake at Mark 6/400°F/200°C for 30 min.
OR
Cook in a saucepan for a further 10 min and serve.

5 **Serve** with spoonfuls of jam or syrup; or with stewed fruit.
VARIATIONS Before baking stir in dried fruit and chopped nuts; or flavour with vanilla, almond, mixed spice, nutmeg or cinnamon.

MERINGUE TOPPING

This is not difficult but adds a luxury touch.
1 Whisk 2 egg whites until they stand in stiff peaks (but do not over whisk or the whites will not fold easily and may break down).
2 Whisk in 1½ oz/40 g caster sugar then fold in another 1½ oz/40 g, using a metal spoon to cut through mixture.
3 Pile the meringue into an ovenproof dish containing stewed fruit, or a pie filling.
4 Bake at Mark 4/350°F/180°C for about 10 min until crisp and light brown. Decorate if wished with glacé cherries and angelica, cut into small shapes.
Do not freeze.

LEMON MERINGUE

The sweetness of the meringue is offset by the tang of the lemon.
1 Mix, in a saucepan, 3 tbsp/45 ml of cornflour with ¼ pt/150 ml water and the grated rind and juice of 2 lemons.
2 Bring to the boil, stirring well, to thicken.
3 Add 3–4 oz/75–100 g of caster sugar.
4 Cool slightly then stir in 2 egg yolks.
5 Pour into a 7 in/18 cm shortcrust pastry case (baked blind, see p. 70).
6 Pile meringue topping over, see above.
7 Cook as above.
Do not freeze.

BAKED ALASKA

This sensational but simple dessert is a sponge base topped with ice-cream, coated with meringue, and baked at Mark 8/450°F/230°C for 3 min until the outside is just browning. Make sure your oven has reached the high temperature required before putting in your pudding.

BAKED EGG CUSTARD

Simple to make, and most nutritious.
1 Warm 1 pt/550 ml milk, but do not boil.
2 Lightly whisk together 3 eggs (size 3 or 4) with 2 tbsp/30 ml caster sugar, then pour the milk over.
3 Strain the mixture into a buttered ovenproof dish (1½ pt/900 ml) and grate some nutmeg over the top.
4 Stand the dish in another shallow dish of cold water (to come half-way up the sides of the inner dish). This makes sure the pudding heats evenly and helps to prevent it separating.
5 Bake at Mark 3/325°F/170°C for 45 min, until the custard is set. A knife inserted in its centre should come out clean.
Do not freeze.

BREAD AND BUTTER PUDDING

A good way to use up stale bread.
1 Cut 4 thin slices of buttered bread into strips and arrange them in a greased ovenproof dish.
2 Sprinkle with 2 oz/50 g sultanas or currants and 1 tbsp/15 ml caster sugar.
3 Heat ¾ pt/400 ml milk without boiling and pour onto 2 lightly whisked eggs (size 3 or 4).
4 Strain the egg mixture over the bread and grate some nutmeg over the top.
5 Bake at Mark 4/350°F/180°C for about 35 min until set and lightly browned.
VARIATIONS Use soft brown or demerara sugar instead of the caster sugar. Replace ¼ of the dried fruit with mixed peel.
Do not freeze.

QUEEN OF PUDDINGS

Use the yolks for the custard and the whites for the meringue topping.
1 Warm, in a saucepan, ¾ pt/400 ml milk, 1 oz/25 g butter and the grated rind ½ lemon.
2 Whisk together 2 egg yolks (size 3 or 4) and 1 oz/25 g caster sugar.
3 Place 3 oz/75 g white breadcrumbs in a lightly buttered ovenproof dish and strain the milk over the top.
4 Bake at Mark 4/350°F/180°C for 25 min until just set.
5 Warm 2–3 tbsp/30–45 ml jam and spread over the top.
6 Top with meringue (see previous recipe) and bake for another 15 min to lightly brown meringue.
Do not freeze.

JUNKET

This pudding is made with rennet (also used for making cheese, see p. 60) which comes from the digestive juices of calves, and sets the milk, forming curds and whey. Rennet contains an enzyme which is most active at blood heat. Overheating destroys it; and if you chill it too quickly, the rennet becomes inactive and the junket fails to set. Never disturb a junket until ready to serve: when cut, the whey runs out from the curds, spoiling the texture.
1 Heat 1 pt/550 ml fresh milk to blood heat.
2 Pour into a serving dish and stir in 1–2 tbsp/15–30 ml caster sugar.
3 When dissolved add the rennet (available as liquid, tablet or powder, and unflavoured or flavoured. Always follow the manufacturer's instructions).
4 Leave in a warm place until set (about ½ hr).
VARIATIONS Sprinkle over nutmeg, cinnamon or mixed spice; or mix in few drops of vanilla or almond essence; or mix in 2 tsp/10 ml coffee essence; or 2 tbsp/30 ml cocoa mixed with 2 tbsp/30 ml boiling water and cooled; or mix in 2 tsp/10 ml rum.
Do not freeze.

TRIFLE

Perfect for special occasions (you can make it in advance) and also popular for family meals.
1 Cut a jam-filled Swiss roll into ½ in/1 cm slices and arrange them in a glass dish.
2 Sprinkle over about 6 tbsp/90 ml medium sherry.
3 Add, if you like, some drained canned fruit such as raspberries or black currants and 2–4 tbsp/30–50 ml of the juice.
4 Pour over a custard sauce made with ¾ pt/400 ml milk (see p. 57). Cover and cool.
5 Decorate with whipped cream which can be piped, flaked almonds and/or glacé cherries and angelica.
Do not freeze.

CHOCOLATE MOUSSE

A light, cold dessert that goes down well after a heavy main course.
1 Melt 8 oz/225 g plain chocolate in a basin over a pan of hot water. Turn off heat.
2 When melted stir in 4 egg yolks, one at a time, then (if you like) 1 tbsp/15 ml rum or brandy and ½ oz/15 g butter.
3 Whisk 4 egg whites in a bowl until stiff and fold them into the chocolate mixture using a metal spoon.
4 Pour into a large serving dish or into individual dishes and chill.
Decorate if you wish with whipped piped cream and grated chocolate.
Freezes well.

JELLY

You can use commercial packet jelly but home-made ones using fresh fruit juice can be more interesting and nutritious. Left-over fruit and juice can be used up in this way.
1 Dissolve 1 packet or 3 tsp/15 ml powdered gelatine in ¼ pt/150 ml hot (not boiling) water. Add gelatine to the water and not the other way round. Stir well to dissolve.
2 Stir in 3 oz/75 g caster sugar and continue stirring until dissolved.
3 Add ½ pt/300 ml fresh fruit juice.
4 Pour into a dish or mould, then cool and chill.
You can use canned fruit juice, or frozen juice or fruit squash, too.
Add fruit just as the jelly is beginning to set. Serve from the dish. Or to turn out from a mould:

1 Draw tip of knife round rim to release edge.
2 Immerse sides in hot water for 2 seconds.
3 Put an inverted plate on top (holding it firmly in place).
4 Turn over and shake gently to release.
Chop up jelly for children's parties, or to use as a decoration.
Do not freeze.

MILK JELLY

Popular with children, and more nutritious than jelly.
1 Dissolve gelatine as above in ¼ pt/150 ml fruit juice.
2 Stir in 3 oz/75 g caster sugar until dissolved.
3 Cool slightly; when just warm, stir in ¾ pt/400 ml cold milk. Set as for jelly.
Do not freeze.

CHRISTMAS PUDDING

1 Sieve together 2 oz/50 g plain flour with ½ tsp/2.5 ml each mixed spice, cinnamon and grated nutmeg.
2 Mix in 2 oz/50 g white breadcrumbs, 5 oz/150 g shredded suet, 4 oz/100 g soft brown sugar, 6 oz/175 g each raisins and sultanas, 1 oz/25 g mixed peel and 1 oz/25 g ground or chopped almonds.
3 Beat together 2 eggs (size 2 or 3), the finely grated peel and juice of an orange, 1 tbsp/15 ml black treacle, 1 tbsp/15 ml brandy and 3 tbsp/45 ml beer.
4 Add the liquid to the dry ingredients and mix well.
5 Put into a buttered 2-pt/1.1-litre pudding basin and cover with a double layer of greased greaseproof paper or foil. Make a pleat in the top to allow for rising, and tie securely with string.
6 Steam for about 9 hrs. (Note: to reheat, steam for about 3 hrs.)
Serve with sweet white sauce or brandy butter. Use a pressure cooker to save time and steam. Makes enough for 6–8 people.
Will keep (and improve) for many months. Wrap in a double layer of greaseproof paper and then with foil.

Please also see fruit (pp. 74–78), pancakes (p. 71) and fritters (p. 72).

Making food look good

Always try and make your meals look as attractive as possible. Give the food you cook eye-appeal, everybody will assume it is going to be delicious, and the battle is half-won.

Part of the secret is in your overall plan: try to choose foods that complement each other on the plate. Avoid a predominance of all one colour – steamed white fish, for example, with mashed potato and boiled parsnips! Contrasting colours can work wonders – a touch of bright green or red or golden brown. Take care, when serving food, to drain fried foods of excess fat, and boiled foods of excess water. Arrange food tidily, and wipe away any splashes from around rims with a clean cloth.

The rest of the art of making food look good comes in the little extras you can add before serving. To save time and effort when cooking and serving the rest of the meal, try to arrange your garnishes in advance so that you can simply pop them into place.

Below we have listed a selection of ideas to transform simple ingredients with attractive finishing touches. But don't go mad: an excess of garnishing will have a reverse effect and detract from the food.

Ideas for garnishes

Lemon Use slices, wedges, or twists, and serve with fish, veal escalopes, or chicken cooked in breadcrumbs.

Orange Use slices, wedges, twists or segments and serve with duck, pork, fruit dishes, or puddings and desserts. Thin slices of orange can be used to line a dish for an orange-flavoured sponge pudding which looks very good when turned out.

Apple Use slices, wedges or rings, dipped in lemon juice or fried, and serve with pork, sausages, fruit dishes, or with puddings and desserts.

Tomato Use wedges, slices, or halves cut into roses, and use for salads or savoury cold dishes, such as cold meats.

Cucumber Use thinly sliced or diced, or cut

into twists for salads and cold savoury dishes, or for hors d'oeuvres.

Radish Use slices or cut into roses for salads, cold savoury dishes or appetizers (see p. 47).

Gherkin Cut into slices or fans and use for salads, cold savoury dishes or appetizers.

Olives Use green or black types, plain or stuffed, in the same dishes as gherkin.

Watercress Use small bunches to garnish whole poultry and game, joints or hot or cold savoury dishes, or salads.

Parsley Use sprigs in the same way as watercress or chop and use for soups, sauces and casseroles. Avoid over-using parsley, as the flavour can become boring.

Mustard and cress Use for salads; also good for dainty dishes such as appetizers and starters.

Bread Use croûtons (see p. 52) sprinkled into a bowl of soup to serve; this adds interest and texture to creamy soups. Or use fried bread – cut into thin slices, or cut bread into shapes with fancy cutters, fry and use to garnish stews, casseroles or savoury foods with a sauce. Or dip one half of a fried shape, e.g. triangle, in beaten egg (but shake off the excess) and then in chopped parsley, to give extra decorative effect for special occasions.

Onion rings Dip rings in milk and flour and fry; serve with soups, casseroles, or with vegetables coated with white sauce.

Bacon curls Serve with roast chicken or poultry or with dishes made from these.

Potatoes These can be mashed and piped round serving dish using a wide nozzle and then filled with meat, vegetables or a sauce-based recipe. Potato nests can hold peas and diced vegetables for serving. Decorate the top of a shepherd's pie with a fork or the end of a palette knife.

Cream Pipe onto cold desserts such as mousse, soufflés, trifles, etc. Use different nozzles to make roses, shells or a lattice. Or swirl into soups and casseroles just before serving for decoration and a creamy taste.

Butter Use for glazing vegetables; simply add small knobs, or brush over melted butter for a more even effect. Make into shapes for serving with bread, etc. Chill and make into curls (to use with bread) with a special tool. Run this along the length of the butter block in a straight line; chill and serve. Or make balls with two small wooden butter pats. Place a small square of butter between these; keep the bottom one still and rotate the top one to shape into balls. Or simply decorate a block of butter by pressing into a wooden mould or use a fork run along the top to make a pattern.

Nuts Serve walnuts and hazelnuts, whole or chopped, on sweet dishes piped with cream. Or use almonds, whole or flaked (toasted or fried in butter) chopped on sweet dishes piped with cream; also on some savoury dishes such as trout (the almonds are usually flaked for

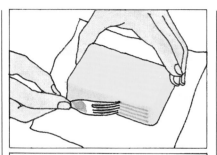

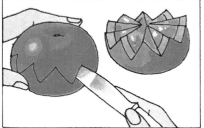

this). Chopped mixed nuts are less expensive and make a good standby for decorating.

Chocolate This can be used to decorate many cold desserts, particularly those with piped cream or those with chocolate as an ingredient. Also use grated chocolate, for example, to decorate cakes. To make chocolate leaves, use washed rose leaves, dried in a tea towel. Dip their upper surface in melted chocolate, place on a small plate, chill, then peel off the real leaves very carefully. To make chocolate curls, chill the chocolate block then run a spoon heated in hot water along the back of the block and chill the curls, spread out on tray. To make chocolate shapes, pour melted chocolate in a thin layer onto waxed paper. Before it is quite set, mark out simple shapes with a knife; chill and lift off.

Angelica Use in strips or cut into shapes (e.g. diamonds) to decorate cakes or cold desserts.

Glacé cherries Use whole, or halved to decorate cold desserts or cakes.

For pastry decorations, see p. 68.
For cake decorations such as sugar glazing and icing, see p. 66.

Tea, coffee and other drinks

Tea, as the whole world knows, is the British national drink, but a 'good cuppa' needs to be made with care; and coffee is considered even trickier.

Drink tea at any time and vary it to suit your tastes: with milk or lemon, hot or cold, weak or strong. It contains a stimulant, caffeine, that makes you feel less tired and more alert. Stewed tea is the result of over-brewing and is caused by bitter-tasting tannin in the tea.

Buying tea

'Black' tea is what we mainly drink, made from leaves mostly from India and Ceylon, fermented then dried. 'Green' tea is unfermented and comes largely from China and is used mostly in blends; in general it is weaker than black with a more delicate 'scented' flavour (serve with lemon slices, not milk). The quality of tea depends on where it is grown and the part of the plant from which the leaves are picked. The teas that most people buy for everyday are usually blended to keep taste and price constant. Unblended speciality teas are usually more expensive. Tea-bags specially developed to infuse quickly are increasingly popular being convenient and easy to dispose of. You should get about 50 cups from $\frac{1}{4}$ lb/100 g loose leaf tea.

Instant tea is brewed tea, dried to powder. Put 1 tsp/5 ml in cup, pour on boiling water, then add milk. Remember that strong tea can always be weakened but weak tea cannot be strengthened.

Storage

Tea is easily spoilt by moisture and strong smells. So keep in a dry place, in an airtight tin or tea-caddy to conserve aroma and strength. Buy in small quantities. Tea and tea-bags will keep for about 3 months, and after this will slowly deteriorate.

To make tea

Always use good quality tea.
1 **Put** cold *fresh* water into kettle (empty out any old water) and bring to boil.
2 **'Warm** the pot' by pouring in a little of the boiling water, and then throw this away.
3 **Put** tea in the pot – for medium strength, allow 1 tsp/5 ml per person plus 1 tsp/5 ml 'for the pot'.
4 **Pour** boiling water onto tea (take the pot to the kettle, not the kettle to the pot), stir, put lid on and allow to infuse or 'brew' for about 4–5 min (some special teas may take longer). Allow 3–4 min for China tea.
One tea-bag makes 2 cups; infuse for 3–4 min and stir well.

Serve tea hot with milk, putting milk in cup first then add sugar to taste, or hot with slice of lemon, or iced with cucumber or mint and orange slices. Tea can also be made into refreshing punches for parties.

Buying coffee

The flavour of coffee varies according to where the coffee comes from. The two most common types found in supermarkets are Brazilian blends which are mild, and Kenya blend which are rich and slightly acid. Other coffee types include Mysore, rich and full-flavoured from southern India; Mocha, a traditional Turkish coffee, served very strong and sweet; Vienna, a blended coffee with a strong, smooth flavour; and strong Continental, a blend of dark roasted coffees. Roasted coffee beans are sold loose, in packets, or in vacuum packs, as light, medium or dark: this describes the coffee strength as well as its colour and depends on the roasting time. You can grind coffee at home with a hand or electric grinder. Vary the grinding time to produce coarse, medium or fine grounds to suit the coffee-making method (see below). Your supplier may be able to grind for you, and some shops have do-it-yourself grinding machines on their premises. The best flavour comes from freshly roasted, freshly ground beans. Ready-ground coffee is not as fresh or as strong and loses flavour quickly when the packet is opened. Sold vacuum-packed, usually medium roast, medium grind.

Instant coffee is powdered or granulated coffee or a liquid with added sweetening. It is made from blended ground and percolated beans. Use 1 tsp/5 ml per cup, and pour on boiling water, or for frothier coffee a mixture of milk and water, or just hot milk. Add sugar to taste.
De-caffeinated types have the caffeine removed and are sold ground or as instant.

To make coffee

Choose from the following methods.

1 Use a percolator, which can be heated on your hotplate, or is available as an electric appliance. Use medium or coarse ground coffee and allow 1½–2 oz/40–50 g per 1 pt/550 ml water. Put water in the percolator and coffee in its metal basket (its position varies according to type). When the water boils it is forced up the centre tube and filters over and through the coffee grounds. Allow to percolate through the coffee for about 10 min. Some electric types have an automatic time control; and once percolated, a thermostat keeps coffee just below boiling point until required.

2 The filter method requires a funnel lined with special filter papers, which fits snugly onto pot or cup. Use finely ground coffee, the same quantities as for percolators, above. Warm pot and pour the boiling water over the filter attachment containing the coffee grounds; the coffee will collect in the jug or cup below. Electric types have a water container, a heater and often a hotplate to keep the coffee warm once made. You spoon the coffee into the filter funnel over the jug, and fill the water container. The water is automatically heated and then is poured through the coffee, and a thermostat switches off the heater.

3 The jug method Put the coffee (medium ground and same amounts as above) into a warmed jug and then pour boiling water onto it. Stir, cover and allow to brew for about 5 min. Strain coffee into another warmed jug to serve, or straight into cups. 'Plunger' coffee pots are available as a refinement of this method; when the coffee has brewed, a perforated plunger is pushed down through the coffee, trapping the grounds at the bottom – no need to strain.

Serve coffee 'white' with milk or cream, or 'black' (no milk). Iced coffee is sweetened, cooled and then chilled; then add an ice cube and a spoonful of whipped cream.

For *Irish* coffee – add whiskey; for *German* coffee – add Kirsch; for *Russian* coffee – add vodka; for *Normandy* coffee – add Calvados; for *Caribbean* coffee – add rum.
For *French* coffee – add Cointreau.

Storage

Keep coffee beans in an airtight container or jar in a dry place for 3 months. Ground coffee, 1 month; instant coffee, 1 year. Vacuum packs keep indefinitely, but once opened store as above.

Milk shakes

Mix milk with fruit juice, concentrates or fruit syrups, or with special milk shake powders, chocolate powder, coffee or with peeled mashed banana. For best results use an electric blender or a rotary whisk. Serve ice cold, and add 2 tbsp/30 ml ice-cream before serving: leave on top or whisk in. Use tall tumblers – special milk shake shapes are available.

Cocoa, drinking chocolate and other branded mixtures

Carefully follow packet instructions. In general, spoon the powder into hot (but not boiling) milk; or pour hot milk onto a spoonful of the mixture. Whisking sometimes improves the consistency.

Soft drinks, fruit drinks, cups, punches

Commercial fruit squashes are generally very sweet, and keep in a bottle with screw top for about 6 months. Unsweetened versions are available from health food shops and from some supermarkets. Natural fruit juices (sweetened or unsweetened) can be bought frozen, in bottles, in cartons or in cans. Once made up or opened use within 1 week. Frozen keeps for 1 year, bottles and cartons for 3 months, canned for 1 year.
You can make more interesting fruit drinks yourself, as follows:

ORANGEADE
1 Finely grate rind of 3 oranges and mix with 3 oz/75 g sugar.
2 Pour over 2 pt/1.1 litres boiling water and stir until sugar dissolves.
3 Cool then stir in juice of the oranges.
4 Serve chilled with ice.
Or for lemonade, use 4 lemons and 6–8 oz/175–225 g sugar.

FIZZY LEMON
1 Put juice of 2 lemons into jug, add sugar to taste and stir to dissolve.
2 Pour over 1½ pt/900 ml soda water and serve immediately.

FRUIT PUNCH
1 Mix together 1½ pt/900 ml fresh orange juice, grated rind and juice of a lemon, 1 tsp 5 ml mixed spice.
2 Heat 1 pt/500 ml water in a saucepan with 4–6 oz/100–175 g sugar and a cinnamon stick to dissolve.
3 Cool and pour over orange mixture.
4 Chill, strain and serve with ice. Float small slices of fresh fruit on top if wished (orange, lemon, banana, etc).

Choosing wines

Serving wine with meals at home has become increasingly popular over the past ten years, with many more foreign wines becoming available at affordable prices. Much has been written or talked about choosing wines, and the articles or conversation tend to be littered with off-putting jargon and formidable-sounding 'rules' which give the subject a quite unnecessary degree of high mystique. The only 'rule' (if, indeed, there are to be any at all) is to buy and drink what you and your family and friends like, on the basis of experimentation. Nevertheless, it is useful to know a little bit about wine types, and the traditions that surround which wine is to be served with which foods.

Table wines

These are 'still' (i.e. non-sparkling, see below) and are usually served with food. They can be red or white, and red wines usually have the highest content of alcohol. Rosés are light-bodied red wines.

Sparkling wines

Sparkling wines are slightly 'fizzy' with bubbles caused by carbon dioxide trapped in the bottles or vats during fermentation. They are white, and can be dry or sweet. The most famous, of course, is champagne, and by law only wines made in the Rheims district can bear this name.

Fortified wines

These include port and sherry, and have their alcoholic content boosted by the addition of brandy. They are normally served before or after meals, or with the cheese or fruit.

Serving wine

Traditionally, wine glasses are curved inwards at the rim to trap the fragrance of the wine, which the drinker savours before progressing to the first sip. For this reason, glasses are only filled half- to two-thirds full at a time. Red wines are brought into the room where they are to be drunk for at least one hour before serving, and the cork is removed so that the wine can 'breathe'. White wines are usually chilled in the fridge (an hour is long enough) or, more grandly, in a bucket with ice.

In general, a light wine is served before a heavier full-bodied wine, and dry wines are served before sweet ones, thus a dry white wine is served before a red wine, and a red wine before a sweet white. To accompany the normal order of a meal, you might serve a dry white wine with your starter or fish course, a red table wine with your meat course and a sweet white wine with dessert. But in practice, of course, people cannot afford to provide such a variety of wines, and it is quite acceptable to offer either a dry white or a medium-bodied red to be drunk throughout the meal. Sweet white wines are not usually drunk throughout a meal as they do tend to cloy the palate.

Pressure cookers

A pressure cooker traps and controls the steam that would normally escape from an ordinary saucepan. As the water inside the cooker boils and turns to steam, the pressure rises and this increases the temperature. Heat is forced through the food to shorten cooking times. A flexible rubber 'gasket' (seal) between the lid and the pan makes sure of a tight seal under pressure. All pressure cookers can be used on any fuel.

Why use a pressure cooker?

1 For speed Most foods are cooked in one-third of the normal time: for some, cooking times are cut by three-quarters. Dried vegetables and fruit do not need to be soaked overnight.

2 For economy To save fuel – only minimum heat is needed to maintain pressure. You can cook a whole meal in a pressure cooker at one go, and it will tenderize cheaper, tougher cuts of meat. You can cook large quantities, eating some the same day, and freezing the rest.

3 For cleanliness It cuts down on steam in the kitchen, and traps smells inside. This is particularly useful when steaming puddings for example, which take a long time to cook in a conventional steamer.

Types available

Three pressures are commonly available.
Low (5 lb pressure) used for steaming mixtures with raising agents (e.g. puddings) and for bottling fruit.
Medium (10 lb pressure) used for softening fruit for jelly, jam and marmalade and for bottling and blanching vegetables.
High (15 lb pressure) used for general everyday cooking.
A pressure cooker which offers all three will be the most versatile, but your normal cooking patterns will decide which pressures you need the most. The size you buy will depend on the size of your family, and whether you wish to cook large quantities of food for the freezer.
In accordance with British Standards, all pressure cookers have safety devices which operate if the pressure becomes too high, or the cooker boils dry or overheats. But if you follow carefully the manufacturers' instructions, these safety devices should never be needed.

Accessories

A trivet or rack is used inside when food is to be cooked by steam rather than by liquid (for example, steamed vegetables or a pot roast). It prevents flavours from intermingling, and can also be used to separate layers of food.
Separators which fit on top of the trivet are metal baskets which may be perforated (for vegetables) or unperforated (for stewing fruits, milk puddings, etc). Separators are used to keep foods apart during cooking and are also useful for getting food out of the cooker.

Advantages of pressure cooking various foods

Soups You save time: soups and stocks are made in minutes instead of hours. You can make stock with less steam and smell. Or cook concentrated soups for freezing; they take up less space and you can always add liquid later.
Meat Tougher cuts are tenderized and moistened, and cooking times are shortened.
Poultry and game Cheaper, tougher birds are tenderized. The results are always moist. Trussed birds keep their shape well. Cooking time is speedy.
Casseroles and stews Maximum concentration and mixing of flavours, to produce tasty, speedy results.
Fish There is no particular gain on speed, but it keeps its shape well in a pressure cooker and the flavour is superb. Fishy smells are reduced in the kitchen.
Vegetables Speedy cooking times. Several vegetables can be cooked together in separators yet each will retain its own individual flavour. Dried vegetables need no overnight soaking.
Fruits These can be cooked whole to keep their shape well, or they can be puréed. Particularly useful for freezing large amounts of fruit in season. You can cook several different fruits in the separators, without their flavours mixing.
Puddings Puddings can be steamed much more quickly with less steam. Milk puddings (rice, egg) are made with delicious creamy results.
Preserves Saves time in making jams, jellies, marmalade and chutney. Fruit for jams, etc, is softened under pressure. When the sugar is added, the pressure cooker is used without its lid, as an ordinary saucepan.

Pressure cooker points

1 Always read thoroughly the maker's instructions, and keep the booklet handy.

2 Always use a liquid which will give off steam, e.g. water, stock, milk, wine or cider, etc. Never use oil or fat.
3 Do not fill the cooker more than half-full with liquids or foods which may normally boil over, e.g. milk, pasta, cereals, soups, casseroles. Do not fill more than two-thirds full with solid food such as vegetables and meat. Leave enough space above the food for steam to circulate; or for the food to rise.
4 To reduce pressure Stand the pressure cooker in a bowl of cold water; use this method when cooking time is crucial, e.g. for vegetables, joints of meat or fruit; or remove the pressure cooker from the heat and allow pressure to reduce in room temperature; use for soups, stews, dried vegetables; for milk puddings; for puddings containing a raising agent; and for bottling. Some pressure cookers automatically release the pressure when cooking time is completed.

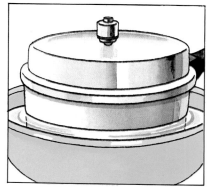

5 Add thickening agents (such as flour or cornflour) after pressure cooking, because otherwise they can break down and the mixture remains thin and runny.
6 Less seasoning is needed, because the flavours tend to be more concentrated, and as less liquid is used, foods retain more of their natural mineral salts.
7 Always use a clockwork timer and start timing from when the pressure cooker has reached the correct pressure, and not from when you first put it on the hotplate.
8 To test if pressure is reduced: follow maker's instructions. Types with 'indicator plungers' will have no 'rings' visible; with others, raise the weight or valve gently with a fork, and if steam still comes out, put it back and leave for short while longer.
9 To cook foods which need different lengths of time, put the food that needs longest in first, then reduce the pressure with cold water at the appropriate time during cooking, and add the food with the shorter cooking time.
10 Always store a pressure cooker open, to allow air to circulate and to avoid musty smells.

Other cooking appliances

New electrical kitchen gadgets are coming onto the market all the time, and it is as well to think carefully about the value of any particular appliance to you and your family before making a purchase.

Choosing electrical appliances

Storage is a most important point to consider. Many appliances will not get used frequently unless kept readily to hand – mixers and liquidizers, for example, are best kept standing on the worktop ready for immediate use.

Always buy models which carry the 'BEAB label' of the British Electrotechnical Approval Board. This means that the appliance has been tested and approved for electrical safety in accordance with British Standards.

It is vital with all electrical appliances to follow carefully the maker's instructions for installation, usage and maintenance. Take time to read their booklets and keep them handy for future reference.

Appliances for preparation

Electrical machines, used correctly, take the elbow grease out of many traditional cooking tasks.

Mixers

These vary in size and power. The larger type can only be used with their own built-in bowl, and have powerful motors rated at about 400 to 450 watts. They can tackle a wide range of cookery tasks and can cope with large quantities and heavy mixtures. Smaller lightweight food mixers have less powerful motors rated at around 100 to 200 watts, and are available with bowl and stand, or they can be hand-held, which is useful for mixing in your own bowls or at a saucepan at the cooker.

Beaters Various types may be available with your machine. For example four-bladed beaters to use for whipping, whisking and creaming. Hook-shaped beaters are for use with heavier ingredients. Sometimes special dough hooks are available for kneading yeast mixtures. Speed controls are usually variable, although some small mixers only have one speed. Follow the maker's recommendations for which speed to use for various recipes.

Attachments These optional extras for your food mixer include blenders (sometimes called liquidizers), coffee grinders, shredder/slicers, bean slicers and pea shellers, potato peelers, juice extractors, juice separators, fruit press, colander and sieve, can-opener, coffee mill, coffee grinder, grinder, mincer and cream-makers.

Food preparation machines

These usually consist of revolving steel cutters in an enclosed bowl, with a funnel down which extra ingredients may be poured. Plastic blades are also supplied, which the makers recommend for some operations. These machines can be used for mixing, rubbing-in, creaming, mincing, puréeing, beating and kneading. Special discs are available which fit in the place of the steel blades which can grate, or shred, or cut chips. They are indeed highly versatile and speedy machines, which can cope with cakes, pastries, bread, soups, batters, pâtés, mincing meat, soups, etc. Many recipes can be made in one operation since the machine can first be used to chop and then mix. But you cannot use them for whisking egg whites and they do not cope with as large quantities as a big food mixer.

Blenders/liquidizers

These vary in power, price and design. Stainless steel motor-driven cutters are enclosed in a goblet of glass or plastic, usually marked off in pints and/or litres, with a lip and handle for easy pouring. A lid fits tightly on top, and some models have a removable central cap so that you can add extra ingredients while the machine is working. Smaller goblet blenders have a capacity of about 1 pint/$\frac{1}{2}$ litre. Take care not to overheat the motor by using only for short periods at a time. Larger $1\frac{3}{4}$ pint/1 litre blenders are more powerful, and can cope with larger, stiffer mixes. A grinder attachment is usually available for both types. They are very versatile machines.

Coffee grinders

These small neat little machines are comparatively inexpensive and take up little space. They can be used for grinding beans to make fresh coffee (see p. 82); also for grinding small quantities of nuts; to make breadcrumbs; even in an emergency for grinding down granulated sugar to make a small quantity of icing sugar!

Appliances for cooking

Many small plug-in 'table-top' (or worktop) cooking appliances have become available in recent years. They are a particular boon to people with limited space available, who perhaps do not have the use of a full-sized cooker. However, many people buy one or more of the following in addition to their cooker. But before you are tempted by a demonstration or a glossy leaflet, make sure that you are really going to use an appliance sufficiently to justify the usual considerable cost.

Electric frypans (or multi-purpose cookers)

Electric frypans can fry, roast or stew. Models are available with non-stick linings, and temperatures are thermostatically controlled. The appliances usually look attractive enough to bring to the table.

Contact grills (or infra-red grills)

Contact grills use infra-red heat to cook food quickly and thoroughly. Will speedily grill a wide range of meats including chops, steaks and chicken pieces. Also can be used for toasted sandwiches, including frozen sandwiches taken straight from the freezer.

Slow cookers

Casseroles are cooked very slowly (in general from 8 to 12 hrs), thus avoiding evaporation and retaining the flavour and most nutrients of the foods. Once cooked, the food can be left in the cooker keeping hot without spoiling for a long time, but do not allow to cool in cooker before reheating. Use for cuts of meat that need long cooking to make them tender, and for fish, soups and sauces. In addition you can poach fruit and steam puddings.

Mixer

Slow cooker

Contact grill

85

Making the most of your oven

A gas oven plays an essential part in catering for family meal-time needs.

Heat zones

Your oven has different heat zones, created as the heat rises from the burners and eventually passes out through the flue. The middle of the oven corresponds to the Gas Mark setting on the oven dial. The top shelf is about one mark higher, and the bottom about one mark lower. You can also make use of the oven base plate. Most ovens have a choice of from 4 to 6 shelf positions, although supplied with two shelves. Always leave one clear runner position between shelves to make sure that there is adequate air circulation.

Some new models can either be used in the conventional way or by the fan-assisted method which produces even temperatures throughout the oven.

Cooking a complete meal

Making use of these different heat zones, you can cook a complete meal at a time in your oven, or use it for a big baking session. In general, choose dishes with the same cooking times to be cooked within a range of three gas marks (see our examples). Set your oven on the middle mark. Make sure that all your cooking containers will fit into the oven. Remember that large items, such as apples, potatoes, will take longer to cook than small ones. Shallow dishes cook more quickly than deep ones, and dishes in aluminium or enamel conduct heat more rapidly and therefore cook more quickly than ovenglass or earthenware. Covering with foil will lengthen cooking time, but prevents browning. If you pre-boil rice or vegetables, they will cook more quickly than if they were left in the oven to cook from cold. The chart gives some ideas for cooking sessions which will help you to make use of the whole of your oven.

Automatic cooking

'Automatic' ovens designed to turn on and off at pre-set times are available on many modern cookers. The food can be prepared for the oven, and the cook is free from the kitchen while the food takes care of itself. A clock control is set to switch the oven on or off (or both) at the chosen time. There is a degree of flexibility.

1 With completely automatic cooking, the oven switches itself on *and* off.

2 You can put the oven *on* yourself, and go out to leave the oven to switch off at a chosen time.

3 You can set the control so that the oven switches itself *on* while you

Dish	Shelf Position	Cover
Sunday lunch – Mark 4 – 2 hrs		
Roast lamb (3 lb/1.4 kg) joint with roast potatoes	Middle	Yes
Braised carrots and cauliflower	Top	Yes
Rice pudding	Base	No
Family meal/supper – Mark 5 – 40 min		
Baked stuffed fish – steak/cutlets	Middle	Yes
Mixed vegetables – frozen	Base	Yes – wrap in foil
Plain or flavoured rice	Top	Yes
Fruit pie	Top	No
Dinner party – Mark 4 –1 hr		
Corn on cob/Sweetcorn	Middle	Yes
Casserole of chicken joints in white wine sauce	Middle	Yes
Broccoli	Top	Yes
Baked potatoes in their jackets	Top	No
Fruit topped with meringue	Base	No
Breakfast – Mark 5 – 30 min		
Baked grapefruit halves	Middle	Yes
Sausages – wrapped in bacon rashers	Top	No
Whole tomatoes	Middle	Yes
Hot rolls (wrap in foil) and coffee	Base	Yes
Baking session – Mark 4 – 1 hr		
Baked egg custard (use bain marie)	Base	No
Fruit crumble, gingerbread	Middle	No
Bakewell tart	Top	No

are out so that you can be present for the end of the cooking for dishes that need attention in their final stages.

The design of automatic cookers varies and it is essential always to follow the manufacturer's instructions carefully. Have a trial run one day while still at home to make sure you understand the oven and that it is working correctly.

Cooker cleaning

For day-to-day cleaning try to wipe over the hotplate after each time of using. Always rub spills up immediately, so that they do not dry or burn on, but be careful not to touch any very hot parts. Use a liquid cleaner to remove stubborn marks, and avoid scouring pads or powder, which can scratch enamels. For more thorough cleaning follow manufacturer's recommendations.

You can usually lift off removable parts (making sure an electric cooker is turned off), and wash them in a hot water and detergent solution. Rinse, dry well and replace. Similarly, it is easier to clean the oven while still warm but not hot. Remove shelves and other movable parts and wash all in a hot water detergent solution. Dirty ovens will need the more drastic use of a proprietary cleaner (see manufacturer's instructions). Use a nylon scourer where necessary, but not a metal one which may harm the oven surface. Self-cleaning ovens are now available with sides specially coated to prevent stains from burning-on. But they still need an occasional wiping-over. The top and base need cleaning as usual. Do not scour self-clean linings. Some ovens have a special high setting for automatic cleaning.

Making the most of your grill

Grilling is a speedy way of cooking tasty food by direct radiant heat with minimum fat, particularly useful for quick breakfasts, suppers and snacks, when the food is to be eaten as soon as it is cooked.

General methods for grilling meat are given on p. 27 (only the best cuts are suitable).

Grill types

Most free-standing cookers incorporate a grill compartment, usually at high level. However, gas 'built-in' cookers usually come in three separate parts: the oven, the hotplate and a separate grill which can be mounted above the hotplate or elsewhere to suit individual kitchen layouts. Grills on modern gas cookers mostly have automatic ignition in common with the burners on the hotplate. Many grill pans (or their supporting shelves) are designed to pull out and then lock securely into position, so that you have two hands free to deal with the food. Many designs have now eliminated projecting handles, and some cookers have grills that neatly fold away after use. Grills frequently incorporate plate-warming facilities, either underneath, at their sides or on top.

Ideas for using your grill

Mixed grills

These can be any combination of chops (lamb or pork), steak, sausages, bacon, kidney, halved tomatoes, mushrooms and/or onions (small, whole or halved). Garnish with watercress. Use small amounts of each and do not put them all on the grill pan at the same time; add the quicker cooking food at a later stage. The juices which collect in the grill pan may be used to make a sauce.

Kebabs

An increasingly popular dish which comes from the Middle East. Use small cubes of lamb, pork, beef, chicken or fish; or small sausages, rolls of bacon, kidneys (halved), prawns, or scampi; or chunks of pepper (red or green), tomatoes (whole or halved), mushrooms (whole if small, halved if large), onion (small, whole or halved, or chunks of large onion), or courgette (thick slices). Bay leaves add extra flavour; thread them between the foods, using about two per skewer, and remove before serving. Use a mixture of meat and vegetables, preferably a combination of dry and fatty foods. Or add fruit, e.g. banana with chicken, pineapple chunks with bacon or apple wedges with pork. Use mint leaves with lamb.
1 Turn grill on to a high setting.
2 Thread even-sized pieces of food onto long flat greased skewers, making sure that these will fit across the grill pan. Ideally one skewer should serve one person. Allow for 2–3 pieces of each food on each skewer.
3 Brush the food with cooking oil or melted fat and place on the grill-pan grid.
4 Grill the kebabs, turning and basting frequently until all the foods are well cooked.
5 To serve: ease the food off the skewers using a fork and place in lines on a bed of plain or flavoured rice, or buttered noodles. Serve with green salad and crusty French bread. You can also serve a sauce, e.g. tomato or curry. For extra flavour, marinate meat, poultry and fish (see marinade on p. 31) adding spices or curry powder to give traditional kebab flavours.

Toasted snacks

Ideas for toasted snacks Welsh rarebit (see p. 64). Seasoned white sauce (see p. 56) with grated cheese or chopped hard-boiled eggs stirred in, spread over toast and grilled. Scrambled eggs (see p. 21) with chopped chives or onions, top with grated cheese and brown under the grill; chopped ham mixed with butter, and mustard, spread over toast and topped with grilled mushrooms. Hamburgers, grilled or fried (first spread toast thinly with mustard or horseradish sauce). Kipper, boned and flaked mixed with melted butter and creamed, spread on toast, grill and serve with lemon wedges. Finely sliced onion or tomato sprinkled with grated cheese, spread on buttered toast and grilled. Baked beans (top with grilled bacon rashers for extra flavour).

Browning foods

Use your grill to brown foods just before serving, for example, meat or poultry which has been roasted in foil, or dishes coated with white sauce; these can be sprinkled with grated cheese and/or breadcrumbs, to serve 'au gratin'.
To make a crunchy glaze on the top of puddings, see crème brulée on p. 66.

Rotisserie cooking

The flavour of food cooked over flames is claimed to be superior to oven roast food. Gas is ideal for this cooking method. A revolving electrically-operated skewer or shaft (running from mains or battery), usually sited in the grill compartment, gives the best results as the food is close to the flames or heat source. Some rotisseries are placed in the oven. Special forks slide along the skewer to hold the food in place; these usually clip or screw on tightly. Some rotisseries have kebab attachments to take several skewers. As the spit turns, the food bastes itself. Because the food is continually turning there is no concentration of heat on one particular area to cause spitting or splashing, and this is quite a clean method of cooking.

Use rotisseries for cooking chicken portions, or truss whole chickens into a neat, tight, compact shape, with or without stuffing. Prick fatty birds (e.g. duck) all over with a fork; there is no need to add extra fat. Whole fish or meat joints are also suitable; choose regular shapes for even cooking. A drip tray at the bottom catches the juices, which can be used to baste food during cooking, and then to make a sauce or gravy so that none of the flavour or food value is wasted.
1 Put the joint or bird onto the greased skewer and secure with the special forks.
2 Brush the food with cooking oil or melted fat. Do not use salt as this dries the surface, but you can add pepper, herbs or spices, etc.
3 Turn the grill or oven on to a high setting (follow manufacturer's instructions for oven temperatures).
4 Place the skewer in position with one end fitting into the motor. Follow instructions carefully: methods vary according to the model.
5 Switch on and make sure the rotisserie is revolving smoothly with nothing in its way.
6 Reduce the heat and cook for the recommended time.
You can add flavour or moisten drier meats such as veal or poultry by basting with a sauce such as barbecue, or with a marinade, or with fruit juice, cider or wine. Garlic and other herbs and spices can be added according to the food being cooked.

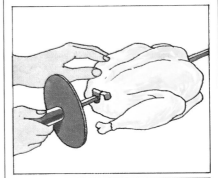

> **TIPS**
> **Try to use tongs for turning food, because when you use a fork the food is pierced, and valuable juices escape. Line your grill pan with foil for easier cleaning, adding a few tablespoons of water to prevent the juices from burning. But never cover the grid with foil.**

Your fridge and freezer

A refrigerator is a kitchen essential, for economy and hygiene. Chilled foods are frequently more pleasant to eat or drink. For the busy cook, the freezer must be one of the most beneficial of modern inventions, enabling you to buy and cook ahead to make best use of precious time and money.

The fridge

A domestic refrigerator keeps the temperature below 7°C. Manufacturers usually indicate a normal setting which should only need adjustment in very hot weather.

Types available

Fridges can be powered by gas or by electricity. Many sizes are available, but 3½ cu ft/100 litres is the smallest practical size for a family of four. Many are designed to fit neatly below a worktop, but make sure there is ventilation at their back. Some are fitted with a worktop themselves to give you extra working space. There are also tall slim models when floor space is at a premium. Doors are usually hinged on the right to open on the left, but some models are available which open the other way round. Doors are usually lined with small racks, but the design of the shelves varies from model to model. Storage compartments may be provided for salads and meat.

Star ratings

These apply to the frozen food compartment.

$*$ The frozen food compartment has a temperature of −6°C and below, and frozen food can be kept for 1 week.

$**$ The frozen food compartment has a temperature below −12°C and frozen food can be kept for 1 month.

$***$ The frozen food compartment has a temperature of −18°C and frozen food can be kept for 3 months.

$*$$***$ Found on fridge-freezers, upright and chest freezers and means that you can freeze down fresh and cooked food yourself, as well as store it for long periods. You can also store ready-frozen foods for 3 months.

New 'larder fridges' are now available without a frozen food compartment, designed to give maximum space for storing fresh or cooked foods for families who also own a freezer.

Food storage

The coldest part of the fridge is below the freezer compartment; the least cold part is the door. As a general guide store raw meat, poultry, offal and wet fish as near to the ice compartment as possible. Keep cooked food, and cooking fats in the middle part, with salads, vegetables and fruit and mushrooms on the base (using special vegetable drawer or 'hydrator' if provided). Milk, butter, eggs and cheese go in the door storage compartments. Food should always be suitably wrapped for the fridge, to prevent it from drying out and exchanging flavours. You can use plastic containers with tight-fitting lids, plastic bags or cling film, or aluminium foil. Or even a bowl with a plate or saucer on top, although these are liable to tip and spill.

Care and cleaning

When ice has built up around the freezer compartment to a thickness of about ¼ in/6 mm, you should defrost. Some models defrost automatically, others have a button you push for defrosting. In others, however, you must turn the fridge off and remove all food. As the ice melts, water will collect in the drip tray beneath the frozen food compartment. A bowl of hot water placed inside the fridge will speed up the process. When all the ice has gone, wipe out the fridge with a clean cloth, using warm water to which has been added a teaspoon of bicarbonate of soda. Dry thoroughly, switch on and replace food.

FRIDGE POINTS

1 Avoid putting hot food into the fridge which raises the temperature and causes rapid icing-up.

2 Try not to store strong-smelling fruits such as melon, strawberries and pineapple, and if you do, make sure they are well wrapped, or their flavours may linger for a long time, and pass to other foods.

3 Do not store bananas in the fridge as they will turn black.

The freezer

The freezing process makes food so cold that chemical changes are slowed down, and harmful micro-organisms become inactive. The food stays in this state providing that the temperature is kept at 0°F/−18°C. When the food is allowed to thaw out at room temperature, or in the oven the chemical changes start up again, and the micro-organisms become active. There are four basic essentials for good freezing. The food must be:

1 Fresh and of good quality.
2 Quickly and correctly 'frozen-down'.
3 Packaged correctly to exclude all air.
4 Stored at the correct temperature for the correct lengths of time.

Choosing a freezer

It is better to choose a model larger than you think you can presently use. As a general guide, allow 3–4 cu ft/85–113 litres of freezer space for each member of the household. There are three basic types:

1 The upright freezer looks like a refrigerator, and takes up similar floor space. It has a front-opening door, and shelves (which may be adjustable), or baskets which can be pulled out; some have shelves on the door for small items. Some models have a 'fast-freeze' shelf or compartment for quickly 'freezing-down' new food. Running costs are slightly higher than for the chest type (see below) because as you open the door, the cold air literally 'falls' or 'rolls' out. You will need to defrost it more often, too.

2 The chest freezer is good for storing large, bulky and difficult shapes, giving maximum capacity for storage. But it takes up to twice as much floor space as an upright, so it may not fit into your kitchen. Consider other sites: the garage? utility room? spare bedroom? under the stairs? the cellar? Running costs are economical and it needs less frequent defrosting than an upright. But be sure you can reach the bottom of the freezer without difficulty. A reliable storage and recording system (see below) is essential for this type of freezer, as packages can easily get mislaid in the bottom or in a corner. Freezer 'baskets' are a great help, as you can simply lift them out to see what frozen foods lie beneath.

3 The fridge–freezer combines a refrigerator and freezer in one upright model, with front-opening doors sitting side-by-side, or one on top of the other. The two-tier type is useful if floor space is limited but it will be fairly tall and if possible should not interrupt a run of work surface. Make sure the freezer compartment has the four-star rating required for freezing food down. Freezing capacity is usually about 7 cu ft/198 litres.

Position of the freezer

1 The kitchen is the most convenient place but it can be stored anywhere so long as the floor is strong enough to support it.
2 An earthed electrical point is required.
3 For maximum efficiency and low running costs, your freezer should be in a cool, dry, well-ventilated position.
4 Avoid damp conditions (e.g. in a garage) which can cause exterior and motor damage.
5 Support your freezer on wooden blocks to avoid contact with the floor, and polish the outside often to prevent rusting. A warning light or buzzer can be fitted to tell you if anything is going wrong.

Freezer maintenance

When using for the first time, and before switching on, wash the freezer out thoroughly with 2 pt/ 1.2 litres warm water containing 1 tbsp/15 ml bicarbonate of soda. Wipe it dry with a clean cloth. Follow carefully your manufacturer's instructions. Turn the freezer on for 12 hours before putting in any food, so that the appliance is working at the correct temperature. A thick layer of frost and ice makes your freezer inefficient, so you should defrost once or twice a year on average, or when the frost is is $\frac{1}{2}$ in/1 cm thick. To defrost, wrap food in thick layers of newspaper (large quantities will be unharmed for about 2 hrs). Pack your parcels closely together, to minimize air circulation. Put some in the fridge on its coldest setting. Switch off the freezer and disconnect it at the mains. You can leave bowls of hot water in it to speed up melting (but never pour hot water in); also leave the door or lid open. Catch the water as the ice melts. You can use a plastic *not* metal spatula to scrape away the ice but *never* use a sharp knife. You will be more comfortable if you wear gloves. Finally, wipe out the freezer as instructed for first-time use, above. Leave it open to dry; and clean the shelves and baskets. Replace them, close the freezer and switch on for $\frac{1}{2}$–1 hour before putting back the frozen food. You should have your freezer serviced once a year. Freezer insurance is available to protect you against power failure.

Making use of your freezer

Use your freezer to store ready-frozen foods or cook and freeze your own dishes. You can freeze garden produce when in season. 'Batch-cooking' involves making large quantities of a particular item so that you can freeze supplies for several weeks, or even months.

Bulk-buy facilities are available from butchers, cash-and-carry stores, supermarkets, farms and freezer centres, but check the quality before making a large financial outlay.

Packaging

To keep food in best condition, air must be eliminated from the food so that no ice forms inside packets and to prevent flavours from passing between foods. Correct packaging prevents drying; on contact with air, food loses moisture, becoming dry and tough when thawed and cooked. In extreme cases, contact with air can cause 'freezer-burn' (particularly on meat), which produces whitish patches on frozen food. Keeping food in the freezer for too long will make it dry and fats; such as bacon, can go rancid so always check on correct storage times. Choose packaging to suit the food and its quantity. And remember that regular shapes take less room, and are easier to stack.

FREEZER CONTAINERS

Foil containers come in many shapes and sizes. Use for casseroles, puddings, pies. You can clean them and use again. Use cardboard lids: with the foil side down. You can cook, freeze and re-heat all in the same container. Avoid using them for fruit, as the acid can make tiny holes, if stored for a long period.
Plastic containers with snap-on lids can be washed and re-used over and over again. Initially, they are expensive. Suitable for storing casseroles, sauces and brittle foods which need protection in the freezer.
Waxed containers are not as strong as foil or plastic containers (see below). Seal them with freezer tape (see above). Fill them only with cold foods, and use as for plastic containers above. Difficult to re-use.
Freezer tape is a special sticky tape which unlike ordinary tape will not come undone at low temperatures. Use it to make packages airtight and to make them secure.
Aluminium foil Used in two layers of the ordinary type; or use one layer and overwrap with a polythene bag; or use heavy-duty 'freezer' foil. See p. 90.
Cling film See p. 90. Use a double layer for wrapping unless you use heavy-duty freezer film. Also use it to interleave foods, e.g. chops.

Polythene bags Heavy-duty types are sold for freezer storage. They come in many sizes and colours and some have an area for labelling; some have gussets to take bulky foods, and they can be self-sealing. Types sold in tear-off strips are very convenient. To remove air from polythene bags; press gently from bottom upwards, twist fold top over and secure with twist ties provides. To re-seal plastic bags of ready-frozen peas, etc, you can use clothes pegs.
Boil-in-bags have the advantage that food can be taken straight from the freezer and put into boiling water to heat up. Expensive and cannot be re-used.
Foil bags Use in the same way as boil-in bags, or as foil bags lined with polythene, which are good for freezing liquids.
Waxed paper is useful for bulky or irregular shapes, but must be used with freezer tape (see above). Or use small pieces to interleave stacks of food, e.g. chops which might otherwise stick together when frozen.
Roasting bags wrap See p. 90.

OTHER CONTAINERS

1 Casseroles, but never use glass unless of the toughened type, as it may crack. They must have airtight rust-proof lids. If straight-sided you can line them with foil (see p. 14) so that once frozen you can use your casserole for other things.
2 Cartons from yoghurt, ice-cream, cottage cheese, etc.
3 Ice cube trays for freezing concentrated stock, herbs, egg whites or yolks (or beaten egg).
4 Food can be frozen in baking tins and pudding bowls ready for storage.
5 Uncooked unwrapped pastry cases can be frozen in their tins, removed and packed for freezing; return to the same tin for cooking. Or open-freeze cooked pastry-cases, jam tarts, etc, in trays, and when frozen remove and pack.

LABELLING

Clear labelling is essential, with name of the food and its quantity, the date of freezing and any special notes concerning thawing, serving or re-heating (e.g. add 2 tbsp/30 ml cream before serving). Use chinagraph or wax pencils, or *waterproof* felt pens on self-adhesive labels, cardboard tops or on the label areas of polythene bags; or label a piece of paper inside the polythene bag. You can use a 'colour-code' for different groups of food. Keep a freezer record in a small notebook to ensure a good rotation of food. List the type of food, the date frozen, its quantity and its position in the freezer. Keep it near the freezer with a pencil attached.

Cooking aids

Numerous 'cooking-aids' are available in the form of aluminium foil, polythene bags, etc. Here we have collected as many hints and tips as we could think of to make your kitchen and cooking run more smoothly.

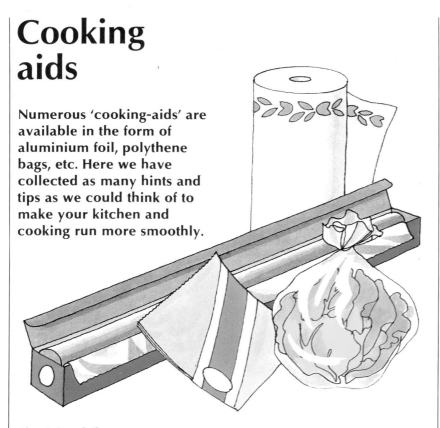

Aluminium foil

This can be re-used several times, but must be absolutely clean.

Storage Foil does not absorb juices, or stick to food. Use to wrap food to keep it fresh and moist in fridge or larder. Wrap tightly otherwise food will go mouldy. Foil can also be used to wrap strong-smelling foods to prevent their flavour passing to other foods. It is especially good for storing foods which must be kept dry, e.g. tea, coffee, salt, brown sugar.

Freezing Use a double layer of ordinary foil to wrap food tightly for the freezer, or use one layer of freezer foil which is thicker. You can line a straight-sided casserole with foil, cook the food, cool and then freeze in the casserole; when frozen lift out of the casserole and wrap.

Cooking Foil helps to keep food like fish in shape during cooking and can also help to keep stuffing in place. Use foil:

1 To wrap meat for roasting to keep it moist.
2 Preserve the flavour and food value of boiled foods. Wrap fish, vegetables, etc, in foil (lightly seasoned), fold over lightly and boil the 'parcels' in water. Twist up the ends to make 'ears' so that you can easily lift them out of the water.

3 Cover steamed puddings, instead of paper or cloth and string.
4 Seal casserole or saucepan lids, when used for pot roasting, etc. Wrap a sheet underneath the lid and press firmly onto the casserole or pan.
5 Cover food or areas of food in the oven to prevent browning, e.g. rich cakes, pastry or poultry.
6 Line a large metal tray with foil for roasting a large item, e.g. a Christmas turkey.
7 Line a dish to be used for biscuit crust (see p. 70) to make, e.g., cheesecake. Fill and chill. Then lift out the cake, holding foil sides, and peel off foil to serve. Keeps dish clean.
You can also cook in the wide variety of foil containers available – e.g. flan cases and loaf tins.
Keeping your grill clean Line your grill pan with foil to catch fat drips, and to help food cook from underneath by reflected heat. But never cover the rack, as this can be dangerous.
Miscellaneous Cover wooden boards or old plates with foil to serve party food, or birthday cakes; make a quick and easy funnel from foil; use circles of foil if you have lost your jam jar lids.

Roasting bags

Heat-resistant, see-through bags or wrappers in which food can be cooked in the oven or boiled on the hotplate. Food is cooked more quickly, the cooking smells are kept in and the natural juices of food retained.

Roasting Meat cooks well with less shrinkage, basting itself; as the natural juices evaporate, they then 'rain' down onto the joint from the top of the bag. This is also suitable for cheaper cuts as the fibres are broken down with long slow cooking. Always dust the inside of bags with flour before using for roasting to prevent a sudden splattering of hot fat.
Boiling Bags are also suitable for 'boil-in-the-bag' recipes, such as stews. Exclude as much air as possible, twist-tie securely, and immerse bag into boiling water for time stated in recipe. Do not cover. Use tongs for lifting the bag out of the water. Several foods can be cooked in separate bags in one pan, reducing smells; saving fuel and pan cleaning.
Freezing and reheating Freeze, for example, a casserole, in a roasting bag for use later. To reheat take the bag from the freezer, and put in pan of boiling water until heated through.
Microwave ovens Ideal for use in microwave ovens, but do not use wrap or bags with a foil edging (used for sealing); also avoid the twist ties provided which have metal inserts. Instead, secure with string, thick cotton or an elastic band.

Cling film

Transparent film which clings to itself or to crockery or glassware.

Storage Use to cover foods in the fridge, larder or kitchen, but the rim of the container must be clean and dry if the film is to stick. The film keeps out dust, flies, etc, and keeps strong smells in. Particularly useful for sandwiches, cheese and meat.
Cooking You cannot use cling film like foil in the oven, but it is excellent for use in microwaves to cover foods which need to be kept moist during cooking. Use the film to line a flan dish for biscuit crumb (see foil), or line a straight-sided dish to hold a cold dessert which you intend to freeze. After freezing, you can lift out the frozen block, using the film, and then overwrap with another layer of film.
Jam-making Use waxed discs plus cling film to cover pots of jam, instead of cellophane circles and rubber bands.
Safety note
Always keep film away from babies and young children because of the danger of suffocation.

Greaseproof paper

Sold in bags or in sheets, this has always been a kitchen essential. As the paper does not absorb grease, any fat present will form a layer between the paper and the food, making it easy to remove.

Wrapping Use for general wrapping purposes, for example, sandwiches. But it is not as easy to seal as foil or cling film. It is not suitable for wrapping for the freezer as it will absorb water. But you·can use it to interleave chops or hamburgers.
Cooking Use to line cake tins – see p. 72. Also to make quick throw-away icing bags – see diagrams. A moistened layer of greaseproof will prevent a skin forming on top of a sauce.

Kitchen paper or paper towels

These are very convenient for general mopping up of kitchen spills, also for wiping your own hands. They are expensive, but as you throw them away you save on the bleach needed for dish cloths.
Cooking Use to dry salads, when a clean tea-towel is not available; drain fried or grilled food on a layer of crumpled paper; use a sheet of kitchen paper to absorb the top layer of fat which may form on gravies or stews, etc. Decorative types can be used for serving food instead of a doily, and, of course, in place of paper napkins.

Plastic (polythene) bags

These are sold in various sizes or more conveniently on pull-off rolls. They usually come complete with twist ties. Buy the heavier duty type for freezer storage. They can be washed and re-used but are rather difficult to dry thoroughly.
Storage Use for general storing in larder or fridge and in particular for washed salads.
Freezing For storing food in the freezer you can use two ordinary polythene bags one inside the other, or a single heavy-duty freezer bag. Or you can line a carton with a polythene bag and pour in cold food for freezing. When frozen, lift out the bag seal and put back in freezer to take up less space than an irregular shape.
Cooking Put a little flour or breadcrumbs into a polythene bag, and then shake foods to be coated inside the bag. Do not use ordinary polythene bags for roasting or boiling.
Safety note
Keep bags away from babies and young children because of the danger of suffocation.

Doilies

These are used for making food attractive for serving and have patterns cut from cloth or paper. Use round shapes for sweet dishes, and oval for savoury.

Waxed paper

Used to interleave foods in the freezer before overwrapping, to make it easy to remove small amounts. Or you can cut this type of paper into discs for jam-making, or use it to line the tins for rich fruit cakes.

Energy saving and safety with Gas

Gas is a safe and economical fuel. By using it wisely, you can save money and help make energy reserves go further.

Economy tips

Simple ways to save fuel in the kitchen.

1 Keep gas flames to the same size as your saucepan bases.

2 Put lids on saucepans.

3 Turn gas down as soon as saucepan contents boil.

4 Do not overfill kettles or pans: boil only the amount of liquid you need.

5 Try cooking more than one vegetable in the same pan, e.g. carrots and potatoes, or steaming one vegetable on top of another one boiling below. Cut vegetables into small pieces to cook them faster.

6 Make use of a pressure cooker, if possible.

7 De-scale kettles regularly.

8 Make full use of your oven whenever possible, cooking extra food for the next day, or for freezing. Vegetables can be cooked in the oven along with the main meal.

9 If possible, avoid opening the oven door while cooking.

10 Do not wash-up under a running hot tap – fill a bowl with water. Repair dripping taps.

11 Defrost fridges and freezers regularly, as recommended by their makers.

12 Do not open fridge and freezer doors unnecessarily.

13 Do not run fridges on a cooler setting than necessary.

14 Cool hot food before putting it in the fridge.

15 Keep freezer well-stocked.

16 When washing clothes or dishes, whether by hand or machine, wait until you have a full load.

In the rest of the house, make sure that you have maximum insulation, using heating only when and where you need it. Reducing room thermostats by 2°C can lower gas consumption by around 10%.

Safety tips

1 All gas appliances need fresh air to work safely and efficiently. Never block grilles or ventilators provided for this purpose in your kitchen.

2 Look for the B.S.I. Safety Mark when buying a new appliance.

3 Make sure that your gas appliances are installed by an expert – either a fitter from your local gas showroom, or a CORGI registered installer. Never try and do it yourself, or allow amateurs to do it for you.

4 Only use appliances for the purpose for which they were designed. Cookers should not be used as room heaters; cupboards around boilers should not be used as airing cupboards.

5 Read carefully the instruction booklets that come with your appliances and keep them in a safe handy place. Re-read them from time to time, and if you lose them, write to the manufacturer for a replacement.

6 Make sure that all your appliances are serviced regularly by qualified service agents. Gas central heating, water heaters and fires should be serviced every year. Other appliances should be serviced every two years. If possible, take advantage of regular maintenance plans.

7 Make sure you know how to turn off your mains gas supply. The tap is usually near the meter. To turn off your supply: first turn off all appliance taps and pilot lights. Then turn the main gas tap to the off position. It is off when the notched line on the spindle of the tap points across the pipe. If your main gas tap is stiff and will not turn, do not force it. Call the gas service, who will loosen it free of charge. Turn off your main supply when you go on holiday or leave your house for any length of time.

8 If you smell gas:

Put out cigarettes.

Do not use matches or naked flames.

Do not operate electrical switches either off or on.

Open doors and windows.

Check to see if a tap has accidentally been left on, or if a pilot has gone out. If not, there is probably a leak.

Turn off the supply at the mains, and call gas service. You will find the number under GAS in the telephone book.

Gas leaks must be repaired by a competent person and you must not turn on your supply again until the leak has been repaired.

A free Home Advice Service is available to give specialist help on the installation and use of gas appliances in your home.

An A–Z of cookery and kitchen terms

Here you will find explanations for any words that puzzled you in our book – or in other recipe books, for that matter!

A

Al dente 'To the teeth', a 'biting' test to see whether a dish is cooked just right; used mainly for pasta, rice and vegetables which should be slightly crisp when cooked.

Appetizer Savoury bits served before a meal to stimulate the appetite, also served with drinks.

Aspic A clear jelly made from the cooked juices of meat, poultry or fish. You can also buy it powdered.

Au gratin A dish coated with a sauce, sprinkled with breadcrumbs and/or grated cheese and grilled to brown before serving.

B

Bake To cook in the oven by dry heat; used for most cakes, biscuits, pastries and other dishes.

Baking blind To bake a pastry case without a filling.

Bain marie A large open dish half-filled with water, which is kept just below boiling point on the hotplate or in the oven. It is used to keep foods hot without further cooking or to prevent the overheating of baked egg custard, etc.

Barbecue A method of cooking over charcoal in the open air.

Bard To cover poultry, game or lean meat with pork or bacon fat; the purpose is to prevent them from drying up during roasting.

Baste To moisten food, e.g. meat, poultry and game, during roasting by spooning over the juices in the pan; it prevents food drying up, adds flavour and improves appearance.

Batter A mixture of flour, eggs and liquid used for pancakes, Yorkshire pudding, fritters, etc.

Beating To turn a mixture over and over with an upward movement using a wooden spoon, fork, whisk or electric mixer. The purpose is to introduce air and lighten.

Béchamel A rich white sauce flavoured with egg yolks or cream.

Beurre manié A mixture of equal quantities of butter and flour mixed. Added little by little to the hot liquid, bringing to the boil each time to thicken.

Bind To hold together or thicken a mixture, using a liquid, egg or melted fat.

Bisque A rich creamy fish or shellfish soup.

Blanch To plunge food in boiling water to preserve its natural colour, or usually to loosen skin (e.g. almonds and tomatoes). Used for preparing vegetables for the freezer.

Blanquette A white meat (e.g. veal) in a white sauce enriched with cream and egg yolk.

Blend To combine ingredients with a little cold liquid to make a smooth even consistency.

Bloom White appearance on surface of fruit (e.g. grapes, plums) indicating that it is fresh.

Boil To cook in a liquid (e.g. water, stock or milk) at 212°F/100°C. Used particularly for vegetables, rice and pasta.

Bolognese Italian dish with tomato-based meat sauce.

Bone To remove bones from meat or poultry before or after cooking. Raw meat is usually boned before rolling or stuffing.

Bottle To preserve fruit or vegetables in a liquid, e.g. syrup or brine.

Bouchée A small puff pastry case with savoury filling, a mouthful to serve as an appetizer.

Bouillabaisse A well-flavoured, thick soup made from a variety of fish and shellfish.

Bouquet garni A small bunch of mixed herbs used to flavour soups, stews, etc, during cooking and then removed.

Bourguignonne A meat dish (usually beef) cooked with red wine.

Braise A method of cooking which is a combination of frying/roasting and stewing.

Brine A salt and water solution in which food is immersed to pickle or preserve.

Brioche A light bun made from yeast dough and served at a continental breakfast.

Brochette Skewers on which meat, poultry, fish or vegetables are grilled.

Broil An American term meaning to grill.

Brown To give a dish (which is usually cooked) a brown finish by putting under a hot grill or placing in a hot oven. Can also mean the addition of commercial food colouring.

Brûlée A French term for a burnt-sugar topping on custard, grilled to a caramel and nearly burned.

C

Calorie A measurement of the energy content in food.

Canapés Small pieces of pastry, biscuit, fried bread or toast with savoury toppings served as appetizers or with drinks, etc.

Canelloni Italian pasta tubes stuffed with savoury filling and coated with sauce.

Caramel Sugar syrup heated very slowly in a thick pan until it is a rich brown colour; it is used for topping custard (to make crème caramel) and puddings, and for flavouring cakes and puddings.

Carbonade A rich casserole made with beer or stout usually from beef.

Carve To cut or slice meat for serving.

Casserole A heatproof container with tightly fitting lid, used for cooking meat and vegetables in the oven. The food is usually served straight from the cooking dish. The term also describes food cooked in this way.

Cassoulet A dried bean dish from France.

Chantilly To serve with whipped cream flavoured with vanilla and slightly sweetened.

Chapatti An Indian flat and unleavened wholewheat bread served with curries.

Charlotte A custard dish set with thin biscuits, e.g. Charlotte Russe. You can use the biscuits as a filling or as a surround.

Chasseur 'Huntsman style', i.e. dishes cooked with mushrooms, shallots, and white wine or brandy, used for meat, poultry, game or fish.

Chaudfroid Cooked cooled fish, poultry or game coated with jelly or glazed with a sauce.

Chill To cool food in the refrigerator, but not to freeze.

Chop To divide food into small pieces, using a sharp knife on a chopping board.

Clarify To clear or purify, e.g. when dripping is melted to strain off the sediment. Clarified butter (or Indian ghee) is sold for frying and for making cakes. The term is also used for 'clearing' jellies and consommés by adding beaten egg white then straining.

Coagulate To turn liquids nearly solid.

Coat To cover food for frying with flour, or egg and breadcrumbs, or batter, etc. Or to cover cooked food with a layer of sauce, or mayonnaise, etc, before serving.

Cocotte A small earthenware ovenproof container, the size of a single portion. Usually used for cooking and serving eggs.

Coddle A method of soft-boiling eggs. Put them into a pan of boiling water, cover, withdraw from heat and allow to stand until set.

Colander A perforated basket (metal or plastic) for draining foods.

Compôte Fruit (fresh or dried) stewed in a sugar syrup, and served hot or cold.

Condé A fruit-and-rice dessert.

Condiment Seasoning served at table, e.g. salt, pepper and mustard.

Conserve Whole fruit preserved as jam.

Consommé A clear meat soup.

Core To remove the centre from fruit or vegetables; or the membranes from kidney.

Court-bouillon 'Briefly boiled'. The seasoned liquid in which fish, meat or vegetables are cooked.

Crackling Pork skin rubbed with salt and baked until crisp.

Cream To beat together fat and sugar until pale and fluffy, used for cakes and puddings.

Crêpe A thin, light and fine pancake.

Crimp To decorate pies, tarts, shortbread, etc. by pinching the edge at regular intervals with fingers to give a fluted effect.

Croissant A crescent-shaped roll.

Croquette A savoury mixture made into cork shapes, then coated with beaten egg and breadcrumbs and deep fried.

Croûte A slice of fried or toasted bread on which a savoury is served. It can also be a pastry case (see 'en croûte').

Croûtons Small cubes of bread, fried or cut from toasted bread, to serve with soups.

Crudités Raw vegetables, usually served with a dip as an appetizer, or as an hors d'oeuvre.

Cruet A combination set of salt, pepper and mustard.

Curd The solid part of soured milk or junket. Or a creamy preserve made from fruit, sugar, eggs and butter, e.g. lemon curd.

Curdle To separate fresh milk into solids (curds) and liquid (whey). It happens when acid is present or under excessive heat. Creamed mixtures (e.g. sugar and fat in creamed mixture) will curdle when the egg is beaten in too quickly or cold from the fridge.

Cure To preserve meat, poultry or fish by salting, drying or smoking.

D

Dariole A small narrow individual mould with sloping sides for steaming puddings or madelaines; and for setting creams and jellies.

Devil To cook meat, poultry or fish with sharp, hot seasonings.

Dice To cut food into small cubes.

Dough A thick mixture of uncooked flour and liquid (plus other ingredients) used to make bread, cake, biscuits, scones, etc.

Doughnut A small round yeast cake with a hole in its middle which is deep fried. Jam doughnuts have no hole.

Dredge To sprinkle lightly and evenly with flour, or sugar, etc.

Dress To pluck, draw and truss poultry and game ready for cooking; or to garnish a cooked dish; or to prepare cooked crab or lobster in shells for serving.

Dressing Usually a sauce for a salad. But it can also mean seasoning or stuffing.

Dripping A fat which comes from roasted meat during cooking or from small pieces of fat that have been rendered down (see rendering).

Drop scones Pancakes cooked on a girdle or griddle (Scottish).

Dumplings Small balls of dough, usually boiled on top of a stew or a casserole.

Drying To preserve food by removing moisture.

Dust See Dredge.

Du Barry A dish with cauliflower as its main ingredient.

E

En croûte Meat or fish which is wrapped or enclosed in pastry before cooking.

Entrée Meat, poultry, fish, eggs or vegetables, hot or cold, served with sauce and garnish.

Enzymes The special proteins in food which accelerate the rate of chemical reaction without being affected themselves – e.g. enzymes cause the browning of potatoes and fruit.

Escalope A thin slice of meat (usually veal), beaten flat, dipped in beaten egg and breadcrumbs and fried.

Espagnole A rich brown sauce.

F

Faggots Savoury cakes made from pork offal, onion and breadcrumbs.

Fibre The indigestible material in food, not absorbed by the body but essential for good health, contained in whole cereal, and fruit and vegetables.

Fillet A tender expensive cut of beef or pork, etc. Or a method of preparing fish by removing bones.

Fines herbes A mixture of chopped herbs, usually parsley, tarragon, chives and chervil.

Flake To separate cooked fish into individual pieces (flakes); or to grate chocolate or cheese into slivers.

Flambé Flamed: alcohol such as brandy or sherry is warmed, added to a dish and then ignited to achieve a concentrated flavour. Used, e.g. for Christmas pudding.

Flan An open pastry or sponge case filled with a savoury or sweet mixture.

Florentine A dish with spinach as its main ingredient.

Florets Cauliflower, broccoli or calabrese, broken into individual pieces, usually from a round mass or head.

Flute A method of decorating pastry.

Foie gras A pâté made from livers of specially fattened geese.

Fold in To combine a whisked or creamed mixture with other ingredients. The purpose is to retain lightness, and it is used for cakes, meringues and soufflés. You cannot fold with an electric mixer; you must use a metal spoon or spatula, with a light circular movement.

Fondue A cheese and wine dish cooked on the table, served with cubes of crispy bread for dunking. Or cubes of meat can be deep fried in oil and served with cold dips or relishes.

Fool A cold dessert made from puréed fruit and whipped cream (and custard).

Forcemeat A stuffing used for meat, fish or vegetables.

Freeze To preserve food by chilling and storing at 0°F/ −18°C.

Fricassée Stewed meat covered with a sauce thickened with eggs and/or cream.

Fritter Batter-covered food (savoury or sweet) deep or shallow fried.

Frosting An American term for icing. Also describes decorating the rim of a glass in which a cold drink is to be served: coat the edge with whipped egg white, dip into caster sugar and allow to dry.

Fry To cook food in hot fat or oil, which can be shallow or deep.

G

Galantine A dish of boned and stuffed poultry, game or meat, pressed and glazed with aspic and served cold.

Garnish An edible decoration added to savoury dish to improve appearance and flavour, e.g. parsley, watercress or lemon.

Gazpacho An iced soup made from tomatoes, cucumber, onion, etc.

Gelatine A jelly used for savoury or sweet dishes.

Genoese A sponge cake, made from a whisked egg mixture, and enriched by adding melted butter.

Glacé Glazed, frozen, iced.

Glaze A glossy finish used e.g. for pastry. Brush on beaten egg or milk before cooking; or use a sugar and water glaze on sweet pies after cooking. Glazing improves the appearance and the flavour.

Gnocchi An Italian dish with small dumplings made from semolina, potatoes or choux pastry.

Goujons Small strips of fish, coated in beaten egg and breadcrumbs and deep fried.

Goulash A Hungarian rice stew flavoured with paprika.

Grate To shave foods, e.g. cheese and vegetables, into small shreds.

Gravy A sauce made from the juices of roast meat or poultry, usually thickened with flour.

Griddle (or girdle) A thick flat metal plate on which scones and cakes can be cooked on the hotplate.

Grill To cook food by direct heat under the grill or over a hot fire.

Grind To reduce hard foods, e.g. coffee beans, nuts, spices, to small fine particles. Use a hand or electric grinder, or a pestle and mortar.

Gut To prepare fish for cooking, by removing innards.

H

Haggis A savoury Scottish pudding made from chopped offal, suet, onions, oatmeal and seasonings, encased in the lining of a sheep's stomach.

Hamburger A minced meat cake, fried or grilled, often served in a bread bun or roll.

Hang To suspend meat or game in a cool dry place for a period of time to tenderize and develop its flavour.

Hash Fried left-over meat and vegetables served with gravy.

Homogenize A method of treating dairy foods to reduce the fat to fine particles and equally distribute them through the liquid.

Hors d'oeuvre Small dishes served cold, usually before the soup, to act as an appetizer; generally small and well-flavoured.

Hot pot An English stew topped with potatoes, and cooked slowly.

Hull To remove the stalk end from soft fruit such as strawberries, raspberries and loganberries.

I

Icing A covering for cakes or pastry which makes them more attractive and adds to the overall flavour. Can be made from sugar and water, sugar and egg white, or sugar and butter, flavoured and coloured to taste.

Infuse To extract flavour by pouring on a boiling liquid. Used, e.g. for tea-making, and for flavoured white sauce.

J

Joint A cut of meat for roasting or to divide meat, poultry or game into smaller pieces before cooking.

Jugged An elaborate cooking method for meat (usually hare) by slow stewing, traditionally actually done in a jug or jar!

Julienne A clear soup with shredded vegetables or a garnish of shredded vegetables.

Junket A dessert made from milk set with rennet and flavoured.

K

Kebab Cubes of meat, marinaded and grilled on a skewer.

Knead To work a dough with your hands so that all the ingredients are smoothly combined.

Kosher Prepared according to the orthodox Jewish law.

L

Ladle A bowl-shaped spoon with a long handle used for serving soup, stew.

Lard To insert, with a special needle, small strips of bacon fat into the flesh of poultry, game birds and meat before cooking. This is to prevent drying out during roasting.

Lasagne Italian dish with layers of pasta leaves, tomato and mince sauce and cheese or cheese sauce.

Lattice A decorative effect achieved by interweaving strips of pastry on top of a tart/flan.

Liaison A thickening agent such as flour, cornflour, arrowroot or egg yolk, etc, used for thickening or binding sauces or soups.

M

Macedoine A diced mixture of fruits or vegetables used as a decoration or a garnish; can be set in gelatine.

Marinade A seasoned liquid in which meat or game, etc, is soaked to tenderize (it softens the fibres) or to give extra flavour. Marinades are usually a blend of oil, wine, vinegar or lemon juice, and seasonings.

Mash To break up food into a smooth consistency.

Meringue Egg white whisked until stiff, mixed with sugar and baked in a cool oven until crisp.

Mill To pulverize or crush, reducing to fine particles.

Mince To break up meat or vegetables into very small pieces, using a hand or electric mincer.

Mirepoix A mixture of lightly fried vegetables used as a bed on which to braise meat.

Mocca/mocha A blend of chocolate and coffee flavouring.

Mousse A light smooth mixture stiffened with egg white, cream or gelatine.

Muesli A mixture of dried fruits, nuts, wheatgerm and rolled oats and served as a breakfast dish – Swiss.

N

Navarin A lamb or mutton stew with vegetables.

Niçoise A cooked dish or salad which usually includes tomatoes, garlic, onions and black olives.

Noisettes Round or oval slices of lamb or beef, ½ in/1 cm thick or more, neatly trimmed.

Non-stick A special lining applied to saucepans and bakeware to prevent food sticking.

Nutrient A component of food, with a specific dietary value for the body.

O

Offal The liver, kidneys and other edible organs of animals.

Omelette Beaten eggs cooked in a frying-pan in a round flat shape, folded over and served with or without a filling, sweet or savoury.

Open freeze Method of freezing foods that are easily damaged, e.g. fruit and vegetables. They are frozen on open trays then packed into rigid polythene containers or polythene bags.

P

Paella A Spanish dish combining saffron-flavoured rice, chicken, shellfish and vegetables.

Panada A thick binding sauce made by the roux method.

Par-boil To cook for part of the cooking time

by boiling; then the food is finished off by another cooking method, which is usually frying, roasting or baking.

Pare To peel vegetables or fruit thinly – using a knife or peeler.

Pasta A flour paste dried into shapes.

Pasteurize A method of heating milk to destroy bacteria.

Pastry A general word for a flour and fat dough baked until crisp.

Pasty A pastry envelope which contains a filling – usually savoury but can be sweet.

Pâté A savoury mixture, minced or finely cut; usually has liver as the main ingredient. It can have a smooth or rough texture, and is cooked in a terrine and served cold.

Paupiettes Thin slices of meat, stuffed, rolled and tied.

Pectin A substance in fruit and vegetables which sets jams and jellies. Can be bought.

Petits fours Tiny fancy pastries, cakes, biscuits and sweetmeats, served with coffee at end of formal meal.

Petit pois Small young green peas.

Pickle To preserve food in salt or in a vinegar solution.

Pilaf Middle East rice dish, can be plain or spicy, usually served as an accompaniment to the main dish.

Pipe To force cream, icing or butter out of special icing bag, through a nozzle, to decorate cakes, etc. You can also pipe meringues, potatoes and biscuits.

Pit To remove a stone or seeds, e.g. cherries.

Pith The white covering next to the flesh of citrus fruits (orange, lemon and grapefruit), just under the rind.

Pizza A flat piece of yeast dough with a savoury topping.

Pluck To remove feathers from poultry or game.

Poach To cook food in enough water to cover in an open pan.

Pot roast To cook meat slowly in a closed saucepan or casserole, in its own juices.

Potage A thick soup.

Praline A crisp confection of nuts and sugar.

Preserve To keep food in good condition by freezing, heating, drying, salting, pickling, bottling, or canning, or by adding chemicals. A preserve can also be a jam or jelly made from fruits or vegetables.

Press To shape meat by pressing under a weight, e.g. tongue.

Prove To allow a yeast dough to rise before cooking.

Pulses Dried peas, beans and lentils.

Punch A drink, hot or cold, with a combination of flavours.

Purée A smooth creamy texture achieved by sieving or blending, usually made with fruit or vegetables.

Q

Quiche A pastry flan with a savoury filling usually made with eggs.

R

Ramekin A small ovenproof dish. Also a small cheese tart.

Raspings Dried breadcrumbs.

Ratatouille A cooked dish of onions, aubergines, courgettes, peppers and tomatoes.

Reduce To boil a liquid in an uncovered pan to evaporate excess liquid and to concentrate.

Relish A sharp, spicy sauce.

Render To extract fat or to clean dripping from fatty meat trimmings by heating in an oven or by boiling in an uncovered pan with a little water, until the water evaporates and the fat is released. The fat is then strained.

Rennet An extract from calves' stomachs, used in cheese-making and to curdle milk for junket.

Rice paper An edible paper, thin, and semi-transparent, used for baking cakes or biscuits which are liable to burn on bottom.

Risotto An Italian savoury rice dish.

Rissoles Cakes of minced meat or flaked fish mixed with breadcrumbs and then fried.

Roast To cook by direct heat in the oven.

Roe Fish eggs. Cod's roe is sold fresh, boiled or smoked.

Rotisserie A roasting spit in the oven or grill compartment, which turns automatically.

Roughage Dietary fibre: the indigestible part of foods.

Roux A mixture, equal amounts of fat and plain flour cooked to form the basis of a sauce and to thicken it.

Rub in To incorporate fat into flour, using the fingertips to rub the two together. Rubbing-in is used for pastry and for some cake-making.

S

Sauté To fry quickly in a little fat.

Schnitzel A thin slice of meat (see escalope), usually veal, dipped in beaten egg and breadcrumbs before cooking.

Score To make shallow parallel cuts in food to improve its appearance and to hasten cooking (e.g. the skin on pork and bacon joints).

Sear To brown meat quickly in a little hot fat before cooking by another method.

Season To improve the flavour of food by adding salt, pepper, herbs, spices and so on. Also a method of preparing saucepans and bakeware before their first use.

Seasoned flour A flour seasoned with salt and pepper, used for coating meat or fish before cooking. It adds flavour and thickens the dish.

Segment To divide the flesh of citrus fruits (orange, lemon, etc) into their natural portions, removing the skin and the pith.

Shred To cut food (usually vegetables and cheese) into very fine pieces, using a sharp knife or a coarse grater.

Shortening A lard or vegetable fat, used for pastry.

Sieve To rub or press through a sieve, food (such as fruit or vegetables) using a wooden spoon.

Sift To pass dry ingredients such as flour, or icing sugar, through a sieve to remove lumps and to introduce air.

Simmer To cook at just below boiling point. A liquid is first brought to the boil, then the heat is lowered so that the surface is nearly bubbling.

Skewer A pointed metal or wooden stick, used to hold the shape of meat, poultry or fish during cooking. Also used to hold small pieces of meat and other foods in place for grilling (e.g. kebabs).

Skin To remove surface fat or scum from stock, soups, etc.

Smoking A method of preserving by exposing food to wood smoke.

Sorbet A flavoured water ice.

Soufflé A light thickened egg dish, which can be sweet or savoury; the egg whites are whisked until stiff and then folded in.

Souse To pickle foods such as fish, pork or veal by cooking in vinegar and spices, then cooling and allowing them to stand in the same liquid.

Spit A rod on which meat, poultry or fish is turned for roasting or grilling or on an open barbecue.

Starter The first course of a meal.

Steam To cook in steam from rapidly boiling water.

Sterilize To remove bacteria from food by applying heat.

Stew A method of long, slow cooking where a liquid is kept at simmering point.

Stir-fry A Chinese method of cooking food quickly in a frying-pan or 'wok'.

Stock A flavoured liquid made by simmering bones (meat, poultry or fish) or vegetables with herbs, etc; used in soups, stews, casseroles and other savoury dishes.

Strain To use a sieve, colander or muslin to separate a liquid from solids.

Stud To insert cloves of garlic, truffles or cloves into or just under the surface of food before cooking.

Stuffing A savoury mixture used to fill poultry, meat, fish or vegetables, usually with a base of rice or breadcrumbs.

Suet White beef fat, can be bought whole from the butcher or shredded in packets.

Sweat To cook vegetables in a covered pan to release their juices without burning, e.g. mushrooms.

Syllabub A rich cold dessert made from cream and sherry or wine.

Syrup A sugar dissolved in water and boiled to thicken; used for fruit salad, drinks, etc.

T

Tenderize To beat meat to make it tender by breaking up the fibres. Tenderizing can also be achieved by marinating.

Terrine An earthenware dish used to cook pâté; this term is also used to describe the pâté itself.

Thicken To alter a consistency by adding flour or other starch or eggs or cream, to make a stiffer mixture.

Truffles A rare expensive fungus, either black or white in colour. Used mainly for garnishing.

Truss To secure poultry or game bird with string or skewers to hold in shape while cooking.

Turn out To remove food from the container in which it has been cooked or the mould in which it has been set. The turned-out food (e.g. cakes, jellies) should hold its shape.

U

Unleavened A flat bread, e.g. chapatti, made without yeast or other raising agent.

V

Velouté A smooth classic white sauce.

Vichysoisse Creamy leek and potato soup, usually served cold.

Vinaigrette A cold oil-and-vinegar dressing used for salads.

Vol-au-vent Large or small, round or oval cases made from puff pastry, with a savoury filling.

W

Waffle A crisp pancake with square holes which is made in a special waffle iron.

Whey The liquid part of curdled milk.

Whip or whisk To beat air into a mixture using a fork, balloon whisk, rotary whisk or electric mixer.

Work To knead with the hands or mix until smooth.

Y

Yeast A living plant used to raise flour doughs, used mainly for bread.

Z

Zest The coloured part of the skin of orange, lemon and grapefruit, containing an oil that gives it its characteristic flavour.

Index